∽ · ∽ · ∽

"This book honors an outstanding scholar, but also makes a contribution of great scholarly and public policy value. It contains important discussions of issues at the forefront of a specialty that began as labor economics, became manpower policy, transformed into human resource economics, and is now often described as workforce development. Under any label, it is a subject at the heart of economic well-being, and the book is required reading for all who want to be up-to-date in the field."

—Garth L. Mangum, Professor of Economics Emeritus, University of Utah

"The work presented here attests to the quality of the scholarship that Vernon Briggs inspires as a teacher and colleague and to the role he has come to play as a model of committed, passionate scholarship, even for those of us who often disagree with the policy changes he wants to introduce. It is a fitting tribute to a man who studies the world in order to change it and make it better and whose research has always come from the heart as well as the head."

—Michael J. Piore, David W. Skinner Professor of Political Economy, Massachusetts Institute of Technology

"The case for an active set of national human resource policies, as supported by Vernon Briggs over his professional life, is greater than at any time in the past 30 years. This book offers much research information and policy analysis that can be used to develop what is needed."

—Andrew M. Sum, Professor of Economics and Director of the Center for Labor Market Studies, Northeastern University

"Vernon Briggs has long been a prolific and influential scholar advocating for progressive and humane labor market policies. This book does full justice to his career by including wide-ranging and useful essays on immigration, education, job training, disability policy, and workforce intermediaries. These chapters will be of interest to both researchers and policymakers as they consider how to rebuild labor market institutions in the face of the dramatic transformations that we have witnessed in recent years."

—Paul Osterman, Nanyang Technological University Professor of Human Resources and Management, Massachusetts Institute of Technology

"With unemployment soaring, it is both pertinent and timely to introduce a new generation of economics students to Vernon Briggs's grand vision of human resources as the source of value creation, stability, and growth. While Briggs's contributions to the immigration policy debate remain controversial, they are clarified and challenged in this volume in ways that are useful in moving that vital conversation forward."

—Eileen Appelbaum, Professor and Director of the Center for Women and Work, Rutgers, the State University of New Jersey

∽ · ∽ · ∽

Human Resource Economics and Public Policy

Human Resource Economics and Public Policy

Essays in Honor of Vernon M. Briggs Jr.

Charles J. Whalen
Editor

2010

W.E. Upjohn Institute for Employment Research
Kalamazoo, Michigan

Library of Congress Cataloging-in-Publication Data

Human resource economics and public policy : essays in honor of Vernon M. Briggs Jr.
/ Charles J. Whalen, editor.
  p. cm.
Includes bibliographical references and index.
ISBN-13: 978-0-88099-359-3 (pbk. : alk. paper)
ISBN-10: 0-88099-359-6 (pbk. : alk. paper)
ISBN-13: 978-0-88099-361-6 (hardcover : alk. paper)
ISBN-10: 0-88099-361-8 (hardcover : alk. paper)
1. Labor economics. 2. Manpower policy. I. Briggs, Vernon M. II. Whalen, Charles J.,
1960-
HD4901.H83 2010
331—dc22

                    2009041858

The facts presented in this study and the observations and viewpoints expressed are
the sole responsibility of the authors. They do not necessarily represent positions of
the W.E. Upjohn Institute for Employment Research.

Cover design by Alcorn Publication Design.
Cover photo by Jim West.
Index prepared by Diane Worden.
Printed in the United States of America.
Printed on recycled paper.

Contents

Acknowledgments

The editor wishes to thank Stephen Mangum for advice on getting this project started and Kevin Hollenbeck and the Upjohn Institute for taking interest in the volume. He also wishes to thank the authors for their valuable contributions, Richard Wyrwa and Bob Wathen for production and copyediting, Stephen Woodbury for valuable input at critical moments, Linda Whalen for reviewing most of the chapters, and, of course, Vernon Briggs for years of inspiration and assistance.

1
Introduction

Charles J. Whalen
Utica College and Cornell University

A few weeks before the start of his senior year at the University of Maryland in September 1958, Vernon M. Briggs Jr. took an all-night drive to visit his college roommate's home in Detroit, Michigan. Arriving with his roommate in downtown Detroit at daybreak, Briggs saw "several blocks where the sidewalks were absolutely filled with people." He recalls:

> I couldn't imagine what they were all doing standing there at this early hour. As we drove further, we came to the building that they were waiting to open. It was an office of the Michigan Employment Commission. The people were lined-up to register for unemployment compensation. I'd never seen unemployed people face to face before. These were not statistics; they were human beings and they were all out of work (quoted in Rohe 2006, p. 228).

Briggs describes the moment as "a life-altering experience." Returning to College Park to complete his undergraduate program, Briggs made a decision to concentrate on labor economics. As he explained in an interview in 2006, "It is the one sub-field of economics that deals directly with people and their wellbeing" (quoted in Rohe 2006, p. 228).

Within a year, Briggs was back in Michigan. This time, he was a graduate student at Michigan State University in East Lansing. Senator John F. Kennedy came to Michigan State during the 1960 presidential campaign and delivered an inspirational speech from the steps of the Student Union Building. "I was there, probably not more than 30 feet from him," Briggs recalls.

A short time later, President Kennedy called on Americans to serve their country—and public-service television advertisements suggested college teaching as one important avenue of service. "It may sound very idealistic today," says Briggs, "but I decided to answer Kennedy's challenge by becoming a college teacher. I have never regretted it" (quoted in Rohe 2006, p. 230).

Today, Briggs is an Emeritus Professor of Industrial and Labor Relations at Cornell University in Ithaca, New York. He began his teaching career while still a graduate student at Michigan State and then moved on to full-time positions at The University of Texas at Austin (1964–1978) and Cornell University (since 1978).[1] In Austin, he received two coveted teaching awards, and there and at Cornell, Briggs shared with countless students his passion for human resource economics and public policy.[2]

This book honors Briggs's professional contributions. Most of the volume's contributors, including this editor, first encountered Briggs in the classroom, either at Texas or Cornell. That is appropriate, of course, because despite his tremendous productivity as a scholar and extensive involvement as a policy analyst, he has always viewed himself as a teacher. Yet the book would be incomplete without contributions from his colleagues as well, and the pages that follow include one chapter by a university colleague who collaborated with Briggs on a number of labor economics projects and another by a professional associate specializing in immigration research.

ECONOMICS FOR THE REAL WORLD

Chapters 2 and 3 examine the development and contours of Briggs's institutional labor economics. Before preparing Chapter 2, William P. Curington, who was inspired to become an economist by Briggs, turned the tables on his University of Texas professor and engaged Briggs in a series of interviews to explore his influences. The resulting chapter traces Briggs's intellectual development from College Park to Ithaca. A number of important influences appear at each stop along the way, including Alan G. Gruchy, a major contributor to the institutionalist tradition; Charles C. Killingsworth, who introduced Briggs (his teaching assistant) and the nation to structural unemployment in the early 1960s; and Ray Marshall, Briggs's Texas colleague and research collaborator. Yet we discover that Briggs also learned from his students. Indeed, it was his Mexican-American students that encouraged Briggs's study of rural labor markets and U.S.–Mexico border issues, which led to his research focus on immigration policy.

Chapter 3—written by the editor, a student of Briggs at Cornell—continues to highlight Briggs's real-world economics. It traces and outlines Briggs's conception of a policy-oriented, human resource economics (HRE) that emerged in the United States and other industrial democracies just after World War II. This HRE received considerable attention from economists and national policymakers for about two decades, until its associated policies were put on the fiscal chopping block during the Reagan–Bush era—and then, due to federal deficit concerns, largely ignored during the Clinton era and beyond (Greider 1981; Thomas 1997).

My chapter shows that, even when the political winds were solidly against him, Briggs continued to forcefully make the case for a revival of active human resource development initiatives. Briggs argued that the nation would likely "pay a high price" for its failure to support human resource development (Briggs 1987, p. 1218), and looking back at a decades-long trend of rising worker insecurity and inequality, it is difficult to disagree with him (Whalen 2008). Moreover, while the United States dragged its feet, China and a number of other nations sought to advance by securing their position as a "knowledge" economy (Grewal et al. 2002; Kao 2007, pp. 83–91).

At the time I am writing this introduction in early 2009, a new U.S. presidential administration is coming into office in the wake of a campaign that gave renewed attention to human resource development. Thus, there is some reason to be hopeful. Yet it remains to be seen whether President Barack Obama and his team will succeed at revitalizing U.S. human resource policies.

IMMIGRATION POLICY

Chapters 4 through 7 are devoted, at least in part, to some aspect of immigration. Philip L. Martin, a distinguished scholar in the field of labor migration, opens the section with a broad examination of the dimensions and impacts of contemporary international migration. Topics addressed include the factors contributing to immigration, government efforts to manage it, and trends in the international migration to the United States. Special attention is given to immigration's labor-market effects and to policy trade-offs. As Martin indicates in the introduction to his essay, its topics "are among those that figure most prominently in Briggs's policy-oriented writings."

Larry Nackerud, another of Briggs's students at Cornell, focuses on political refugee and asylee policy. Noting that Briggs wanted immigration policy to be driven by three considerations—economic accountability for each entry decision into the United States, neutrality with respect to political ideology, and societal equity—Nackerud considers the extent to which this is possible. Nackerud is not as sanguine as Briggs about the possibility, or even the desirability, of using these three considerations as a foundation for policy, but he offers a sympathetic assessment of the Briggs position and makes a number of constructive suggestions that advance the position by means of clarification and extension.

Ernesto Cortés Jr. is the only contributor to the volume who has devoted himself entirely to the world of practice, rather than to a career in the academy. For most of the more than 40 years since he attended Briggs's University of Texas classes, Cortés has worked to build community organizations, especially in the Southwestern United States. Still, as Cortés writes, Briggs's insights echo in his work every day—and Briggs's economics has always been about moving beyond theory and into the realm of action and concrete problem solving.

Cortés addresses two subjects—training and immigration. In discussing training, Cortés explains that his organizations have relied on Briggs's ideas and input when establishing labor-market training intermediaries. In discussing immigration, Cortés outlines a policy stance that diverges from the one held by Briggs, yet he acknowledges that it still remains fully in the Briggs tradition, which gives special attention to unintended consequences and issues of practical policy implementation.

Among the points made by Cortés is that immigration policy should be considered as part of a broader discussion that includes attention to international economic-development policies. This view is developed further in Chapter 7 by James T. Peach. According to Peach, who was also a student of Briggs in Austin, traditional approaches to immigration should be augmented by policies that accelerate economic development within migrant-sending nations. Such policies would be not only compatible with the Briggs immigration strategy, but as Peach notes, also consistent with Briggs's recommendations for over three decades.

LABOR MARKETS

Chapters 8 and 9 examine labor markets and worker well-being. Marta Tienda—who audited Briggs's courses in Texas and co-edited a book with him in the 1980s—teams up with V. Joseph Hotz, Avner Ahituv, and Michelle Bellessa Frost to report on the labor-market experience of women in Chapter 8.

Tienda and her colleagues study the education and employment patterns of young black, white, and Hispanic women in the United States between the late 1970s and early 1990s. (At the start of the period examined, the women were aged 13–16, and at the end of the period, they were aged 28–31.) The chapter sheds light on how women's investments in education and work experience—and their family formation choices—vary along racial and ethnic lines. It also considers the implications of these differences for workforce behavior and adult wage inequality, as well as the sensitivity of young women's labor-force decisions to local labor-market conditions.

A notable finding of Tienda, Hotz, Ahituv, and Frost is that young women enjoyed a substantial wage return for acquiring college degrees but none for completing high school or obtaining its GED equivalent. As they note, this is consistent with numerous studies indicating rising returns on skill during the 1980s. That finding—and another that suggests life-cycle earnings are optimized by "maximizing formal schooling before acquiring work experience"—is also consistent with Briggs's longstanding belief in the importance of human resource development in an age of increasing technological complexity and economic internationalization.

In Chapter 9, Seth D. Harris, a Briggs student from Cornell, focuses on the employment of people with disabilities after the enactment of the Americans with Disabilities Act of 1990. Harris suggests the importance of human capital investments as well, but he also underscores another theme of Briggs's writing and teaching: the persistence of discrimination and the need for government regulation to ensure equal employment opportunity for all workers. By unmasking the faulty assumptions that have misdirected the debate over the economics of workplace disabilities accommodation, Harris seeks to get the debate back on the right track to include attention to matters such as educational opportunities and attainment, job discrimination, and the availability of employee health insurance.

PUBLIC POLICY

The book concludes with two chapters that look at broad and vital parts of the public policy terrain. In Chapter 10, Ray Marshall, Briggs's Texas colleague and collaborator, focuses on the need to modernize the nation's education and workforce-development policies and institutions. The discussion is based on his work with the bipartisan Commission on the Skills of the American Workforce in the late 1980s and the New Commission on the Skills of the American Workforce in the mid 2000s. Marshall calls for far-reaching, systemic changes in the nation's learning systems in the face of what he describes as serious and growing economic difficulties that threaten the nation's ability to restore broadly shared prosperity. His chapter underlines the important human resource problems and policies that Briggs has been discussing for decades and further confirms Briggs's prediction that the country would pay a high price for inaction.

Robert W. Glover and Christopher T. King, who both studied with Briggs in Austin, bring the volume to a close in Chapter 11 by complementing Marshall's contribution with an examination of existing labor-market policies and a discussion of the new policies that are required to address the current situation. Like Briggs and Marshall, Glover and King stress the need to rethink U.S. labor-market policy for a global economy. They focus on a new direction for such policy, one involving sectoral approaches that connect workforce- and economic-development strategies at the regional level.

PEOPLE AND THEIR WELL-BEING

It has been just over a half-century since Vernon Briggs's life-altering experience in downtown Detroit. In the intervening years, he has in turn altered the lives of many others and, by example, has even encouraged some to follow his footsteps into a career of service through college-level teaching. Economics is often criticized for being overly abstract and out of touch with the real world, but as long as there are labor economists drawn to the profession by Briggs and others like him, there will always be at least one sub-field that "deals directly with people and their well-being."

Notes

1. Briggs also taught at Michigan State University (as a visiting associate professor) in the summer of 1969 and at the John F. Kennedy School of Government at Harvard University (in the Institute for Employment and Training) during the summers from 1972 to 1981 (Briggs 2008).
2. Briggs won a teaching excellence award from the University of Texas student yearbook in 1971 and another from the university's College of Arts and Sciences and the Ex-Students Association in 1974 (Briggs 2008). Consistent with his modest nature, Briggs never mentioned these awards (or having been elected student government president as a senior at the University of Maryland) during extensive interviews with William P. Curington as part of this book project. It should also be noted there is really no need to add "and public policy" when discussing human resource economics from Briggs's vantage point; as I discuss later in this volume, public policy is an inherent part of his human resource economics.

References

Briggs, Vernon M. 1987. "Human Resource Development and the Formulation of National Economic Policy." *Journal of Economic Issues* 21(3): 1207–1240.

———. 2008. "Curriculum Vitae for Professor Vernon M. Briggs Jr." Ithaca, NY: School of Industrial and Labor Relations, Cornell University. http://www.ilr.cornell.edu/directory/vmb2/download/vita/vita_vmb2.pdf (accessed June 26, 2009).

Greider, William. 1981. "The Education of David Stockman." *Atlantic* 247(12): 27–54. http://www.theatlantic.com/politics/budget/stockman.htm (accessed February 14, 2009).

Grewal, Bhajan, Lan Xue, Peter Sheehan, and Fiona Sun. 2002. *China's Future in the Knowledge Economy: Engaging the New World*. Melbourne: Centre for Strategic Economic Studies, Victoria University of Technology.

Kao, John. 2007. *Innovation Nation: How America Is Losing Its Innovation Edge, Why It Matters, and What We Can Do to Get It Back*. New York: Free Press.

Rohe, John F. 2006. "Living Standards, Scarce Resources and Immigration: An Interview with Labor Economist Vernon M. Briggs Jr." *Social Contract* 16(4): 227–236.

Thomas, Evan. 1997. "Inside the Beltway but Out of the Loop." *New York Times*, April 27, 7:8. http://www.nytimes.com/books/97/04/27/reviews/970427.27thomast.html (accessed February 14, 2009).

Whalen, Charles J. 2008. "Post-Keynesian Institutionalism and the Anxious Society." In *Alternative Institutional Structures: Evolution and Impact*, Sandra S. Batie and Nicholas Mercuro, eds. London: Routledge, pp. 273–299.

2
Vernon Briggs:
Real-World Labor Economist

William P. Curington
University of Arkansas

Vernon Briggs stepped into a wastebasket and launched my career as a labor economist. In the spring of 1969, I was sleepwalking through the undergraduate economics program at the University of Texas and sitting in Dr. Briggs's labor economics class. He was vigorously making a point when his misstep off the small classroom stage produced a roar of laughter but did not break his train of thought. He woke me up; I thought, "Man, I want to be as passionate about my life's work as this guy."[1]

When I earned an "A" in the course, not the dominant grade on my transcript at that time, Briggs sent a letter congratulating me and inviting me to visit during his office hours. This is the only such letter I ever have received in my academic career. When I did visit the next semester, conversations led to discussion of the graduate program at Michigan State University's School of Labor and Industrial Relations, and I was on my way.

My story is not unique. Briggs was an important influence on many students. Therefore, it seems appropriate to begin this chapter's discussion of his career by turning the clock back a bit and focusing on the people who had a significant influence on him. It was with this intent that I initiated a series of conversations with him in May 2007. We started with a discussion of his years as a student at the University of Maryland and Michigan State University, and then we focused on his work as a faculty member at the University of Texas and Cornell University. This chapter is based on those discussions (Curington 2007).

MARYLAND AND INSTITUTIONAL ECONOMICS

Briggs was born in 1937 in Washington, D.C., and grew up in the Washington suburbs of Silver Spring and Bethesda, Maryland. After high school, he enrolled in the College of Business and Public Administration at the University of Maryland, from which he received a bachelor's degree in economics in 1959. Asked to reflect on his undergraduate experience, Briggs focused on two economics professors whom he found "extremely influential," Dudley Dillard and Alan Gruchy.[2]

Dillard, who was chairman of the university's economics department at the time, taught Briggs's first economics course. It was a yearlong, first-year course on European and United States economic history. The course emphasized the rise of the market system and a historical perspective on the role of government, business, and labor.

Dillard's course indicated the importance of history as a part of the field of economics. "In many ways, economics should be guided by what historically has happened and does happen, not by what is theoretically supposed to happen," says Briggs, drawing on Dillard's core message. "Since then, I have always thought that the proper way to study economics is to take a year of economic history during your beginning year. Dillard was an enormous influence on my view that economics and history are linked."

Even more influential than Dillard was Alan Gruchy, with whom Briggs had three courses. Gruchy was an institutional economist, who introduced Briggs to "a great perspective" rarely found in economics departments these days. "The vital role that institutions play has almost been factored out of the equation in most economics courses—as has economic history." In Gruchy's "Comparative Economic Systems" course, Briggs was introduced to "a critical analysis of neoclassical, mainstream economics as well as of socialist and communist systems of economic organization."

In Gruchy's "Modern Economic Thought" course, Briggs was exposed to the institutionalist writings of Thorstein B. Veblen, John R. Commons, John M. Clark, Wesley C. Mitchell, Rexford G. Tugwell, John Kenneth Galbraith, and Clarence E. Ayres, all of whom were critical of mainstream economics due to "its predilection for theoretical, abstract reasoning rather than dealing with real policy issues." The institutionalist perspective made an indelible impression on Briggs. "My career has been all about trying to apply economics to real issues and trying to deal with public policy responses."

In Gruchy's "National Economic Planning" course, Briggs studied the type of planning found in the Scandinavian market economies. "You can have free, civilized societies in which there is planning that sets priorities for an economy to achieve," says Briggs. "When you seek to set priorities, you really are planning. This perspective influences my thinking to this day."

In short, Dillard's course pointed Briggs in the direction of economics, while Gruchy's masterful teaching "locked in" his decision to major in the field. In the early 1990s, Briggs was asked to speak at memorial services for both professors. The remarks demonstrate the long-lasting influence of these two undergraduate influences (Briggs 1990, 1993). Reflecting on Gruchy, for example, Briggs wrote: "It was the power of his ideas, the breadth of his knowledge, and the manner of his delivery that held us in his sway—then and since" (Briggs 1990, p. 9).

MICHIGAN STATE AND LABOR ECONOMICS

Briggs became interested in labor economics after seeing thousands of unemployed people on a 1958 trip to his college roommate's hometown of Detroit, Michigan. They filled the sidewalk for several blocks in a wait to register for unemployment compensation. "Of all the areas of economics, I thought that labor issues were the most important because labor economics was the one area that most directly involved the welfare of human beings."

Dillard advised studying in Michigan, which would allow the chance to study near an industrial environment. "I had never been around big factories or unions or anything like that, so I applied to Michigan State University (MSU)." Briggs believes Dillard gave him excellent advice. "Part of the process of becoming a scholar is more than mastery of a technique and theory. It's beginning to have some genuine feeling for the subject matter . . . I was able to begin to understand how big business, big labor, and big government functioned."

At MSU, Briggs had an "outstanding" doctoral committee. Charles Killingsworth, a professor of both economics and labor and industrial relations, served as the committee's chair. The other members were John Henderson, Abba Lerner, and Walter Adams. Henderson taught the history of economic thought, which Briggs sees as an essential area of study because it provides "the intellectual foundation" for the entire field. Lerner, a student of John Maynard Keynes and one of the great macroeconomists of the twentieth century, taught economic theory. Adams, "one of the most inspiring teachers you could ever imagine," taught industrial organization.

Briggs recalls that Lerner was "world-class" as both a theoretician and a professor. Lerner's classes were not a battleground for disputes between various schools of thought over the way the world actually operates. Instead, he offered philosophy-oriented courses that probed economic principles and assumptions. "All of his courses were like that—about a theoretical world of markets, economic decisions, and resource allocation. I had four wonderful graduate courses with him in macro- and microeconomics."

Adams coordinated the graduate program while Briggs was at MSU. He used the Socratic form of teaching, which gave him a reputation for being "rough and tough in class," but he also had a gentle heart. "The students could always tell he had our well-being first in mind."[3]

In addition to majoring in economics, Briggs had a minor field in twentieth century U.S. history with Madison Kuhn from the MSU history department. "I don't think economics doctoral students have a minor field anymore or, if they do, it would probably be in statistics or mathematics."[4] Consistent with the perspective he acquired as an undergraduate, Briggs explains his decision to study history as follows: "History is a check on theory in that it gives you real data and real events to try to explain . . . You deal with what actually happens when you have wars, plagues, oil boycotts, strikes, and all the kind of things that make studying economics so important and interesting to me."

It was a combination of Briggs's interest in public policy and some good fortune that led to Killingsworth becoming the chair of his dissertation committee. In the 1962–1963 academic year, when Briggs was scheduled to take his doctoral exams and select his thesis topic, he was assigned to serve as Killingsworth's grading assistant. "That was probably the only time in his career that Killingsworth taught the economics department's introductory labor course for the whole year," says Briggs. "It was taught in a large lecture format of around 300 students in each of the fall, winter, and spring quarters." Briggs was the class's only graduate assistant.

Briggs recalls that Killingsworth's course was a blur between labor economics and industrial relations, which is the way all labor courses used to be taught in economics departments. "You were expected to know not just microeconomic theory pertaining to labor markets but also labor history, labor law, collective bargaining, and all of the institutional applications of public policy to the labor market."

The timing of the assignment to Killingsworth's course was fortunate because it came in the same year that the structural unemployment issue exploded onto the national agenda. The administration of President John F. Kennedy had proposed tax cuts to stimulate demand. Republican legislators vigorously opposed the cuts because they believed the result would be an unbalanced budget.[5] Killingsworth was the leading critic of the administration's tax-cut proposals from the left—not because he thought they could be harmful, just that they "were likely to be insufficient."

Killingsworth's criticism of the tax cuts stemmed from a concern over the effects of structural economic change associated with the coming of the computer, which he saw as having the potential to cause revolutionary labor-market changes. He argued that coping with such a major impact on labor markets would require policies to help the supply of labor adjust to the coming shift in demand for labor. The structural change that Killingsworth anticipated involved the demand for a more highly skilled and educated workforce, combined with fewer opportunities for unskilled, poorly educated workers.

In those days, "there were probably only 100 computers in the entire United States" and few students had even seen one.[6] Nevertheless, Killingsworth insisted that education, training, labor mobility, and antidiscrimination policies were crucial to dealing with the coming structural shift. "He was a 'real' supply-side economist," says Briggs.

Shortly after President Kennedy's assassination, the nation got both the tax cuts and employment policies. The latter—called manpower programs—were enacted as part of Lyndon Johnson's "War on Poverty." There was also federal aid to education, including the Elementary and Secondary School Act and the Higher Education Act. This federal involvement in education is often taken for granted today, "but these were enormous issues in the 1960s because there was no precedent for them."

In the midst of this major policy controversy, Briggs became well acquainted with Killingsworth and acquired valuable teaching experience. Regarding Killingsworth, Briggs recalls:

> The class was way down on the southern part of the campus, so I would meet him at the classroom before class and then he'd drive me back to the economics department after class. That gave us a chance to talk before and after class three times a week. It was an opportunity few graduate students have with their professor. So I got to know him quite well.

This relationship led to Killingsworth's supervision of Briggs's dissertation and provided the foundation for Briggs's teaching career:

> Over the course of the year, he had to miss several classes to testify or give advice to policymakers in Washington. On these occasions he would let me do the teaching. That's how I got started teaching a junior-senior-level labor economics course that incorporated many of Killingsworth's ideas. I would have to write the substitute lectures, but I knew what he wanted to be said.

Looking back, Briggs considers Killingsworth "a brilliant master of the issues of those changing times." Briggs explains:

> I think everyone now recognizes how the structure of the economy has changed so dramatically. The structural shift has been toward mounting employment in the service sector and a rapid decline in manufacturing and mining employment...Killingsworth was one of the first to predict this massive shift in the economy and to propose policy remedies. He was light years ahead of the profession, and I don't think he's ever gotten the credit that he deserves. He took a lot of criticism in those days, but by the 1970s, most people began to realize that he was right.

In time, economists, policymakers, and the public began to recognize "the importance of human resource policies as a necessary part of the nation's arsenal of economic policies."

Killingsworth's influence stuck with Briggs throughout his career. One stream of influence leads into the classroom: "Over the years, my students have heard a lot of Killingsworth's ideas, and they probably gave me a lot of the credit for things I learned from him firsthand." Another channel leads to professional service, especially Briggs's involvement in the National Council on Employment Policy. Killingsworth was an early member, along with labor economists such as George P. Shultz, John T. Dunlop, Ray Marshall, Juanita Kreps, and Eli Ginzberg. Briggs became an associate member of the Council in the late 1960s, along other young economists, including Michael Piore, Peter Doeringer, and Orley Ashenfelter. He became a full member of the Council in 1977 and served as chair of the organization from 1985 to 1987.

Despite Killingsworth's impact on Briggs's thinking, Briggs's dissertation did not deal with structural unemployment. "It was a study of strike subsidies, which was a straight collective bargaining issue at the time."[7] The human resource economics that Killingsworth was teaching his undergraduates was so new that it had not yet been incorporated into the graduate labor courses. Briggs's doctoral thesis led to his first two academic articles, one on an employers' mutual aid pact in the airline industry and the other on the railroad industry's "strike insurance plan" (Briggs 1965, 1967).

TEXAS AND LABOR MARKET STUDIES

Briggs began his first full-time teaching job, with the University of Texas, at the start of the 1964–1965 academic year.[8] The Texas department chair, Carey Thompson, was looking for someone in the labor area because Ray Marshall, the only labor economist at Texas at the time, was going on a two-year leave of absence. Thompson contacted Briggs on the recommendation of Roger Bowlby, who studied economics in Austin and taught labor law at MSU. Although there were other candidates, Briggs believes he was chosen in part because he had "institutionalist training going back to Maryland." He adds: "Texas was an institutionalist department at the time, a real center of it. Clarence Ayres [one of the nation's leading institutionalists] was still actively teaching in the department."

In each semester during his first year at Texas, Briggs taught a labor course, a principles course, and an intermediate micro-theory course. He was assigned the intermediate microeconomics course because he had studied with Lerner, who was widely considered "one of the great gods of economic theory." In the spring of 1965, he began to teach a course called "Manpower Economics and Public Policy"—one of the earliest courses in the nation on human resource economics. It was, of course, "what Killingsworth was working on all these years. I was continuing his tradition with this course," Briggs explains.

"Manpower Economics and Public Policy" examined the importance of the "employability" of the nation's labor force. Topics included education, training, labor mobility, labor-market information, and antidiscrimination policies: "All the things which were now becoming so prominent a part of President Lyndon Johnson's 'Great Society' program—and I was right in Lyndon Johnson's backyard," says Briggs. "It was an exciting time."

When Marshall returned to Austin, Briggs collaborated with him on a variety of labor-market projects. "Ray Marshall was one of the great influences on me . . . And he and I made a wonderful team. We wrote several books and articles together."[9]

Their first project involved developing a national apprenticeship outreach program. Apprenticeship—which combines classroom instruction and hands-on experience—seemed like the ideal form of training for skilled labor, and yet it was an exclusionary system. "It was an enormous civil rights issue. The labor movement had supported the Civil Rights bill, but most craft unions were simply closed to black members," says Briggs. With a U.S. Department of Labor grant, he and Marshall showed how the apprenticeship system could be retained in a nondiscriminatory manner.[10]

The key was reaching out to find people who could meet an apprenticeship program's qualifications but who had no idea that these job opportunities were available. "Simply saying 'we don't discriminate anymore' wasn't going to cut it," Briggs explains. He adds: "Bobby

Kennedy, who was a senator at the time, praised the study as the most worthwhile study he'd ever seen from academia, dealing with a real problem and coming up with a real solution." In the end, the labor movement endorsed the program and the federal government financed its operation nationwide.

Briggs and Marshall then worked on studies of African-American employment in the South. One project looked at the labor market in Houston, Texas. "Houston had a very tight labor market at the time, but there was no improvement in the economic status of black Americans," Briggs recalls. His conclusion was that tight labor markets alone would not change racial patterns of employment or eradicate job discrimination. Policy intervention was essential: "Not only to see to it that antidiscrimination policies were enforced, but also to deal with the fact that many blacks needed to have the educational skills that unequal schools and traditions of discrimination had denied them for over a century." This research caused the Equal Employment Opportunity Commission to convene public hearings in Houston in June 1970, and the testimony reinforced the findings and conclusions of Marshall and Briggs.[11]

Briggs was soon teaching undergraduates, graduate students, and union members on a regular basis. "Labor unions often needed speakers to come in to do training sessions. Well, it was either Ray or me, or both of us . . . Quite often they wanted Ray, but he was so busy that he started sending me—some people even began to think I was Ray. They would write an invitation letter to him and I'd show up." Despite the heavy demands on his time, Briggs considers the work with unionists a valuable experience: "I was actually seeing people who were doing negotiating, being involved with arbitration, and dealing with labor law and the rest of the things you just talk about in the classroom."

At the same time, Briggs's students encouraged him to study the South's rural labor markets. He recalls:

> In those early years at Texas, when I was working on this apprenticeship study, a number of Chicano students I had in class were asking why I didn't talk about issues of Texas and Mexican Americans. And of course, I didn't know anything about either . . . Several of these Chicano students were instrumental in introducing me to Cesar Chavez when he came through Texas on his way down to organize farm workers in the spring and summer of 1966 . . . My

students were instrumental in getting me involved with the Farm
Workers' Assistance Committee that year.[12]

The 1966 struggle centered on an organizational strike at La Casita
Farms in rural Starr County, located on the Mexico border. The Assistance Committee gathered money or food in Austin during the week,
and then on the weekends someone would drive it down to the Rio
Grande Valley. "One day it came my turn to drive the food down and
to spend the weekend in Starr County . . . On a Saturday morning, I
went to the border, and I saw buses picking up strikebreakers, driving
them to La Casita Farms and then taking them right through the picket
lines. I knew immediately that the strike was lost," Briggs recalls.[13]
The experience impressed upon him the need "to learn about the border
and influence of the border on the labor supply of South Texas." Upon
returning home, Briggs began to include immigration and border issues
in his manpower course.

In the early 1970s, Briggs participated in a three-year study of the
Starr County labor market as part of a rural labor-markets consortium
project with three other southern universities. He found that the rural
labor supply was in constant surplus, largely due to border commuters and immigration, which prevented most wages from rising beyond
the legal minimum. In fact, says Briggs, "Even with these low wage
levels, there was a lot of corruption by employers demanding wage
kickbacks if you wanted to get a job. If they paid the minimum wage,
they expected people to kick back 20 cents an hour as a reward for being hired." His University of Texas work on this subject culminated in
a 1977 book, *The Chicano Worker*, coauthored with two professors at
UCLA, Fred Schmidt and Walter Fogel. It was one of the first books to
address the topic (Briggs, Fogel, and Schmidt 1977).

The Chicano Worker represents a beginning as well as an ending.
"My interest in immigration started with this work, and the issue has
become the dominant concern of my work in the last couple of decades," Briggs observes. "I gradually got more and more interested in
immigration primarily because of my interest in the economic status
of Chicanos and in trying to understand why it didn't seem to make
any difference whether most of them had any education or training or
not." For those not attending college, it did not matter whether they
completed high school or dropped out; their wage would still be at just

about the legal minimum. "The whole human capital model was being refuted because you couldn't prove that there was any real reward to education or training for most of this rural workforce."[14]

CORNELL AND IMMIGRATION POLICY

Briggs moved to Cornell University's New York State School of Industrial and Labor Relations in time to begin the fall semester of 1978. It was not easy to leave Austin, and he still misses Texas. There were, however, some frustrations and attractions that contributed to the decision to move northward.

One frustration was an ongoing conflict that the Texas faculty and students had with Frank Erwin, chairman of the university's Board of Regents. Erwin "constantly harangued the faculty" and broke up the College of Arts and Sciences in 1970, leading to the departure of John Silber, who had been dean of the College, and many prominent faculty members. "There were also constant confrontations between the students and the Regents over a large range of issues," Briggs recalls.

Even more important were the attractions associated with Cornell. The flagship institution in labor and industrial relations had invited him to teach the human resource economics course he pioneered at Texas, provided him access to outstanding research facilities, and offered him an opportunity to teach elective courses such as immigration policy. "I probably never would have gotten the chance to teach a course in immigration at Texas" because the department was spread so thin. In fact, when the Cornell offer came, Ray Marshall was serving in Washington, D.C., as Secretary of Labor in the Carter administration. "I envisioned that he wasn't coming back for eight years . . . So, when the Cornell offer came I thought maybe I should take the chance and go." Looking back, he concludes the decision was a good one; "I've had a wonderful career at Cornell."

For a number of years, Briggs continued to address human resource issues such as youth employment, apprenticeship, and public service employment, but his research gradually shifted to a focus almost exclusively on immigration. "Immigration is one of those fields that you can never learn enough about," he explains. "It's so complicated with illegal immigration, legal immigration, refugees, asylum seekers, border commuters, non-immigrant temporary workers, and the list goes on." While human resource economics remained the mainstay of his teaching, Briggs added a course called "Immigration and the American Labor Force" to his regular course offerings starting in 1981.

Briggs became an emeritus professor at Cornell in 2006, but he continues to follow and write about U.S. immigration policy debates. Indeed, he believes the topic is perhaps more important than ever. Briggs explained:

> Immigration has an enormous influence on the labor force in the United States, and it's got an enormous influence on the nation's future in a sense that now we're not getting much growth from demography anymore. The "baby boom" generation is heading into retirement and the movement of women into the labor market is probably not going to go up much more. So the major source of growth of the labor force is going to be from immigration.

Looking at immigration reform bills on the horizon in 2007, Briggs was concerned that low-wage workers would be adversely affected by the proposed legislation:

> We have about a third to a half of the growth of the labor force right now coming from immigration—and the percentage is going to go up enormously should any of the pending immigration reform bills pass, with all the amnesties and the family reunification that will ensue. There will be an enormous growth in size of the labor force, and most of the new entrants are going to be poorly educated, poorly skilled, and non-English speaking job seekers. This is going to be a nightmare for public policy to deal with should this legislation pass.

Briggs wants an immigration policy "that's consistent and congruent with the national interests." That means decisions would be driven by employment-based considerations—labor-market needs and immigrant skills—rather than the recent emphasis on family unification. And he is "not very optimistic" that Congress will move in this direction. Briggs believes that immigration policy and immigration reform efforts are so heavily shaped by political expedience that there's little chance for much progress in low-wage markets. "The policy is being formed by special interests seeking cheap labor or trying to get immigration or amnesty priority for their particular groups."[15]

LEGACY OF TEACHING AND SCHOLARSHIP

Since Briggs is quite modest, I knew he would be reluctant to say much about his legacy. Still, Briggs mentioned two areas where he hopes he has been successful. One is in the realm of university teaching. Recalling Dillard, Gruchy, Killingsworth, Lerner, Marshall, Grubbs, and the other professors and colleagues that influenced his own thinking, Briggs said he hopes his legacy as a teacher would be "first and foremost." His primary aim, Briggs says, has been "to stimulate minds like the people who stimulated mine when I was a student . . . [and] to inspire others as I was inspired."

The other area he mentioned is that of applied research. "I hope I have mastered my subject matter and done my research in a way that is not just for the advancement of my own career, but also for the advancement public policy," Briggs says. He adds:

> I've always tried to select subjects that were important to the public and to the nation. For me, that's what economics is about. It's an operational field that should be dealing with the real world and real world issues, and coming up with public policies that can be actually implemented. I have sought to address public policies that have an influence on the nation's welfare.

True to form, however, Briggs concluded that his ability to succeed as a teacher and real-world labor economist would be for others to judge. Well, let there be no mistake: as a former student and fellow economist, I can report that Vernon Briggs has not merely succeeded; he has also set a high bar for those he inspired.[16]

Notes

1. While I am most comfortable addressing him as Dr. Briggs (during the course of this project, I have had to force myself to call him Vernon), subsequent references to Vernon Briggs in this chapter yield to the conventions of academic writing and refer to him as Briggs. I would like to thank Dr. Briggs for helpful comments and edits of the interview transcript, the Sam M. Walton College of Business for financial support, and Charles Whalen for the opportunity to participate in this volume. Any remaining errors are my own. A copy of the full transcript has been deposited in the Kheel Center for Labor-Management Documentation and Archives, located at the Martin P. Catherwood Library, School of Industrial and Labor Relations, Cornell University, Ithaca, New York.
2. Unless otherwise indicated, all quotes in this chapter are Briggs's remarks in response to the interview conducted by this author in May 2007 (Curington 2007).
3. The affection MSU economics graduate students had for Adams was particularly evident when he took a leave of absence to serve in the administration of President John F. Kennedy. "We were petrified when he went to Washington in January 1961," says Briggs, who also recalls that upon his return, Adams said, "The duty of a professor is to profess in the classroom." Since Briggs holds the same view, it is not surprising that he and Adams became great friends over the later years.
4. "We had to have the statistics courses in those days too," Briggs adds. "Econometrics was not an independent field of study as it has become today. You had to take statistics courses as part of your doctoral program, but they weren't considered to be a field . . . I had to take four courses in statistics taught by the statistics department, not the economics department." In addition to statistics and a field outside economics, Briggs's doctoral degree required four fields within economics (his were economic theory, labor economics, industrial organization, and the history of economic thought) and two foreign languages (his were Spanish and German).
5. Reflecting on the Republican opposition to Kennedy's proposal, Briggs says, "It is ironic that every Republican since Ronald Reagan has based their rationale for cutting taxes to stimulate the economy on the Kennedy experience." (Of course, the Kennedy tax cuts were enacted three months after his death.)
6. The computer at MSU, constructed in 1956, "occupied a 25 foot by 30 foot room on the fifth floor of the Electrical Engineering Building" (Ball 2006).
7. The strike subsidy was a defensive device that companies used in strike-prone sectors of the economy, such as the airline, railroad, and newspaper industries. The tendency was for unions to strike one employer and then use the settlement as a "whipsaw" to get the same benefits from the industry's other companies. In response, companies devised agreements that provided assistance to the company that was shut down.
8. Briggs defended his dissertation in 1965.
9. Regarding Ray Marshall's influence on his thinking, Briggs says:

> He was a true pioneer in the study of the economics of discrimination and a real critic of Gary Becker's theoretical propositions. Ray dealt with dis-

crimination as it was—noting that it is often institutionalized and covert in its manifestations. It often involves the lack of the opportunity to be prepared for jobs and the lack of information and all the rest of the really hardcore issues that Becker's thesis ignores. Becker's thesis is a pretty narrow definition of discrimination: only if people are equally productive but paid differently can there be discrimination. It is more a theory of wages than a theory of discrimination.

10. On the decision of Briggs and Marshall to address labor-market discrimination, Briggs says, "One thing we both had in common was an understanding of segregation, discrimination, and the South. He was from Mississippi . . . I grew up in the suburbs of Washington, D.C., when it was a totally segregated city as were all the public institutions in Maryland . . . We knew first-hand how terrible and cruel that was, how unfair it was."

11. In addition to Marshall, the other "enormous influence" on Briggs while at Texas was his economics-department colleague, Cliff (Clifton M.) Grubbs. Although Grubbs was hired to teach mathematical economics, he was mainly interested in how the economy of the West developed and how the United States had become such a technologically advanced society. As a result, Briggs had lengthy discussions with Grubbs that "fed right into the Killingsworth emphasis on computers and technology as guiding forces affecting the labor market." Grubbs was an outstanding teacher; after winning the highest teaching honors in Austin, he eventually received the Danforth prize, awarded to the finest college teacher in the nation. "He was a great inspiration to me about the importance of teaching and the importance of science and technology on the development of the American economy . . . Our families bought some land together in Colorado. We spent many summer evenings discussing issues from [his] reading lists." For remarks delivered at Grubbs's memorial service, see Briggs (1995).

12. Briggs adds that Chicano, not Hispanic or Mexican American, "was the preferred term at the time."

13. The strikebreakers lived in Mexico but were permanent resident aliens. They had "green cards" that permitted them to work in the United States. Briggs adds, "Technically, it is illegal to do this, but laws do not enforce themselves."

14. Briggs adds that the Kerner Commission (the National Advisory Commission on Civil Disorders) found that many African Americans had a similar labor-market experience in the nation's urban centers: "For those who didn't go on to college, it really didn't make any difference whether they stayed in high school or dropped out of school."

15. For Briggs, "It is very unfortunate that the recommendations of the Commission on Immigration Reform have never been followed." He explains:

> Barbara Jordan, who I got to know through my work in Houston back in the late 1960s when she was a Senator in the Texas legislature, chaired the commission in the 1990s. I testified before them several times and their recommendations are consistent with my views . . . However, today

you have massive immigration without any regard for the human capital endowments of the entrants.

16. For additional personal reflections on Briggs's influences and academic contributions, see Rohe (2006).

References

Ball, Katherine. 2006. "MSU Exhibit Showcases 50 Years of Computing at MSU." News release, October 12. East Lansing, MI: Michigan State University. http://computing.msu.edu/events/?m=200610 (accessed January 26, 2009).

Briggs, Vernon M. Jr. 1965. "The Mutual Aid Pact of the Airline Industry." *Industrial and Labor Relations Review* 19(1): 3–20.

———. 1967. "The Strike Insurance Plan of the Railroad Industry." *Industrial Relations* 6(2): 205–212.

———. 1990. "Allan G. Gruchy: Master Teacher of Undergraduate Economics." *Briggs Papers and Speeches*, Vol. 4, Paper No. 56. Ithaca, NY: Cornell University, School of Industrial and Labor Relations. http://digitalcommons.ilr.cornell.edu/briggsIV/1 (accessed January 26, 2009).

———. 1993. "Reflections on Dudley Dillard's Career." *Journal of Economic Issues* 27(2): 593–596.

———. 1995. "Colorado Clif." *Briggs Papers and Speeches*, Vol. 4, Paper No. 60. Ithaca, NY: Cornell University, School of Industrial and Labor Relations. http://digitalcommons.ilr.cornell.edu/briggsIV/5 (accessed January 26, 2009).

Briggs, Vernon M. Jr., Walter A. Fogel, and Fred H. Schmidt. 1977. *The Chicano Worker*. Austin, TX: University of Texas Press.

Curington, William P. 2007. "Interview with Vernon M. Briggs Jr." Copy deposited in the Kheel Center for Labor-Management Documentation and Archives, Martin P. Catherwood Library. Ithaca, NY: Cornell University, School of Industrial and Labor Relations.

Rohe, John F. 2006. "Living Standards, Scarce Resources, and Immigration." *The Social Contract* 16(4): 227–236.

3

The Human Resource Economics of Vernon Briggs

Charles J. Whalen
Utica College and Cornell University

According to a Cornell University Web site, Vernon M. Briggs Jr. came to that university's School of Industrial and Labor Relations in 1978 "as a professor who specializes in human resource economics and public policy" (Cornell University 2009). In fact, Briggs's research and teaching helped establish that specialty, which I will simply refer to as human resource economics (HRE) in recognition of the fact that public policy is already inherent in Briggs's conception of those words. HRE resides at the intersection of the academic fields of economics, industrial relations, and public affairs.

This chapter traces and explores Briggs's conception of HRE. It probes the history of economic thought for the intellectual roots of this area of specialization. It examines how HRE emerged to address the issues of economic growth, stabilization, and efficiency, and to contribute to the public discourse on matters of social equity, economic opportunity, and government regulation. It explains the clash between human capital theory and HRE. And it outlines Briggs's five dimensions of human resource development (HRD), which is his term for HRE that manifests itself in public policy; although Briggs developed his conceptualization decades ago, each dimension continues to warrant our attention.

I base the chapter largely on a combination of Briggs's writings (especially Briggs 1987a,b, 1996), biographical interviews (Curington 2007; Rohe 2006), and my notes to his fall 1980 course, "Public Policy and the Development of Human Resources" (later renamed "Human Resource Economics and Public Policy") (Briggs 1980).[1] However, my essay is also colored by countless opportunities to read his works, listen to him lecture, or talk with him informally over nearly 30 years.

SMITH, MARX, AND COMMONS

Briggs sees HRE as a policy-oriented field that considers human resources as a key—indeed, as *the* key—to economic progress and personal development. Adam Smith recognized that worker "skill, dexterity and judgment" is at the heart of the wealth of nations (Smith 1935, p. lvii). In fact, a labor theory of value is a cornerstone in the writings of classical economists from Smith to Karl Marx. Nevertheless, Briggs argues that HRE is a product of conditions found in post–World War II advanced industrial democracies.

Adam Smith's *The Wealth of Nations* came close to establishing HRE. According to Robert Heilbroner, "To see that labor, not nature, was the source of 'value' was one of Smith's greatest insights" (Heilbroner 1986, p. 49). Smith was even a pioneer in recognizing the harmful effects of routine work upon labor: "[T]he understandings of the greater part of men are necessarily formed by their ordinary employments. The man whose life is spent performing a few simple operations . . . generally becomes as stupid and ignorant as it is possible for a human creature to become" (Smith 1935, p. 734). Smith's solution? Public education, which would help counteract those effects (Smith 1935, pp. 734–738).

Yet Smith veered sharply away from Briggs's HRE by stressing the self-regulating nature of markets. Smith argued that self-interested individuals, engaging in market transactions, are led "by an invisible hand" to promote the interests of society as a whole (Smith 1935, p. 423). The result of that emphasis, intended or not, was an economic science that saw very little room for government intervention in economic life.

Marx also waded into territory that might have led to HRE, but taking a different turn than Smith, he concluded that "the proletarianization of the work force" would inevitably result in "a new socialist society" (Briggs 1987b, pp. 1208–1209). Briggs was not persuaded to follow Marx down that path. In the first chapter of the main textbook used in Briggs's fall 1980 course, "Public Policy and the Development of Human Resources," Garth L. Mangum writes, "Those who criticize American capitalism suggest no better alternative" (Mangum 1976, p. 27). Briggs was open to learning from other advanced industrialized nations, especially those in Western Europe (Briggs 1987a, p. 8; 1987b), but he definitely shared Mangum's preference for capitalism over socialism.

Looking for a "third way" between Smith and Marx, Briggs saw a foundation for HRE in the institutional economics of John R. Commons. It is from Commons's "Wisconsin School" brand of institutionalism that Briggs's HRE gets its reformist bent. Rejecting centralized planning, institutionalism seeks "pragmatic ways to address the inevitable human adjustment problems associated with the advances of industrialization." The aim is practical problem solving, "designed to achieve a 'reasonable' and harmonious society" (Briggs 1987b, p. 1209).

Institutionalism is sometimes called evolutionary economics. This is because institutionalists recognize that societal institutions are always in an "evolving" state. Thus, any economics based on an institutionalist foundation must aim to deal with changing circumstances in a dynamic setting (Briggs 2007). Moreover, evolutionary economists must accept that such changes place certain limitations on their work: Briggs approvingly quotes Edwin Witte—a student and colleague of Commons at the University of Wisconsin—who notes that, in dealing with public-policy questions, the institutionalists "seek not universal laws, but solutions applicable to a particular time, place and situation" (Briggs 1996, p. 373).

Although Commons provided HRE with an intellectual grounding, Briggs argues that economists did not begin to treat national public policies in this realm as a coherent and unified whole until the 1960s. In the opening paragraph to a 1987 article on HRD, Briggs writes, "One of the most insightful explanations for economic progress in industrialized nations during the last half of the twentieth century has been the recognition of 'human resources as the wealth of nations.'" He continues: "The notion has long enjoyed rhetorical appeal by politicians in democratic societies. But awareness that the principle has enormous implications for national and international well-being has essentially been a post–World War II phenomenon." In particular, Briggs maintains it was only then that many economists and policymakers began to realize that HRD could play a central role in "efforts to address such difficult issues as efficiency, equity, stabilization, and growth" (Briggs 1987b, p. 1207).

GROWTH, STABILIZATION, AND EFFICIENCY

Briggs's reference to "human resources as the wealth of nations" comes from a 1973 Frederick H. Harbison book with that title (Harbison 1973). However, one can trace this literature back to the 1964 book by Harbison and Charles A. Myers, *Education, Manpower, and Economic Growth*.[2] Harbison and Myers examined 75 countries on the basis of a composite HRD index and compared those findings with national indicators of economic development and growth. Their main conclusion was that, to make the greatest strides in terms of growth and development, each nation needs to develop and implement a coherent HRD strategy that sets clear priorities and integrates them into an overall national economic-development agenda (one that recognizes and reflects broad social goals, not merely narrow economic objectives) (Harbison and Myers 1964).

Decades after publication of *Education, Manpower, and Economic Growth*, Briggs continued to stress the link between human resources and aggregate economic growth. Citing the work of both Edward Denison and Anthony Carnavale, Briggs demonstrated in 1987 that "while economists in general and public policymakers in particular have focused upon physical capital as the explanation for [productivity increases and] long-term growth, it has actually been human resource development that has been the major contributor . . . It is a fact of economic life that deserves prominence in policy formulation" (Briggs 1987b, pp. 1213–1214).

While economists' attention to the link between human resources and growth can be traced to the 1960s, the place of human resources in economic stabilization took center stage in the 1970s. In 1971, Sar A. Levitan, Garth L. Mangum, and Ray Marshall produced a textbook entitled *Human Resources and Labor Markets: Labor and Manpower in the American Economy*. In one of its final chapters, the authors wrote, "Manpower expenditures and programs expanded continuously throughout the 1960s, but were applied without any countercyclical intent." Still, they concluded that such human resource policies could constructively play a more active role in addressing economic fluctuations (Levitan, Mangum, and Marshall 1972, p. 517).[3] In fact, another chapter in their book mentions the just-enacted Emergency Employment Act (EEA) of 1971, which did indeed seek to address the business cycle by offering temporary positions in periods of high unemployment (Levitan, Mangum, and Marshall 1972, p. 359).[4]

The nation's first experiment with countercyclical job creation since the Great Depression ran from 1971 to 1978, first under the EEA and then under the Comprehensive Employment and Training Act (CETA).[5] This direct job-creation initiative involved public-service employment: local governments (and later also nonprofits) hired the unemployed to serve in any of a range of positions, including teacher's assistant, home-health aide, and police dispatcher, or to work on community conservation and weatherization projects. Studies by Briggs and others assessing this experiment concluded that "concerns about local governments substituting public service employment for local funds were largely unfounded." They also found that the public-service employment programs "accomplished their desired fiscal effects," namely that they boosted aggregate spending and employment more quickly than tax cuts and that they directly targeted the unemployed (Marshall and Briggs 1989, pp. 598–601). President Ronald Reagan brought the public-service employment experiment to an end in 1981, but the experience of the 1970s demonstrates that Levitan, Mangum, and Marshall had been right when suggesting that human resource policy could serve as an "important adjunct to monetary and fiscal policies" (Levitan, Mangum, and Marshall 1972, p. 517).

Although Briggs discussed the countercyclical aspects of public-service employment when I was his student in 1980, I recall more vividly his suggestion that human resource policy can serve as an anti-inflationary device. Conventional fiscal policy addresses unemployment by increasing aggregate demand. From the vantage point of 1980, however, there was considerable anxiety that employing such a strategy would exacerbate an already serious inflation problem. In other words, the fear was that more demand stimulus would simply yield a movement along the Phillips Curve (which depicts an inverse relation-ship between unemployment and inflation). At a time when a number of politicians and economists were actively promoting permanent tax cuts as "supply-side" economics, Briggs was offering a genuine supply-side solution: attacking joblessness in a way that reduces labor bottlenecks in the economy, thereby *shifting* the Phillips Curve in a manner that lowers the inflation rate associated with any given level of unemploy-ment (Briggs 1980).[6] In short, Briggs's HRE draws attention to training and labor-market services that have the potential to enhance both eco-nomic efficiency and stability in the face of rising prices.

In attempting to enlist labor-market policies in the fight against in-flation, Briggs and other human resource economists underscored the distinction between cyclical, frictional, and structural unemployment. Cyclical unemployment—long explained with reference to a manufac-turer who temporarily "lays off" employees during a recession and fully intends to rehire them when the slump abates—is the sort of joblessness that responds best to an aggregate-demand stimulus.[7] Frictional unem-ployment, in contrast, is joblessness that signals a less than perfectly efficient labor market in the sense that, although appropriate work is available for job seekers, the unemployed and employers with vacancies have not yet located each other. To address this sort of unemployment and simultaneously combat price increases, human resource economists advocate not only better placement services, job-search counseling, and outreach programs that let workers know about employment opportu-nities, but also relocation assistance and other measures that enhance worker mobility (Levitan, Mangum, and Marhsall 1972, p. 515; Briggs 1980). Structural unemployment, meanwhile, involves a mismatch be-tween the skills or characteristics of the jobless and the requirements of available positions; remedying this problem can also help attenuate inflation, but it often requires training and other interventions that reach beyond what is required to tackle frictional unemployment.

Labor economists were addressing frictional and cyclical unemploy-ment long before the Great Depression (see, for example, Commons and Andrews 1916, pp. 261–290), but structural unemployment received considerably less attention until after World War II.[8] In the early 1960s, though, the problem of structural unemployment was thrust into the national policy spotlight. Indeed, according to Briggs, this development is a major reason for the emergence of HRE as an academic area of specialization (Briggs 1980, 1987b, p. 1214–1218; Marshall and Briggs 1989, pp. 590–593).[9]

Careful observers of the early post–World War II economy noted that the average U.S. unemployment rate was rising with each successive period of cyclical prosperity. This "creeping prosperity unemployment" triggered a "full-scale debate among economists over whether structural changes in the economy had become more severe than in the past" (Marshall and Briggs 1989, p. 590). At the core of this debate was the concern expressed by a number of economists (most notably Briggs's professor at Michigan State University, Charles C. Killingsworth) that automation, the emergence of computers, and associated technological change was eliminating the need for many unskilled workers and increasing the demand for skilled workers—such as "engineers, statisticians, programmers, mathematicians, and repairmen"—in "a broad array of industries" (Marshall and Briggs 1989, p. 591). If these economists were right, then stimulating aggregate demand would be an inefficient and perhaps even ineffective way of addressing the resulting unemployment. Thus, they argued, with some success, for "interventionist human resource policy . . . especially for government-financed training, education, labor-mobility programs, and job-information systems that could focus on the groups who needed special assistance" (Marshall and Briggs 1989, p. 592).[10]

Soon after the notion of structural unemployment caught their attention, a group of labor economists—especially those most heavily influenced by the institutionalist tradition and its appreciation of incessant economic change—began to realize that "other structural changes were also transforming the labor force" (Marshall and Briggs 1989, p. 591). These changes included the shift from an economy heavily dependent on goods production to one more focused on services; a geographic movement of economic activity from the Northeast and Midwest and toward the South; an accelerated decline in agricultural employment; and the transition of baby boomers from school to work in the 1960s and 1970s. Still other changes appeared as well, along with a new term—the "dislocated" worker (Marshall and Briggs 1989, pp. 591–593). Thus, HRE began as, and continues to be, an area that gives attention to structural economic change and its implications for the study of employment, and it couples that attention with a discussion of pragmatic policies that can foster more efficient and smoothly functioning markets.[11]

EQUITY, OPPORTUNITY, AND REGULATION

The civil rights movement is another major development contributing to the emergence of HRE and national human resource policy in the United States. Briggs addressed this in his 1980 course and in his textbook with Ray Marshall (Briggs 1980; Marshall and Briggs 1989, pp. 593–594). From those sources, it is clear that he views civil rights as a matter of human rights, social equity, individual economic opportunity, and national economic efficiency. For Briggs, ensuring equal opportunity means that government needs to tackle not only overt discrimination, but also institutional forms of discrimination, which range from procedural matters that affect hiring decisions to "the preparation of people for jobs" (Marshall and Briggs 1989, p. 593). He also sees this matter as moving HRE beyond Keynesianism's single-minded focus on the *level* of employment and toward the study of both the level and *composition* of employment (Marshall and Briggs 1989, p. 594).[12]

Of course, Briggs has never been interested in equity and opportunity for racial and ethnic minorities alone; he has consistently been an advocate of equal opportunity for all. Thus, he was supportive of the "new" structuralist research of the 1970s. It demonstrated that minorities, women, and youth were entering the labor force in larger numbers and often faced employment challenges, which put upward pressure on the unemployment rate. Briggs stressed that the "original" and "new" structuralist positions dovetailed. According to Marshall and Briggs, both structuralist variants are united in that they "stress the necessity of human-resource policies as the most equitable and efficient way to reduce aggregate unemployment rates" (Marshall and Briggs 1989, p. 592).

The preceding quote indicates Briggs's HRE rejects the common assertion that equity and efficiency confront society in the form of an inescapable trade-off. Like Robert Kuttner, author of *The Economic Il-*

lusion: False Choices between Prosperity and Social Justice, Briggs has argued instead that this trade-off is often an "economic illusion" and that equity and efficiency are frequently "mutually reinforcing" (Kuttner 1984, p. 1). His essay "Efficiency and Equity as Goals for Contemporary U.S. Immigration Policy" provides just one of many examples of this, as even its title indicates (Briggs 1989).

Nevertheless, Briggs does not have a slavish devotion to markets. As an institutionalist, he rejects the mainstream economists' conventional assumption that economic efficiency is a "value neutral" concept. He also rejects their assertion that the neoclassical model of perfectly competitive markets is the only appropriate professional standard against which real-world markets should be judged.

Thus, Briggs's HRE is explicitly and unapologetically normative. In 1980, the final topic examined in his human resources course was "The Relationship of Research and Policy in the Human Resource Field," and one of the assigned readings was *Objectivity in Social Research*, by the institutionalist Gunnar Myrdal. The main point of Myrdal's slim volume is that there is no such thing as "objective" social research and that the closest a researcher can come to "objectivity" is to make value premises explicit—that is, to "expose the valuations to full light," and "make them conscious, specific, and explicit" in both theoretical and policy research (Myrdal 1969, pp. 55–56).[13]

The institutionalist way of thinking shapes Briggs's approach to the entire subject of labor-market regulation. Although Briggs has often called on the state to help labor markets operate more efficiently, he believes there are situations that require government to step in as a regulator, not merely as a facilitator. Policy views must be informed by theory but also by one's values—and (consistent with the institutionalist appreciation of a dynamic world) by an understanding of history.

This approach to regulation surfaced unmistakably in the mid 1980s during the fortieth anniversary celebration at the Cornell University School of Industrial and Labor Relations (ILR). Participating in a panel devoted to examining the role of government in the workplace, Briggs began his remarks by reminding his audience why labor markets have become regulated: experience has shown that labor-market competition can often have serious adverse effects on workers. As a result, "[W]e now have a battery of worker protections sanctioned by laws and regulations. I think this is a very fundamental and justifiable outcome." In short, Briggs based his support for regulation on history and on a value judgment about what is the right way to operate an industrial society. "We don't want inadequate health and dangerous safety conditions, regardless of what any benefit–cost study might say . . . We cannot let exposure of workers to cancer-causing substances be determined by what happens in the marketplace. Period!" Briggs concluded: "As I see the world from my ivory tower, these interventions in labor markets—which may end up distorting the perfectly competitive market model (the standard often used to evaluate deviations by these policy interventions)—serve to improve the imperfect world in which I live and in which our workers work" (Briggs 1987a, p. 8).[14]

HUMAN CAPITAL THEORY VERSUS HUMAN RESOURCE ECONOMICS

HRE was not the economics profession's only post–World War II development that focused on the importance of human skills and knowledge. The other tradition, called human capital theory, emanated from the department of economics at the University of Chicago. Much of that work can be traced to the influence of Theodore W. Schultz, whose 1960 presidential address before the American Economic Association was entitled "Investment in Human Capital" (Schultz 1961).

A human resource economist in the Briggs tradition would probably quarrel with little in Schultz's address. His main point was to stress that investments in people are perhaps the most important of all determinants of economic growth, a notion that served as the point of departure for the work of Harbison and Myers (1964) and many others. The address does contain a brief discussion of research by Gary Becker regarding on-the-job training, which suggests that Becker's reliance on a competitive-market model sets the stage for "meaningful economic studies" on that subject (Schultz 1961, p. 10). Still, Marshall and Briggs present Schultz's contributions without much critical commentary in their labor economics text (Marshall and Briggs 1989, pp. 24–25 and 213–214).

In contrast, Becker and other human capital theorists receive much more critical scrutiny from Marshall and Briggs (1989, pp. 177–192) and from Briggs on his own (1987b, pp. 1210–1213). Part of that critique relies on an essay by Michael J. Piore, which stresses that there is a huge gulf between the endeavors of human capital theorists and human resource economists. According to Piore, human capital theory is "applied theory concerned with the application of certain principles" derived from neoclassical economics (such as principles related to maximizing behavior and, as seen in the previous paragraph, the functioning of competitive markets). In contrast, HRE, rooted in institutional labor economics and informed by the manpower policy experience of the 1960s and 1970s, is "an applied field concerned with the solution of particular problems" (Piore 1974, p. 253).

Of course, Briggs's concern is not simply over the highly flawed nature of the assumptions of human capital theory. It is also that those assumptions lead to analyses that claim to be relevant to the real world. Building on a neoclassical foundation, human capital theory does not recognize "the significance of complex institutional practices and historical factors that influence labor-market operations," writes Briggs (1987b, p. 1211). He continues:

> There is no allowance made for the ways that societal institutions (for example, schools, businesses, unions, government, or the military) can limit through their customs, practices, and policies the efforts of individuals to maximize opportunities to improve themselves. Nor is there any recognition of the historical barriers that have been placed in the paths of subgroups of the labor force to attain levels of human capital or to apply equally those human capital attributes that they do possess. Studies, for example, have found that many such workers often already have human capital endowments that exceed the limited range of jobs that are generally available to them. (Briggs 1987b, p. 1211)

DIMENSIONS OF HUMAN RESOURCE DEVELOPMENT

Drawing on a 1987 essay by Briggs entitled "Human Resource Development and the Formulation of National Economic Policy," one can identify five HRD dimensions. The first three are national and economic in nature: workforce quantity, quality, and opportunity. The other two are personal development and international well-being.

Workforce Quantity

One way to look at the quantitative dimension of HRD is to begin with the number of employed people in the United States. In January 2009, the official number was just under 142.1 million. To be counted among the employed by the U.S. Bureau of Labor Statistics (BLS), a person must first be viewed as part of the civilian labor force. To be included in the labor force, one must be 16 years of age or older, reside in one of the 50 States or the District of Columbia, and not be confined to an institution (home for the aged, prison, or mental-health facility). There were 153.7 million people in the U.S. labor force in January 2009 (U.S. BLS 2009).

Of course, not everyone in the labor force is counted as employed, a category that requires a minimum number of hours worked within a certain BLS reference period. A member of the labor force can also be "unemployed," which requires one to be available and either searching for work or waiting to be recalled by an employer. There were 11.6 million unemployed people in the United States in January 2009, 7.6 percent of the labor force (U.S. BLS 2009).

The 7.6 percent unemployment rate of January 2009 is one measure of unutilized labor, but there are also potential workers who are part of the U.S. population and not currently part of the labor force. Many of those potential workers fall within a BLS category of people who are "marginally attached" to the labor force. These are "persons not in the labor force who want and are available for work, and who have looked for a job sometime in the prior 12 months (or since the end of their last job if they held one within the past 12 months), but were not counted as unemployed because they had not searched for work in the 4 weeks preceding the [most recent BLS employment] survey" (U.S. BLS 2008). There were about 2.1 million marginally attached workers in January 2009, including 734,000 "discouraged workers," who were no longer looking because they believed no jobs were available to them (U.S. BLS 2009).[15]

There is also underutilized labor. For example, the BLS identified 7.8 million of the employed labor force as involuntary part-time workers in January 2009. These people would like to work full time but had their hours cut back or were unable to find full-time jobs (U.S. BLS 2009). Another category of underutilized labor is underemployment, which involves people working in positions that require less skill and education than they possess.

Looking over this terrain, Briggs has often called for a comprehensive national human resource strategy that would include a commitment to full employment. He envisions a strategy that would address not just the unemployment rate but also the challenges surrounding marginal attachment and underutilization. This strategy would have a macroeconomic component involving fiscal and monetary policies, but it would also include a battery of labor-market and education policies that recognize the need for remedies tailored to fit different circumstances. He writes: "Different groups in the labor force have different needs. Hence, a menu of policy options needs to be offered" (Briggs 1987b, pp. 1216–1217).

Immigration is also an important part of the quantitative dimension of HRD. In fact, its role has been growing for decades. In the 1980s and 1990s, immigration accounted for 37 and 47 percent of the growth in the U.S. population, respectively. In the first half of the twenty-first century, two-thirds of the nation's population growth "will be the consequence of the arrival of immigrants themselves and of their future children who will be born in this country" (Briggs 2003, p. 4). Quoting from a National Research Council report, Briggs writes that immigration to the United States "will obviously play the dominant role in our future population growth" (Briggs 2003, p. 4).

According to Briggs, there are few nations in the world that accept significant numbers of immigrants each year, and the tendency among these nations is to adjust the numbers annually according to labor-market conditions. In contrast, immigration policy in the United States focuses heavily on family unification and "has been allowed to function independently of its economic consequences" (Briggs 1987b, p. 1221; 2003).

The United States is also the destination for many illegal immigrants. "An estimated 11.8 million unauthorized immigrants were living in the United States in January 2007 compared to 8.5 million in 2000," according to a U.S. Department of Homeland Security report (Hoefer, Rytina, and Baker 2008, p. 1).

In his presidential address before the institutionalist Association for Evolutionary Economics, Briggs explained his concerns about the impact of immigration upon the U.S. economy:

> The flow of immigrants into the United States has tended to be bimodal in terms of human capital attributes (as measured by educational attainment), but the highest concentration by far is in the lowest end of the nation's human capital distribution . . . In the low-skilled labor market, immigration has increased the competition for whatever jobs are available . . . As for skilled jobs, immigration can be useful in the short run as a means of providing qualified workers where shortages of qualified domestic workers exist. But, the long-term objective should be that these jobs should go to citizens and resident aliens. (Briggs 1996, p. 381)[16]

Thus, Briggs believes that immigration policy must be treated as an integral part of the nation's human resource strategy. During an interview in 2006, for example, he summarized his position as follows: "Immigration should primarily be linked to filling skill gaps in the labor force until the nation's own education and training system can meet those needs. The human capital of immigrants should not run counter to these needs" (quoted in Rohe 2006, p. 233).[17]

Workforce Quality

In addition to a quantitative dimension, HRD must also have a qualitative dimension. For Briggs, a nation interested in the qualitative dimension of human resources must address the needs of its most economically disadvantaged residents, but it must also do more, including engage in "preventive maintenance" and embrace the notion of "long-run educational development" (Briggs 1987b).

In the case of those who cannot find employment on a regular and self-supporting basis, or who must rely on the underground economy, Briggs stresses that society must "provide a *lifeline of opportunity* to prepare for legitimate employment" (Briggs 1987b, p. 1225, emphasis added). Doing so is both just and economically pragmatic, he argues. His 1987 essay on HRD illustrates this need with a discussion of three

U.S. economic problems: the declining labor-force participation of black males, the poverty challenge facing female-headed households, and increasing adult illiteracy (Briggs 1987b, pp. 1225–1227).

The problems facing black males have not receded. A 2006 volume edited by Ronald B. Mincy for the Urban Institute finds the labor-force participation rate for black men continued to decline even during the economic boom of the 1990s (Mincy 2006). A 2004 report by Andrew Sum and his colleagues at Northeastern University, meanwhile, finds a decline in the employment-to-population ratio of black men that began in the mid 1950s and continues into the mid 2000s. It also finds a high and rising rate of year-round joblessness among black men (one out of every four were idle all year in 2002) (Sum et al. 2004b). Moreover, both of these recent studies advocate the sort of targeted education and workforce-development strategies that Briggs has been promoting for decades.

Poverty among female-headed households and the illiteracy problem also remain serious. Briggs's HRD essay indicated that "one out of every three families headed by a woman was living in poverty" in 1985 (Briggs 1987b, pp. 1225–1226). In mid 2005, the poverty rate for such families was 29 percent—10 times the rate found in two-parent families (Gosling 2008, pp. 175–176). A 2002 report on an adult literacy survey, sponsored by the U.S. Department of Education, concluded that about 44 million of the 191 million adults in the United States have skills that place them in the lowest of five possible levels on prose, document, and quantitative proficiency. Many respondents "had such limited skills that they were unable to respond to much of the survey" (Kirsch et al. 2002, p. 18). The following year, another literacy program estimated that 50 million Americans cannot read or comprehend above the eighth-grade level and that nearly 75 percent of the unemployed are illiterate (Morry 2003).

Along with a lifeline for the unemployed and working poor, Briggs's national system of HRD would have a *preventive maintenance* component that offers assistance to anyone who becomes vulnerable to unemployment, regardless of salary history. In his 1987 essay on HRD, Briggs stressed the increasingly dynamic nature of the workforce in addition to the increased skill and educational requirements associated with the fast-emerging service-based economy. He also highlighted the inefficiency and impracticality of depending entirely on individuals to adjust to these changing employment patterns on their own. Thus, he called on government to develop a network of programs that would assist individuals with this readjustment process by providing reliable information on labor-market trends and job requirements and by offering workers ample opportunities for educational upgrading, job retraining, employment counseling, and even relocation when appropriate (Briggs 1987b, pp. 1227–1230).

Since education is the cornerstone of Briggs's strategy for achieving national success in a dynamic, global economy, long-run educational development is also essential to his conception of the qualitative dimension of HRD. In particular, he has often called for a major national effort toward five educational objectives: preventing students from dropping out of school; boosting the average literacy and educational proficiency level across American society; ensuring that education is contingent on ability to learn, not ability to pay; making educational opportunities accessible to adults throughout their working lives; and linking education reform to a national industrial policy.[18] Briggs recognizes this will require extensive changes within U.S. educational institutions (affecting administrative practices, teacher certification and compensation, decision-making within schools, student assessment methods, and more), but he insists such changes are needed for education "to contribute to the answer and not worsen the problem of contemporary labor-force adjustment" (Briggs 1987b, pp. 1230–1231).

Equal Employment Opportunity

A workforce-opportunity dimension to HRD exists alongside the quantitative and qualitative dimensions. As with labor-market regulation in general (discussed earlier), Briggs addresses employment opportunity by beginning with the historical record. Whereas conventional economics argues that discrimination is irrational and thus should not persist, Briggs responds, "Experience, however, has demonstrated that it cannot be realistically assumed that labor markets function solely on the basis of merit and productivity." Instead, he argues, "It has been revealed that the roots of discrimination run deep into the institutional practices that prepare workers to compete in the labor market" (Briggs 1987b, p. 1231).

In Briggs's view, equal employment opportunity must begin by requiring antidiscrimination mechanisms that not only monitor hiring practices and patterns but also offer redress in the event of discriminatory actions. As he wrote in 1987, for some women and minorities, it is enough to ask for hiring requirements to be job related and for employment practices to be fair. This alone can sometimes "open up employment opportunities where they previously did not exist" (Briggs 1987b, pp. 1231 and 1234).

Other times, however, biases and discrimination go much deeper and help explain why certain groups within the labor force might not appear in the applicant pool of a fair-minded employer. For example, recruitment and job-posting practices can be structured (even inadvertently) in a way that favors some groups over others. In addition, inequality and discrimination can shape the institutions that educate, train, and prepare people for employment, and past patterns of discrimination can cause even those with educational or training opportunities to temper their occupational aspirations and forego such opportunities out of discouragement. Thus, Briggs has always believed that active outreach, training, apprenticeship, and placement programs are indispensable tools in the pursuit of equal employment opportunity (Briggs 1987b, pp. 1231–1234).[19]

Personal Development and International Well-Being

Briggs's final two HRD dimensions look beyond the national economy and focus on personal development and international well-being. As mentioned at the outset of this chapter, Briggs believes human resources are the key to personal development as well as to a healthy national economy. Thus, it is not surprising that part of the benefit accruing to an individual from HRD is economic and comes from opportunities associated with being adequately prepared for employment (Briggs 1987b, p. 1235). At the same time, another part of the individual benefit of developing one's human resources is that it provides the chance to be a more informed member of society—in Briggs's words, HRD heightens "one's broader awareness of the quality of the society of which he or she is a part" (Briggs 1987b, p. 1235).

Of course, economists have long recognized there are social as well as individual implications of an investment in human resources (indeed, education offers the classic case of a good with a positive external-. ity), and Briggs believes the civic benefits of an educated and informed citizenry can be as potent as the economic ones. He surveys the awesome ability of science and technology to create, destroy, and "reshape the relationship of human beings to their natural environment," and he writes, "It is imperative that the uses of these forces be the result of the decisions made by an informed citizenry and not by an opinionated or indifferent society" (Briggs 1987b, p. 1235).

That last point connects the personal to the political, but it also connects the individual to the rest of humanity. Much of Briggs's work has focused on well-being at the national level, but he has always viewed a prosperous and humane U.S. economy as providing us with the best position from which to address problems on an international scale. Moreover, over the years, he has given increasing attention to international issues. Not surprisingly, his message centers on leveling the playing field in a way that brings up those at the bottom, rather than encouraging a global race to the bottom.

I recall finding evidence of this in his remarks delivered as part of the ILR School's fortieth anniversary celebration. Toward the end of his talk on government regulation, Briggs noted: "In the 1980s, we have seen the coming of the internationalization of our economy. This raises a whole new series of concerns about regulation . . . The next step will be the need to establish international labor standards. It is a difficult task, but I do think it is possible" (Briggs 1987a, p. 7).

Briggs returned to this theme more recently in an e-mail message. Responding to the draft of an article I composed for the sixtieth anniversary of the Labor and Employment Relations Association, he wrote: "In the conclusion, you might consider adding something to the effect that the reality in this present era of globalization is that many of the identical issues that confronted the founders of our organization and resulted in their focus on the national economy of the United States are rapidly becoming international issues. Whereas our organization helped set the buoys for intellectual inquiry [that involved] national studies, the challenge now is to try to do the same at the international level" (Briggs 2007).

HUMAN RESOURCES: THE WEALTH OF NATIONS

Briggs's quantitative, qualitative, and opportunity dimensions of HRD have always focused on national economic well-being. His personal development and international dimensions, however, address broader themes of individual fulfillment, civic virtue, and global responsibility. Reflecting on all of this, it is easy to see what I have found so compelling about Briggs's brand of economics. It is fitting, of course, to give him the last word, and what better way to do so than with a quote that ties together each of these dimensions and themes? "If human resources are truly 'the wealth of nations,' their development carries with it the parallel responsibility to recognize that their contribution to the economy must enhance the quality of life on this planet and not lead to its enslavement, impoverishment, or extinction" (Briggs 1987b, p. 1236).

Notes

1. Rather than rely on my course notes as a definitive source, I have tried to use them (and the course syllabus) primarily as a "road map" to further reading on the origin and development of HRE.
2. The book by Harbison and Myers is a direct precursor to the 1973 Harbison volume. Still, Eli Ginzberg, an early pioneer in HRE, stressed the importance of human resources to the wealth of a nation in an even earlier volume (Ginzberg 1958).
3. In the final edition of the Marshall and Briggs textbook, *Labor Economics*, they explain that the term "manpower policy" came into being in the 1960s "to define the new set of labor market policies designed to develop the employment potential of the nation's human resources . . . The European nations referred to these endeavors as 'active labor-market policies.' By the [late] 1970s, the term *manpower* itself had been replaced (it was felt to be a sexist term) by *employment and training policies* or *human resource policies*" (Marshall and Briggs 1989, p. 588).
4. The second edition of *Human Resources and Labor Markets: Labor and Manpower in the American Economy* (1976) was one of two books listed as "general background references" in Briggs's 1980 course syllabus (the other was *CETA: Decentralization on Trial*, by Bonnie B. Snedeker and David M. Snedeker, 1978) (Briggs 1980).
5. According to Briggs, CETA's public-service employment programs "were essentially counterstructural," not countercyclical, from 1978 to 1981, when funding

was eliminated in the first year of the presidential administration of Ronald Reagan (Briggs 1982, p. 260).

6. The suggestion of shifting the Phillips Curve through human resource policies was also put forth in the early 1970s by Levitan, Mangum, and Marshall (1972, pp. 514–515). In addition, see Marshall and Briggs (1989, p. 594).

7. Indeed, Levitan, Mangum, and Marshall (1972, p. 515) called cyclical unemployment "demand-deficient unemployment."

8. To be sure, discussions of structural unemployment and its remedies are not absent from the pre–World War II economics literature; see, for example, Watkins (1922, pp. 222 and 234).

9. For a discussion of structural unemployment in the context of HRE, see also Levitan, Mangum, and Marshall (1972, pp. 515–517). For early discussions of structural unemployment, see Killingsworth (1965a,b); for a later reexamination, see Killingsworth (1979).

10. In the wake of the early 1960s debate between structuralists and advocates of an aggregate-demand stimulus in the form of tax cuts, Congress passed the Economic Opportunity Act (EOA) of 1964 in addition to tax cuts. The EOA included "a number of experimental human resource programs" (Marshall and Briggs 1989, p. 595). Other programs with structural components would follow, including CETA.

11. For my own analysis of recent U.S. economic performance from a perspective emphasizing economic change and focusing on implications for working families, see Whalen (2009).

12. Reflecting on the civil rights era from the vantage point of the mid 1980s, Briggs wrote: "There had to be changes in the racial and gender composition of employment patterns, as opposed to an exclusive policy focus merely on the level of employment. As a black leader once expressed it, 'After all, we had full employment back on the plantations.'" At the same time, an equal-employment opportunity strategy must be accompanied by a full-employment strategy or the former will only heighten job-security concerns among groups that previously benefited from exclusionary employment practices (Briggs 1987b, pp. 1233–1234).

13. Myrdal's book also stresses that real-world problems often cut across the boundaries of academic disciplines: "In reality, there are not economic, sociological, or psychological problems, but simply problems, and . . . as a rule they are all complex" (Myrdal 1969, p. 10). Still another point offered in the same section of Briggs's course is Robert A. Gordon's call for economic scholarship that has "'[real-world] relevance with as much rigor as possible' and not 'rigor regardless of relevance'" (quoted in Dunlop 1977, p. 282). Briggs, of course, accepts both of these points.

14. Even when defending regulation regardless of the extent to which it causes a market to deviate from the perfectly competitive model, Briggs still stressed the possibility that workplace efficiency and equity may be compatible objectives: "In many ways, the coming of regulation . . . has probably led to more efficient labor markets in the process, because they are now more equitable . . . Companies which have strong social consciences should not be forced to compete with those that have the least social conscience" (Briggs 1987a, p. 7). Briggs also recognized

there are limits to government's ability to regulate effectively. His solution was squarely in the John R. Commons tradition: "What needs to be done in the health and safety area, for example, is to establish health and safety committees in the workplace and empower these committees to close down or stop production if they think there are violations. At the enterprise level, they know better than some inspectors if there is some danger or violation" (Briggs 1987a, p. 8).

15. Other marginally attached workers indicate they have not recently looked for work due to reasons such as family responsibilities and school attendance (U.S. BLS 2009).

16. For evidence that supports Briggs's concern about the harmful impact of immigrants upon low-skill U.S. labor markets, see Sum et al. (2004a).

17. For more on Briggs's view on immigration policy, see Chapter 2 by William P. Curington (which is based on Curington 2007). See also Briggs (1996, especially p. 381), which indicates a wariness regarding short-term immigration measures designed to relieve shortages (because such measures may cause us to "miss the opportunity to draw additional U.S. workers into the economic mainstream").

18. On linking education and training with industrial policy, Briggs writes: "There can be little purposeful long-term educational preparation of the labor force for employment if there is little direction provided as to where the economy is thought to be going" (Briggs 1987b, p. 1231).

19. Writing in 1987, Briggs argued that antidiscrimination policies must continue because "it is unlikely that the principles of equal employment opportunity have yet been fully institutionalized to the degree that they can be taken for granted" (Briggs 1987b, p. 1234). Even with the passage of more than 20 years and the recent election of an African-American president, I suspect Briggs continues to hold the same view today. Indeed, in Chapter 9, Seth D. Harris provides evidence that would support Briggs in this stance.

References

Briggs, Vernon M. Jr. 1980. "Public Policy and the Development of Human Resources." School of Industrial and Labor Relations course 261, Cornell University. Course syllabus and class notes as transcribed by the author (Whalen).

———. 1982. "The Revival of Job Creation Programs in the 1970s: Lessons for the 1980s." In *Proceedings of the Thirty-Fourth Annual Meeting*, Barbara D. Dennis, ed. Madison, WI: Industrial Relations Research Association, pp. 258–265.

———. 1987a. "The Role of Government in the Workplace." *ILR Report* 24(2): 7–8.

———.1987b. "Human Resource Development and the Formulation of National Economic Policy." *Journal of Economic Issues* 21(3): 1207–1240.

————. 1989. "Efficiency and Equity as Goals for Contemporary U.S. Immigration Policy." Center for Advanced Human Resource Studies Working Paper no. 89-02. Ithaca, NY: School of Industrial and Labor Relations, Cornell University.

————. 1996. "Immigration Policy and the U.S. Economy: An Institutionalist Perspective." *Journal of Economic Issues* 30(2): 371–387.

————. 2003. *Mass Immigration and the National Interest: Policy Directions for the New Century.* 3d ed. Armonk, NY: M.E. Sharpe.

————. 2007. E-mail message to the author. August 27.

Commons, John R., and John B. Andrews. 1916. *Principles of Labor Legislation.* New York: Harper and Brothers.

Cornell University. 2009. *Vernon Briggs: Biography.* Ithaca, NY: School of Industrial and Labor Relations, Cornell University. http://www.ilr.cornell.edu/directory/vmb2/biography.htm (accessed February 13, 2009).

Curington, William P. 2007. "Interview with Vernon M. Briggs Jr." Copy deposited in the Kheel Center for Labor-Management Documentation and Archives, Martin P. Catherwood Library. Ithaca, NY: School of Industrial and Labor Relations, Cornell University.

Dunlop, John T. 1977. "Policy Decisions and Research in Economics and Industrial Relations." *Industrial and Labor Relations Review* 30(3): 275–282.

Ginzberg, Eli. 1958. *Human Resources: The Wealth of a Nation.* New York: Simon and Schuster.

Gosling, James J. 2008. *Economics, Politics, and American Public Policy.* Armonk, NY: M.E. Sharpe.

Harbison, Frederick H. 1973. *Human Resources as the Wealth of Nations.* New York: Oxford University Press.

Harbison, Frederick H., and Charles A. Myers. 1964. *Education, Manpower, and Economic Growth: Strategies of Human Resource Development.* New York: McGraw-Hill.

Heilbroner, Robert. 1986. *The Worldly Philosophers: The Lives, Times and Ideas of the Great Economic Thinkers.* New York: Simon and Schuster.

Hoefer, Michael, Nancy Rytina, and Bryan C. Baker. 2008. *Estimates of the Unauthorized Immigrant Population Residing in the United States: January 2007.* Washington, DC: Office of Immigration Statistics, U.S. Department of Homeland Security.

Killingsworth, Charles. C. 1965a. "Automation, Jobs, and Manpower: The Case for Structural Unemployment." In *The Manpower Revolution: Its Policy Consequences*, Garth L. Mangum, ed. Garden City, NY: Anchor Books, pp. 97–117.

————. 1965b. "Unemployment after the Tax Cut." In *Unemployment in a*

Prosperous Economy, William G. Bowen and Frederick H. Harbison, eds. Princeton, NJ: Industrial Relations Section, Princeton University, pp. 82–97.

———. 1979. "The Fall and Rise of Structural Unemployment." In *Proceedings of the Thirty-First Annual Meeting*, Barbara D. Dennis, ed. Madison, WI: Industrial Relations Research Association, pp. 1–13.

Kirsch, Irwin S., Ann Jungeblut, Lynn Jenkins, and Andrew Kolstad. 2002. *Adult Literacy in America: A First Look at the Findings of the National Adult Literacy Survey.* 3d ed. NCES 1993-275. Washington, DC: National Center for Education Statistics, Office of Educational Research and Improvement, U.S. Department of Education.

Kuttner, Robert. 1984. *The Economic Illusion: False Choices between Prosperity and Social Justice.* Boston: Houghton Mifflin.

Levitan, Sar A., Garth L. Mangum, and Ray Marshall. 1972. *Human Resources and Labor Markets: Labor and Manpower in the American Economy.* New York: Harper and Row.

Mangum, Garth L. 1976. *Employability, Employment, and Income: A Reassessment of Manpower Policy.* Salt Lake City, UT: Olympus Publishing.

Marshall, Ray, and Vernon M. Briggs Jr. 1989. *Labor Economics: Theory, Institutions, and Public Policy.* 6th ed. Homewood, IL: Irwin.

Mincy, Ronald B, ed. 2006. *Black Males Left Behind.* Washington, DC: Urban Institute Press.

Morry, Chris. 2003. *Illiteracy in the United States: Summary of Findings of the "Words Are Your Wheels" Literacy Program.* Victoria, British Columbia, Canada: Communication Initiative Network.

Myrdal, Gunnar. 1969. *Objectivity in Social Research.* Middletown, CT: Wesleyan University Press.

Piore, Michael J. 1974. "The Importance of Human Capital Theory to Labor Economics: A Dissenting View." In *Proceedings of the Twenty-Sixth Annual Winter Meeting*, Barbara D. Dennis, ed. Madison, WI: Industrial Relations Research Association, pp. 251–258.

Rohe, John F. 2006. "Living Standards, Scarce Resources, and Immigration: An Interview with Labor Economist Vernon M. Briggs Jr." *Social Contract* 16(4): 227–236.

Schultz, Theodore W. 1961. "Investment in Human Capital." *American Economic Review* 50(1): 1–17.

Smith, Adam. 1935. *An Inquiry into the Nature and Causes of the Wealth of Nations.* Originally published in 1776. New York: Modern Library.

Snedeker, Bonnie B., and David M. Snedeker. 1978. *CETA: Decentralization on Trial.* Salt Lake City, UT: Olympus Publishing.

Sum, Andrew, Neeta Fogg, Ishwar Khatiwada, and Sheila Palma. 2004a. *For-*

eign Immigration and the Labor Force of the United States: The Contributions of New Foreign Immigration to the Growth of the Nation's Labor Force and Its Employed Population, 2000 to 2004. Boston: Center for Labor Market Studies, Northeastern University.

Sum, Andrew, Ishwar Khatiwada, Frimpomaa Ampaw, Paulo Tobar, and Sheila Palma. 2004b. "Trends in Black Male Joblessness and Year-Round Idleness: An Employment Crisis Ignored." Prepared for Alternative Schools Network, Chicago, Illinois. Boston: Center for Labor Market Studies, Northeastern University. http://www.nlc.org/ASSETS/223BA7C42D964A32A2CAC31E28DDFAFC/IYEF_DY_Black_Males_Report.pdf (accessed June 26, 2009).

U.S. Bureau of Labor Statistics. 2008. "Marginally Attached Workers (Current Population Survey)." Defined in BLS Information Glossary. Washington, DC: U.S. Department of Labor. http://www.bls.gov/bls/glossary.htm (accessed February 13, 2009).

———. 2009. "The Employment Situation: January 2009." Washington, DC: U.S. Department of Labor. http://www.bls.gov/news.release/empsit.nr0.htm (accessed February 13, 2009).

Watkins, Gordon S. 1922. *An Introduction to the Study of Labor Problems.* New York: Thomas Y. Crowell Company.

Whalen, Charles J. 2009. "An Institutionalist Perspective on the Global Financial Crisis." School of Industrial and Labor Relations working paper. Ithaca, NY: School of Industrial and Labor Relations, Cornell University. http://digitalcommons.ilr.cornell.edu/intlvf/27 (accessed June 14, 2009).

4

Immigration and the U.S. Labor Market

Philip L. Martin
University of California, Davis

On a typical day, about 100,000 foreigners arrive in the United States. Most are temporary migrants or visitors, including tourists, business people, students, and workers, who are welcomed at airports and border crossings. About 2,600 are legal immigrants or refugees who have been invited to become permanent residents of the United States, 94,000 are temporary visitors, and 3,200 are unauthorized foreigners, usually Mexicans, about half of whom are apprehended just inside the Mexico–U.S. border.

Vernon Briggs's career has focused on low-wage U.S. workers. Briggs consistently urged enactment and enforcement of policies that would help low-wage workers to help themselves. The self-evident truth that "a tight labor market is a worker's best friend" has been a cornerstone of Briggs's analysis of immigration policy, which stresses that periods of less immigration in U.S. history were associated with faster increases in wages for low-wage U.S. workers.

This chapter provides a global and national perspective on contemporary immigration patterns. It does not prescribe but aims to show the dimensions and impacts of migration. Among the topics covered are the factors contributing to international migration, government efforts to manage immigration, trends in the types of migrants entering the United States, migration's labor-market effects, and immigration policy trade-offs. The topics addressed are among those that figure most prominently in Briggs's policy-oriented writings.

GLOBAL MIGRATION

Migration is the movement of people from one place to another. Migration is as old as humankind wandering in search of food, but international migration is a relatively recent development. It was only in the early twentieth century that the system of nation-states, passports, and visas developed to regulate the flow of people across borders (Torpey 1999).

International migration is the exception, not the rule. The most significant form of migration control is inertia—most people do not want to move away from family and friends. The use of passports, visas, and border controls has also given modern governments significant capacity to regulate migration, and they do. One item considered by many governments when deciding whether to recognize a new entity that declares itself a nation-state is whether it is able to regulate who crosses and who remains within its borders.

There were 190 million international migrants in 2005, meaning that 3 percent of the world's people left their country of birth or citizenship for a year or more (Table 4.1). The number of international migrants increased by almost 4 million a year between 1995 and 2005, with almost all of the increase in high-income countries.

Most of the world's 6.7 billion people never cross a national border; most live and die near their place of birth. Those who cross national borders usually move to nearby countries, such as from Mexico to the United States or from Turkey to Germany. There were 62 million migrants from developing countries in industrial countries in 2005, but almost as many migrants, 61 million, had moved from one developing country to another, such as from Indonesia to Malaysia. There are also large flows of people from one industrial country to another, for ex-

Table 4.1 International Migrants in 2005 (millions)

	Destination country	
Origin country	Industrial	Developing
Industrial	53	14
Developing	62	61

SOURCE: United Nations Population Division (2006).

ample, from Canada to the United States, and much smaller flows from industrial to developing countries, such as Japanese who work or retire in Thailand (United Nations Population Division 2006).

PERSPECTIVES ON MIGRATION

International migration is likely to increase for reasons that range from persisting demographic and economic inequalities to improvements in communications and transportation that increase mobility. There are also more borders to cross. There were 193 generally recognized nation-states in 2000, four times more than the 43 in 1900.[1] Each nation-state distinguishes citizens and foreigners, has border controls to inspect those seeking entry, and determines what foreigners can do while inside the country, whether they are tourists, students, guest workers, or immigrants.

Most countries discourage immigration, meaning that they do not encourage foreigners to settle and become naturalized citizens. Some also discourage emigration; for example, Communist nations attempted to prevent emigration between 1961 and 1989, and North Korea continues to try to keep its citizens from leaving.

There are five major countries that do plan for the arrival of immigrants: the United States, which accepted 1.2 million immigrants in 2006; Canada (250,000); Australia (125,000); New Zealand (50,000); and Israel (25,000).[2] The number of newcomers arriving in industrial countries exceeds the planned 1.6 million a year, suggesting that many of these newcomers are temporary visitors or unauthorized foreigners who find ways to settle despite not arriving as immigrants.

Perspectives on the rising number of migrants can be framed by two extremes. At one extreme, the *Wall Street Journal* advocates a five-word amendment to the U.S. constitution: "There shall be open borders."[3] Organizations ranging from the Catholic Church to the World Bank have called for more migration, arguing that people should not be confined to their countries of birth by national borders and that more migration would speed economic growth and development in both the sending and the receiving countries.

At the other extreme, virtually every industrial country has organizations such as the U.S.-based Federation for American Immigration
Reform (FAIR), which calls for sharp reductions in immigration on
the grounds that unskilled newcomers hurt low-skilled U.S. workers,
have negative environmental effects, and threaten established U.S. cultural values. Many European countries have political parties that call
for reducing immigration, such as the National Front in France, which
proposed (during the 1995 presidential campaign) removing up to 3
million non-Europeans from France to reduce the number of Muslim
residents.[4]

The first step toward making migration a manageable challenge is
to understand why people migrate. Most people do not want to cross
national borders to settle in another country, and, even though the number of migrants is at an all-time high, international migrants are (as
mentioned above) just 3 percent of the world's residents. Furthermore,
economic growth can turn origination nations into destination nations,
as has been seen recently in Ireland, Italy, and Korea. The challenge
is to manage migration in a way that reduces the differences that encourage people to cross borders and to understand how investment,
remittances, and aid can stimulate economic development and reduce
migration pressures.

DIFFERENCES AND NETWORKS

Differences in demographic and economic conditions encourage
people to cross national borders, and their movements have been eased
by revolutions in communications, transportation, and rights.

Most of the world's people and most of the population growth are
in developing countries. The world's population, which reached 6 billion in October 1999, is growing by 1.3 percent or 80 million a year,
with 97 percent of the growth in developing countries.[5] In the past, significant demographic differences between areas prompted large-scale
migration. For example, Europe had 21 percent of the world's almost
1 billion residents in 1800 and the Americas had only 4 percent (Table
4.2). When there were five Europeans for every American, millions of

Table 4.2 World Population by Continent, 1800, 2000, and 2050 (percent shares)

	1800	1999	2050[a]
World (millions)	978	5,978	8,909
Africa	11	13	20
Asia	65	61	59
Europe	21	12	7
South America, Latin America, and Caribbean	3	9	9
North America	1	5	4
Oceania	0	1	1

NOTE: Columns may not total 100 due to rounding.
[a] Projected.
SOURCE: United Nations Population Division (1999, table 2).

Europeans emigrated to North and South America in search of economic opportunity as well as religious and political freedom.

Will history repeat itself? Africa and Europe have roughly equal populations today, but by 2050, Africa is projected to have three times more residents. If Africa remains poorer than Europe, the two continents' diverging demographic trajectories may propel young people from overcrowded cities such as Cairo and Lagos to move to Berlin and Rome.

The economic differences that encourage international migration have two dimensions, one fostered by inequality between countries and the other by inequality within. The world's almost 200 nation-states have annual per-capita incomes that range from less than $250 per person to more than $50,000, a difference that provides a significant incentive (especially for young people) to migrate for higher wages and more opportunities (World Bank 2009).[6]

The 30 highest income countries had a total of 1 billion residents in 2005, about one-sixth of the world's population; their combined gross national income was $36 trillion, about 80 percent of the global $45 trillion.[7] The resulting average per-capita income of $35,000 in high-income countries was 21 times the average of $1,750 in low- and middle-income countries. Despite rapid economic growth in some developing countries, including the East Asian "Tigers" in the 1990s and

China and India more recently, the ratio in per-capita incomes between high-income and other countries rose between 1975 and 2000 and shrank only marginally since 2000. In 2005, average per-capita income in high-income countries was 61 times higher than that in low-income countries and 13 times higher than that in middle-income countries (Table 4.3).

Another aspect of economic inequality between nation-states also adds to international migration pressures—international differences in labor force growth. The world's labor force of 3.1 billion in 2005 included 600 million workers in the high-income countries and 2.5 billion in the low-income countries. Almost all labor force growth is projected to be in lower income countries; their labor force is projected to increase by about 425 million between 2005 and 2015, whereas the labor force in high-income countries is projected to remain stable at just over 600 million (Table 4.4).

Internal inequality related to rural–urban migrations also can encourage international migration. In lower income countries, 40 percent of workers are employed in agriculture, a sector often heavily taxed despite the fact that farmers and farm workers usually have lower than average incomes.[8] With taxes helping to keep farm incomes less than nonfarm incomes, there is often migration from rural areas to urban areas, one of the reasons why the urban share of the world's population surpassed 50 percent for the first time in 2008 (United Nations Population Fund 2007).

Industrial countries had "Great Migrations" off the land, which provided workers for expanding factories, fueled population growth in cities, and added to emigration pressures. Similar Great Migrations are under way today in countries from China to Mexico, and this rural–urban migration has three implications for international migration. First, ex-farmers and farm workers are most likely to accept 3-D (dirty, dangerous, and difficult) jobs inside their countries or abroad (Martin and Midgley 2006).[9] Second, rural–urban migrants often have to make cultural as well as physical transitions, and many of them find the transition is as easy abroad as at home; for example, rural Mexicans may find it as easy to adapt to Los Angeles as to Mexico City. Third, domestic rural–urban migrants get one step closer to a country's exits because it

Table 4.3 Global Migrants and Per-Capita Income Gaps, 1975–2005

Year	Migrants (millions)	World pop. (billions)	Migrants (%)	Annual increase (millions)	Countries grouped by per capita GDP ($)			Ratio	
					Low	Middle	High	High-low	High-mid
1975	85	4.1	2.1	1	150	750	6,200	41	8
1985	105	4.8	2.2	2	270	1,290	11,810	44	9
1990	154	5.3	2.9	10	350	2,220	19,590	56	9
1995	164	5.7	2.9	2	430	2,390	24,930	58	10
2000	175	6.1	2.9	2	420	1,970	27,510	66	14
2005	191	6.4	3.0	3	580	2,640	35,131	61	13

NOTE: The 1990 migrant stock was raised from 120 million to 154 million, largely to reflect the breakup of the USSR; 1975 income data are for 1976. 2005 data are gross national income.

SOURCE: United Nations Population Division and World Bank Development Indicators.

Table 4.4 World, Developed Country, and Less Developed Country Economically Active Populations (EAP), 1980–2020

	1980	1985	1990	1995	2000	2005	2010	2015	2020
World EAP	1,929,556	2,160,150	2,405,619	2,604,941	2,818,456	3,050,420	3,279,373	3,481,270	3,651,283
More dev. EAP	522,683	544,271	568,832	573,626	589,151	604,521	613,388	611,392	602,977
Less dev. EAP	1,406,873	1,615,879	1,836,787	2,031,315	2,229,305	2,445,899	2,665,986	2,869,878	3,048,307

Change (%)	1980–1990	1990–2000	2000–2010	2010–2020
World EAP	25	21	17	17
More dev. EAP	9	5	4	5
Less dev. EAP	31	26	21	20

SOURCE: International Labour Office (2009).

is usually easier to obtain visas and documents for legal migration—and to make arrangements for illegal migration—in the cities.

Differences encourage migration, but it takes networks or links between areas to encourage people to move. Migration networks are a broad concept, and they include communication factors that enable people to learn about opportunities abroad as well as the migration infrastructure that actually transports migrants over national borders and even the rights regime that allows them to remain abroad. Migration networks have been shaped and strengthened by revolutionary changes in each of these areas (communications, transportation, and rights) during the past half-century.

Communications and Transportation

The communications revolution helps potential migrants to learn about opportunities abroad. The best information comes from migrants that are already established abroad because they can provide family and friends with information in an understandable context. Cheaper communications enable migrants to quickly transmit job information as well as advice on how to cross national borders to friends and relatives at home. For example, information about vacant California farm jobs may be received in rural Mexico, thousands of miles away, before it spreads to nearby cities that have unemployment rates of over 20 percent.[10] Meanwhile, films and television programs depicting life in high-income countries may encourage people (especially younger people) to assume that the grass is greener abroad and that migration will lead to economic betterment.[11]

The transportation revolution highlights the declining cost of travel. British migrants unable to pay one-way passage to North American colonies in the eighteenth century often indentured themselves, signing contracts that obliged them to work for three to six years for whoever met the ship and paid the captain. Transportation costs today are far less, typically less than $2,500 to travel anywhere in the world legally, and $1,000 to $20,000 for unauthorized migration. Most studies suggest faster payback times for migrants today, so that even migrants who pay high smuggling fees can usually repay them within two or three years.

Managing Migration via Rights

The communications and transportation revolutions help migrants to learn about opportunities and to cross national borders, while the rights revolution affects their ability to stay abroad. After World War II, most industrial countries strengthened the constitutional and political rights of people within their borders to prevent a recurrence of fascism, and most granted social or economic rights to residents in their evolving welfare states without distinguishing citizens from migrants.

As migration increased in the 1990s, policymakers began to roll back certain rights, especially socioeconomic rights, for migrants in an effort to manage migration. For example, many European governments (Germany, for example) put liberal asylum provisions into their post-war constitutions to avoid another situation similar to when refugees perished because other countries returned them to Nazi Germany. In the early 1990s, over 1,000 foreigners a day were applying for asylum in Germany. The government distributed them throughout the country and required local communities to provide them with housing and food. Because more than 90 percent of these were eventually found not to be in need of protection, there was a backlash that included attacks on foreigners.

The German government responded in three ways: 1) it required nationals of the countries of origin of asylum seekers (such as Turkey) to obtain visas, allowing pre-screening; 2) it imposed fines on airlines bringing foreigners to Germany without visas and other documents; and 3) it and other European Union countries agreed to make it diffi-cult for foreigners from "safe" countries (or who transited through safe countries en route to Germany) to apply for asylum.[12] In this way, the constitutional protection of asylum was maintained, but by making it harder to apply, they reduced the number of applicants.

In the 1990s, the United States debated the cost of providing wel-fare or social assistance to legal and unauthorized migrants. The North American Free Trade Agreement was expected to speed up econom-ic and job growth in Mexico, reducing migration between the United States and Mexico. Instead, Mexico–U.S. migration surged during the U.S. recession of 1991–1992, prompting California voters to approve Proposition 187 in 1994 over the objections of almost all statewide political and opinion leaders (*Migration News* 1994). The proposition called for establishment of a state-funded screening mechanism to ensure that unauthorized foreigners did not obtain state-funded services, including public-school education.[13]

Proposition 187 led to a national debate over immigrant numbers and rights, especially about the access of newcomers to social assistance. President Bill Clinton and those who wanted to "end welfare as we know it" argued that the number of needy migrants should be reduced to ensure continued access to welfare benefits among legal immigrants. However, employers argued that the better solution was to allow immigration to remain at high levels and reduce their access to social assistance. Employers won—immigration remained high and welfare benefits were curbed, but benefits to poor children and elderly immigrants were restored during the economic boom of the late 1990s.[14]

Balancing migrant numbers and migrant rights is a major challenge. Countries with the highest shares of migrants in their labor forces, such as the Gulf oil exporters, tend to extend few rights to migrants—it is very hard for a guest worker to win immigrant status and naturalize in Saudi Arabia or the United Arab Emirates. Countries with fewer guest workers, such as Sweden and other Scandinavian countries, tend to grant more rights to foreigners. The numbers-rights trade-off is apparent in World Trade Organization negotiations, where some developing countries argue that their migrant "service providers" should not have to earn the minimum wage in the destination country. Requiring payment of the minimum wage, they reason, will reduce the number of migrant workers employed (Ruhs and Martin 2008).

U.S. MIGRATION

The United States is a nation of immigrants. Under the motto "*e pluribus unum*" (from many one), U.S. presidents frequently remind Americans that, with a few exceptions, they or their forebears share the experience of beginning anew in the land of opportunity.[15] Immigration is widely considered to be in the national interest since it permits immigrants to better themselves and strengthen the United States.

For its first 100 years, the United States facilitated immigration, welcoming foreigners to settle a vast country. Beginning in the 1880s, certain types of foreigners were barred, including prostitutes, workers who arrived with contracts that tied them to a particular employer for several years, and Chinese, beginning an era of qualitative restrictions. In the 1920s, quantitative restrictions or quotas set a ceiling on the number of immigrants accepted each year.

Amendments in 1965 switched preferences from those wishing to migrate from countries in northwestern Europe to those who had relatives in the United States and those desired by U.S. employers. The origins of immigrants were not expected to change, but they did. In the 1960s, half of U.S. immigrants were from Latin America and Asia; between 2000 and 2005, 73 percent were from these regions (Martin and Midgley 2006, p. 3). Illegal immigration began rising in the 1970s, rose faster after immigration reforms in 1986, and was the first major immigration issue debated in Congress in the twenty-first century, as exemplified by debates in the Senate in 2006 and 2007 (*Migration News* 2006, 2007a).

Immigration occurs in waves, and the United States is in the midst of its fourth wave of immigrants. The first wave arrived before records were kept beginning in 1820, and most newcomers were from the British Isles. The second wave, dominated by Irish and German immigrants in the 1840s and 1850s, challenged the dominance of the Protestant church and led to a nativist backlash against Catholics and immigrants.

The third wave, between 1880 and 1914, brought more than 20 million immigrants to the United States, an average of 650,000 a year. Most of these southern and eastern European immigrants found jobs in factories in the cities of the Northeast and Midwest, where Americans leaving the farm sometimes joined them. Third-wave immigration was slowed first by World War I and then by quotas in the 1920s.

The fourth and current wave began with immigration reforms put in place in 1965. Since then, immigration has increased at an accelerating rate. The average annual inflow of legal immigrants was 250,000 in the 1950s, 330,000 in the 1960s, 450,000 in the 1970s, 735,000 in the

1980s, and more than a million since the 1990s (U.S. Department of Homeland Security 2009).

Types of Migrants

Foreigners enter the United States through a front door for legal permanent immigrants, a side door for legal temporary migrants, and a back door for unauthorized entrants. About two-thirds of legal immigrants are family sponsored, which means that family members in the United States asked the government to admit their relatives. There are no limits on the number of immigrant visas available for immediate relatives of U.S. citizens, and 580,000 were admitted in Fiscal Year 2006, but there is a cap on the number of immigrant visas available to relatives of permanent residents and more distant relatives of U.S. citizens (only 222,000 were admitted in 2006), resulting in long waits for visas. For example, Mexican spouses of U.S. immigrants had to wait six years for immigrant visas in 2008, and the wait for Mexican adult brothers and sisters of U.S. citizens was 13 years.[16]

Legal temporary migrants are foreigners who come to the United States to visit, work, or study. There are no limits on most types; the United States willingly accepted more than 30 million tourists and business visitors in 2006. Temporary foreign students and workers are more controversial. In the aftermath of the terrorist attacks of September 11, 2001, the U.S. government required foreign students to be interviewed personally before receiving visas to study in the United States and to pay a fee to support a database that tracks them while they are studying in the states.

Guest workers receive visas that tie them to a U.S. employer and specify how long they can stay. Holders of H-1B visas have at least a college degree and fill a job that normally requires a college degree. Most H-1B guest workers are Indians employed in computer-related jobs. Each can stay up to six years and "adjust" to regular immigrant status if their U.S. employer deems them uniquely qualified to fill the job.

It is easy for U.S. employers to have H-1B guest workers admitted; they simply attest that they are paying the prevailing wage and satisfying other conditions, and their request is almost automatically approved.

In 2001, Congress set an annual cap of 65,000 on the number of H-1B visas available to most employers, but there is no limit on the number for workers employed by nonprofit organizations such as universities. The number admitted on H-1B visas doubled from about 100,000 to 200,000 in the 1990s and almost doubled again to just under 400,000 in 2004, as Congress raised the cap temporarily at the request of high-tech firms.[17] Employers want far more than 65,000 H-1B visas to be available, and Microsoft founder Bill Gates has joined the chorus of those who say the cap should be eliminated entirely (McCullagh 2005). Critics of the H-1B program say that the easy availability of H-1B visas has discouraged Americans from studying and working in science and engineering fields (Teitelbaum 2003).

Unauthorized foreigners are persons in the country in violation of U.S. immigration laws. Demographer Jeff Passel estimated there were 11 million unauthorized foreigners in 2005, with the number increasing by 525,000 a year (Passel 2006a). There were 37 million foreign-born U.S. residents in 2005, of which 31 percent were naturalized U.S. citizens, 39 percent were legal immigrants and temporary visitors, and 30 percent were unauthorized. Somewhat over half of the unauthorized foreigners entered the country by evading border controls, and the rest entered legally but did not leave as required (Passel 2006b).

The Department of Homeland Security (DHS) is responsible for preventing unauthorized foreigners from entering the nation and for finding and removing those here illegally. The department's Customs and Border Protection agency includes the Border Patrol, which has more than 12,000 agents to apprehend foreigners attempting to enter the United States between designated ports of entry. In recent years, Border Patrol agents have been apprehending about 1.3 million foreigners a year, and 85 percent of these are Mexicans caught just inside the Mexico–U.S. border. In addition, some 208,500 foreigners were removed or deported from the United States in 2005, 70 percent of which were Mexican.[18]

Economic Impacts

Most immigrants come to the United States for economic opportunity. As they go to work, immigrants affect the U.S. economy and labor market. Most working-age immigrants find jobs, earn and spend most of their wages, pay taxes, and consume public services. In doing so, immigrants expand employment and the economy while slightly depressing wages or the growth in wages, especially for workers similar to the immigrants. With more workers, profits rise, and the entire economy is larger as a result of immigration.

In 1997, the National Research Council emphasized that the main beneficiaries of immigration are the immigrants themselves, who earn higher wages than they could in their home countries, followed by their U.S. employers. Skilled U.S. workers and affluent consumers also benefit from the presence of unskilled immigrants, for example, when professionals hire migrants to do household work or pay slightly less in restaurants because migrants hold down wages. The net economic benefits of legal and illegal immigration were estimated to be $1 billion to $10 billion in the mid 1990s, meaning that U.S. gross domestic product was increased by this amount because of immigration (Smith and Edmonston 1997). Proponents of immigration stress that the immigrant effect was positive; opponents stress that the overall impact was negligible because the then $8 trillion economy was expanding by 3 percent, growing by $240 billion a year or by $10 billion every two weeks.[19]

Immigration has a small, yet positive overall economic effect, making the major economic questions about immigration distributional, such as who benefits and who suffers from immigration? In general, immigrants are different from those born in the United States in their level of education, so they will have uneven effects on U.S.-born workers.

The best single predictor of U.S. income is years of education. Some 30 percent of immigrants who arrived since 1990 and were 25 or older in 2002 had at least a college degree, compared with 24 percent of U.S.-born Americans in the same age category. At the other end of the education distribution, 34 percent of the immigrants did not finish high school as compared with 16 percent of U.S.-born adults (U.S. Census Bureau 2005).

The differences between immigrants and those born in the United States are clear: the educational profile of U.S.-born adults features a bulge in the middle, reflecting the 62 percent of Americans with a high-school diploma but no college degree. Immigrants, on the other hand, divide into three distinct groups of about equal size: college graduates, high-school graduates, and those with less than a high-school diploma. The large share of immigrants with less than a high-school diploma has raised concerns about the impact of immigrants on low-skilled U.S. workers and about the balance of their taxes paid relative to tax-supported benefits received.

LABOR-MARKET EFFECTS

Immigration adds workers who change U.S. wages, prices, and profits. The President's Council of Economic Advisers summarized the labor-market effects of immigrants as follows: "Although immigrant workers increase output, their addition to the supply of labor . . . [causes] wage rates in the immediately affected market [to be] bid down . . . Thus, native-born workers who compete with immigrants for jobs may experience reduced earnings or reduced employment" (Council of Economic Advisers 1986, p. 221).

Most research interest and policy concerns focus on how immigrants affect those near the bottom of the labor market. Governments have long protected vulnerable low-wage workers by establishing minimum wages, regulating hours of work, and allowing workers to join unions and bargain for higher wages with their employers. The 1960s War on Poverty and civil rights movement reinforced the U.S. commitment to improving conditions at the bottom of the labor market, which resulted in the creation of employment and training programs that enable workers to improve their skills and earnings as well as affirmative-action programs for groups that suffered discrimination in the past.

Economic Studies

Economists and other social scientists have used three kinds of studies to examine the labor-market effects of immigrants in detail: 1) case studies, 2) econometric studies, and 3) economic-mobility or integration studies.

Case studies examine the impacts of immigrants in a particular industry or occupation, not the overall economy. When unionized farm workers in southern California went on strike for a wage increase in 1982, many were replaced by unauthorized newcomers recruited to break the strike by labor contractors. The displacement of union workers in this case was a result of a competition between employers. The unionized harvesting association lost business and laid off workers as growers turned to labor contractors who hired non-union and often unauthorized workers to get their lemons picked. Eventually, the unionized harvesting association went out of business, and the wages of lemon pickers declined (Mines and Martin 1984).

Case studies show that immigrants can displace workers and depress wages by adding vulnerable workers to the labor force. This scenario conforms to accepted labor-market theory, but as the lemon example shows, immigration's effects on wages and employment can be indirect and thus hard to measure. One reason is that many workers are hired via networks, meaning that current workers bring friends and family to fill vacant jobs. Once a cross-border network takes over the recruitment of new workers to fill job vacancies in a particular workplace, local workers may not learn about them as immigrants recruit new workers from abroad. An example of network hiring via contractors was when the owners of office buildings in Los Angeles replaced unionized black janitors with immigrants hired through cleaning contractors in the 1980s and 1990s (General Accounting Office 1988, pp. 39–41).

Other case studies show how an industry can introduce immigrants to an area via recruitment networks. The U.S. meat industry employs about 500,000 workers to turn cattle, hogs, sheep, and poultry into meat and other products, and it has shifted from cities such as Chicago to more rural areas in the Midwest and Southeast over the past quarter century. Plants became fewer and larger, and they often sought to operate 16 hours a day with two "disassembly" shifts in areas with relatively few workers, and wages were much lower than those paid in cities, where workers had other job options. Many of these plants recruited immigrants, and today about half of the workers in meatpacking are Hispanic (Equal Employment Opportunity Commission 2008).

Case studies emphasize how contractor recruitment, networks, and industry shifts interact to transform particular workplaces or industries, whereas econometric studies consider how immigration, wages, and employment interact in a city's labor market, usually by comparing cities with higher and lower shares of immigrant workers. Econometric studies begin with the assumption that, if the presence of immigrants depresses wages or displaces workers, cities with a higher share of immigrants in their labor forces should have lower wages or higher unemployment rates, especially for similar U.S. workers. Thus, econometric studies typically compare wages and unemployment rates for blacks, Hispanics, and women in cities with relatively more and fewer immigrants, such as Los Angeles and Minneapolis, expecting to find lower wages or higher unemployment in the area with more immigrants (Los Angeles in this example).

During the 1980s, to the surprise of economists, econometric studies found few of these expected negative labor-market effects. For example, a comparison of the wages and unemployment rates of black workers in Miami and other cities such as Atlanta and Tampa found no significant differences, even though the 1980 Mariel boatlift increased the Miami labor force by 7 percent in just four months (Card 1990). Several reasons for finding no adverse effects were offered, including the fact that jobs were created to build housing for the newcomers and that Cuban newcomers and local blacks did not compete for the same jobs; for example, few Cuban newcomers got government jobs. Economist George Borjas summarized the 1980s research literature by concluding, "Modern econometrics cannot detect a single shred of evidence that immigrants have a sizable adverse impact on the earnings and employment opportunities of natives in the United States" (Borjas 1990, p. 81).

As more data became available in the 1990s, researchers began to realize that, instead of staying in "immigrant cities," U.S. workers who competed most directly with immigrants moved away from immigrant cities or did not move to them. As a result, the effects of immigration on wages or unemployment were quickly diffused throughout the country rather than being measurable in an immigrant city such as Los Angeles or Houston. Furthermore, the "similar U.S. workers" who remained in "immigrant cities" often did not compete directly with immigrant workers, such as when blacks and women worked for government agencies at wages negotiated by collective bargaining or set by federal, state, or local governments that did not respond immediately to an influx of immigrant workers. If some of the U.S. workers who compete with newcomer immigrants move away, and the workers who remain are sheltered from immigrant wage effects, it is very hard to detect the expected effects of immigrants in comparisons of city labor markets (Borjas 1994a, 1999).

Measuring the impacts of 22 million foreign-born workers on 127 million U.S.-born workers is no easier when foreign-born workers differ significantly in education and location. The expected labor-market effects of adding immigrants to the labor force—slower wage growth and higher unemployment among similar workers—tend to be small and very hard to measure, especially because U.S. residents are mobile and labor markets are flexible. Indeed, if immigrants move to fast-growing cities, city comparison studies may suggest that immigration benefits similar U.S. workers (Borjas and Katz 2005). The difficulty in measuring immigrant impacts, and the different conclusions reached by economists such as George Borjas, who believes that immigrants reduce the wages of similar U.S. workers, and David Card, who does not, ensures a continuing debate on their effects (Lowenstein 2006).

Economic-mobility or integration studies examine how immigrants and their children are faring in the United States. Immigrants earn just over 75 percent as much as U.S.-born workers. In 2007, their median weekly earnings were $554 versus $722 for U.S.-born workers (U.S. Department of Labor 2008). Lower earnings for newcomers who may not know English or have U.S. work experience are not surprising; the question is whether the earnings of immigrants catch up to those of U.S.-born workers over time, suggesting economic integration.

Economist Barry Chiswick studied the earnings trajectories of immigrant men who were in the United States in 1970. Chiswick found that the earnings of immigrant men were initially 10 percent lower than those of U.S.-born men of similar age and level of education. However, the earnings of immigrant men rose faster, and after an average 13 years in the United States, they had earnings equal to those of similar U.S.-born men, and after 23 years, the immigrants earned 6 percent more (Chiswick 1978). Chiswick's study provided evidence for the fresh-blood argument that immigration benefits the United States because the extra drive and ambition that leads people to cross national borders and begin anew expands the U.S. economy and raises average earnings.

A decade later, economist George Borjas concluded that Chiswick's findings applied to a unique set of circumstances. Most of the immigrants in the United States in 1970 were Europeans or well-educated Asians who initially earned less than comparably educated U.S. men, but they caught up as they learned English and gained U.S. work experience. However, later cohorts of immigrants who arrived with far less education, such as legal and unauthorized Mexican immigrants, started their American journeys with much lower earnings than earlier immigrants. The earnings of Mexicans did not rise as fast, leading Borjas to conclude that continued Latin American immigration would lead to widening gaps between immigrants and native-born Americans (Borjas 1994b).[20]

Entrepreneurship

Economists tend to look at earnings to measure economic integration, but some social scientists emphasize other indicators, such as entrepreneurship and the creation of new businesses. Immigrant-owned businesses are highly visible in many cities, from ethnic restaurants and shops to gardening and cleaning services. With immigrants often willing to work long hours, sometimes creating jobs for family members and other immigrants from their countries of origin, some commentators say that immigrant energy can revitalize cities (Aronson 1997, pp. 11–12; Portes 1995, p. 29). Many Cubans in Miami, for example, began businesses to serve other Cubans in an "ethnic enclave" that is now seen as an economic incubator (Portes and Bach 1985).

Entrepreneurship is hard to measure, and self-employment is often used as a proxy measure for those who begin their own businesses. About 13 percent of U.S.-born workers were self-employed in 2005 (a broad category including, for example, farmers, doctors, and lawyers), as were 11 percent of foreign-born workers. Rates of self-employment were especially high among some groups: 28 percent of those born in Korea were self-employed in the United States, as were 20 percent or more of those born in Russia and Iran (Camarota 2005). Self-employment normally declines with economic development, especially as farmers leave the land for urban jobs in factories and offices. However, in the new service economy, it has become easier to be self-employed, and immigrants may be in a unique position to spot opportunities (Camarota 2005).

In the end, though, it is not clear that self-employment is a sign of immigrant economic success. In fact, self-employment tends to increase during recessions, as some ex-farmers return to the land in developing countries and some laid-off executives become self-employed consultants in more developed countries (Borjas 1990; Filer, Hamermesh, and Rees 1996).

IMMIGRATION TRADE-OFFS

Immigration is often characterized as either good or bad for the country, but public policy choices are rarely contests between good and bad. They are instead arguments about which "good" deserves higher priority. For example, raising interest rates can lead to lower inflation, a desirable result, but away from fuller employment, a competing good. Similarly, reducing trade barriers can stimulate exports, helping some employers and workers, but it also increases imports, which can lead to the failure of other businesses and a loss of jobs.

There is no easy way to balance the trade-offs between competing outcomes, and the United States has found it especially hard to deal with trade-offs inherent in the three basic immigration questions:

1) How many immigrants should be allowed to enter?

2) From which countries and in what status should they come?

3) How should the government enforce immigration rules?

Immigrant farm workers provide an example. Americans want to pay low prices for food. They also want farm workers, like other U.S. workers, to have decent wages and working conditions. Congress permitted Mexican farm workers to enter as immigrants and guest workers and tolerated unauthorized migrants, which helped to keep farm wages low but also increased poverty among farm workers. To alleviate this poverty, the federal government spends about $1 billion a year on special education, health, and housing programs for farm workers and their children.[21]

What is the trade-off between cheap food and decent farm wages? According to the U.S. Bureau of Labor Statistics' Consumer Expenditure Survey, there were 120 million "consumer units" in 2007, and they had an average of 2.5 persons, 1.3 earners, and 1.9 vehicles. These consumer units or households had average annual incomes of $63,100 before taxes, and their expenditures averaged $49,600 (U.S. Bureau of Labor Statistics 2008). These household expenditures included $6,100 for food (12 percent). Food spending was split 57–43 percent, including $3,500 for food eaten at home ($67 a week) and $2,700 for food bought away from home. To put food spending in perspective, other significant expenditures were $17,000 for housing and utilities, $8,800 for transportation, $2,900 for health care, $1,900 for apparel, and $2,700 for entertainment (U.S. Bureau of Labor Statistics 2008).

The largest at-home food expenditures were for meat and poultry, totaling $777. Expenditures on cereal and bakery products, $460, exceeded the $387 spent on dairy products. Expenditures on fresh fruits ($202) and fresh vegetables ($190) totaled $392, or $7.50 a week (consumer units spent an additional $112 on processed fruits and $96 on processed vegetables). The average consumer unit spent more on alcoholic beverages, $457 (or $8.75 a week), than on fresh fruits and vegetables (U.S. Bureau of Labor Statistics 2008).

Farmers get a small share of the retail food dollar, an average of 19 percent. In 2006, farmers received an average 30 percent of the retail price of fresh fruits and 25 percent of the retail price of fresh vegetables, so consumer expenditures of $392 meant $109 to the farmer ([0.3 × $202 = $61] + [0.25 × $190 = $48] = $109). Farm labor costs are typically less than a third of farm revenue for fresh fruits and vegetables, meaning that farm worker wages and benefits for fresh fruits and vegetables cost the average consumer unit $36 a year (U.S Department of Agriculture 2008a).

Although strawberries are picked directly into the containers in which they are sold, and iceberg lettuce gets its film wrapper in the field, farmers and farm workers get a very small share of the retail dollar. Consumers who pay $1 for a pound of apples are giving 30 cents to the farmer of which 10 cents goes to the farm worker; those spending $2 for a head of lettuce are giving 42 cents to the farmer and 10 cents to the farm worker (U.S. Department of Agriculture 2008a).

If the influx of immigrant workers was slowed or stopped and farm wages rose, what would happen to expenditures on fresh fruits and vegetables? In 1966, the fledgling United Farm Workers union won a 40 percent wage increase for table grape harvesters, largely because Bracero workers (temporary contract laborers from Mexico) were not available. The average earnings of field workers were $9.40 an hour in 2007, according to a U.S. Department of Agriculture survey of farm employers, and a 40 percent increase would raise the average to $13.15 an hour. If this wage increase were passed on to consumers, the 10-cent farm labor cost of a pound of apples would rise to 14 cents, and the retail price would rise to $1.04 (U.S. Department of Agriculture 2008b).

For a typical household, a 40 percent increase in farm labor costs translates into about a 4 percent (3.6 percent) increase in retail prices for fresh fruits and vegetables.[22] If farm wages rose 40 percent and were passed fully to consumers, average spending on fruits and vegetables would rise by $14 a year (3.6 percent × $392). However, for a typical seasonal farm worker, a 40 percent wage increase could raise earnings from $9,400 for 1,000 hours of work to $13,150, lifting him or her above the federal poverty line for an individual.

Are the savings on fresh produce due to immigration worthwhile? Under the present arrangement, the migrants are better off, earning more in the United States than they would at home. U.S. farmers and their bankers are also better off, enjoying higher profits and higher land prices. Consumers of U.S. commodities pay less for fresh produce. The critical question is whether these benefits are more valuable than having farm work performed and rewarded like other work in America. The way this question is answered affects U.S. immigration policy, espe cially with respect to Mexico.

CONCLUSIONS: IMMIGRATION AND VERNON BRIGGS

Immigration means change—in the number and type of people and workers in a country, in the structure and functioning of labor markets, and in the welfare of residents and workers. Migration has interrelated cultural and political as well as economic dimensions, as demonstrated by this chapter's discussion of recruiting networks and migration management. At the same time, the economic and labor-market effects of migrants are often difficult to measure, which prompts some to conclude that there are few such effects.

Vernon Briggs has long been concerned about low-wage and minority workers. His scholarship demonstrates that periods of low immigration and rapid economic growth, such as the 1960s, reinforce governmental poverty-reduction efforts and enable a rising tide to lift most U.S. workers up the U.S. job ladder (Briggs 2003). His work also documents that unauthorized migration surged in the 1990s, in part a consequence of flawed policy initiatives, as the real wages of U.S. workers with little education and few skills declined, even as their share of the labor force diminished (Briggs 2005).

Briggs deserves our gratitude for pioneering efforts to analyze these trends and to educate and inform policymakers and the public about the links between increased immigration and low-wage workers. The unauthorized foreigners who arrived in the 1990s are having U.S.-born (and thus U.S.-citizen) children, and a future Vernon Briggs will likely develop policy options to help them climb the U.S. job ladder.

Notes

1. Charles C. Lemert says there were fewer than 50 nation-states in 1900 (Lemert 2005, p. 176).
2. Data were obtained from the Web sites of government immigration agencies that were accessed in August 2007.
3. A *Wall Street Journal* editorial on July 3, 1986, first made the open borders proposal, which was repeated in an editorial on July 3, 1990.
4. The National Front candidate, Jean Marie Le Pen, received 15 percent of the vote in the first round of presidential voting in 1995 (Fekete 1995).
5. The average woman in developing countries has 3.5 children (excluding China), versus 1.5 children per woman in developed countries. According to the Population Reference Bureau (http://www.prb.org), the world's fastest growing population is in Gaza, where the population growth rate is 4.5 percent a year, and the fastest shrinking population is in Russia, where the population is declining by 0.5 percent a year.
6. Young people are most likely to move over borders because they have the least invested in jobs and careers at home and the most time to recoup their "investment in migration" abroad.

7. Average global per-capita income was $7,000 per person. At purchasing power parity, which takes into account national differences in the cost of living, the world's gross national income was $56 trillion or $9,400 per capita—$32,500 per capita in the high-income countries and $5,200 in low- and middle-income countries (World Bank 2009).

8. Taxes are extracted from agriculture by monopoly input suppliers who sell seeds or fertilizers at high prices or by monopoly purchasers of farm commodities who buy from farmers at less-than-world prices and pocket the difference when the coffee, cocoa, or other commodity is exported. In high-income countries, farmers' incomes are generally higher than those of nonfarmers, in part because high-income countries transfer funds to producers of food and fiber.

9. For example, this is evident in Chinese coastal cities, where internal rural–urban migrants fill 3-D jobs, and abroad, where Chinese migrants are employed in industries that range from services to sweatshops (*Migration News* 2008).

10. These farm worker recruitment networks are examined in *Rural Migration News*. See http://migration.ucdavis.edu/rmn/index.php.

11. Even if migrants know that movies and TV shows portray exaggerated lifestyles, migrants who find themselves in slave-like conditions abroad sometimes say they did not believe things in rich countries could be "that bad."

12. The goal is to prevent so-called asylum shopping, such as when an asylum seeker from Turkey passes through Bulgaria and Romania en route to Germany and applies for asylum because conditions for asylum applicants and rates of recognition are better in Germany (Da Lomba 2004).

13. A federal judge stopped implementation of Proposition 187 (which was approved by a 59 to 41 percent margin in November 1994), but some of its provisions were included in 1996 federal immigration reforms (see *Migration News* 1994).

14. Details of the three U.S. laws enacted in 1996 can be found at *Migration News* (http://migration.ucdavis.edu). One provision that was eventually dropped would have made legal immigrants deportable if they received more than 12 months of welfare benefits.

15. The exceptions are Native Americans, slaves, and those who became U.S. citizens by purchase or conquest, such as French nationals who became Americans with the Louisiana Purchase, Mexicans who became Americans with the settlement ending the Mexican War, and Puerto Ricans who became U.S. citizens as a result of the American victory over Spain in 1898.

16. Waiting lists are published in the Department of State *Visa Bulletin*, available at http://travel.state.gov/visa/frvi/bulletin/bulletin_1360.html.

17. In addition to the H-1B cap exemption for certain nonprofits, up to 20,000 foreign students a year who earn master's degrees and doctorates from U.S. universities can receive H-1B visas. As a result, the number admitted each year exceeds 100,000. An H-1B visa holder can later become an immigrant if he or she qualifies on the basis of family unification or employment.

18. Annual DHS reports entitled "Immigration Enforcement Actions" can be found at http://www.dhs.gov/ximgtn/statistics/publications/index.shtm. Almost all apprehended Mexicans "volunteer" to return to Mexico. Those caught so many times

they appear to be smugglers may be prosecuted by U.S. authorities. In the investigation of the firings of eight U.S. attorneys in December 2006, it was reported that, in most border districts, the same individual had to be apprehended at least six times before being prosecuted by the U.S. Attorney's office (see *Migration News* 2007b).

19. By 2005, the U.S. economy was growing by about $15 billion in two weeks.
20. Between 1970 and 1990, the share of U.S. men without a high-school diploma by age 25 fell from 40 percent to 15 percent; the share of immigrant men without a high-school diploma fell from 48 percent to 37 percent (Borjas 1994b).
21. The evolution and effectiveness of these programs is examined in Martin and Martin (1993).
22. The calculation is as follows. If farmers receive an average 27.8 percent of the retail price of fresh fruits and vegetables ($109/$392), and give a third of what they get to farm workers, then the farm worker share of the retail dollar is 9 percent ($0.278 \times 0.33 = 9$ percent). If farm labor costs rise 40 percent, then 0.4×9 percent yields a 3.6 percent rise in retail prices.

References

Aronson, David. 1997. "Immigrant Entrepreneurs." *Research Perspectives on Migration* 1(2): 1–15.

Borjas, George J. 1990. *Friends or Strangers: The Impact of Immigrants on the U.S. Economy.* New York: Basic Books.

———. 1994a. "The Economics of Immigration." *Journal of Economic Literature* 32(4): 1667–1717.

———. 1994b. "Assimilation and Changes in Cohort Quality Revisited: What Happened to Immigrant Earnings in the 1980s?" NBER Working Paper no. 4866. Cambridge, MA: National Bureau of Economic Research.

———. 1999. "The Economic Analysis of Immigration." In *Handbook of Labor Economics, Volume 3A*, Orley Ashenfelter and David Card, eds. Amsterdam: Elsevier, pp. 1697–1760.

Borjas, George J., and Lawrence F. Katz. 2005. "The Evolution of the Mexican-Born Workforce in the United States." NBER Working Paper no. 11281. Cambridge, MA: National Bureau of Economic Research.

Briggs, Vernon. 2003. *Mass Immigration and the National Interest: Policy Directions for the New Century*. Armonk, NY: M.E. Sharpe.

———. 2005. "Immigration and Poverty Reduction: Policy Making on a Squirrel Wheel." *Journal of Economic Issues* 37(2): 325–332.

Camarota, Steven A. 2005. *Immigrants at Mid-Decade: A Snapshot of America's Foreign-Born Population in 2005*. Washington, DC: Center for Immigration Studies. http://www.cis.org/articles/2005/back1405.html (accessed January 31, 2009).

Card, David. 1990. "The Impact of the Mariel Boatlift on the Miami Labor Market." *Industrial and Labor Relations Review* 43(2): 245–257.

Chiswick, Barry. 1978. "The Effect of Americanization on the Earnings of Foreign-Born Men." *Journal of Political Economy* 86(5): 897–921.

Council of Economic Advisers. 1986. "The Economic Effects of Immigration." In *Economic Report of the President, 1986.* Washington, DC: U.S. Government Printing Office, pp. 213–234.

Da Lomba, Sylvie. 2004. *The Right to Seek Refugee Status in the European Union.* Antwerp: Intersentia.

Equal Employment Opportunity Commission. 2008. *Job Patterns for Minorities and Women in Private Industry (EEO-1).* Washington, DC: Equal Employment Opportunity Commission. http://www.eeoc.gov/stats/jobpat/jobpat.html (accessed January 31, 2009).

Fekete, Liz. 1995. "Issues in the French Presidential Elections." Independent Race and Refugee News Network news release, June 1. http://www.irr.org.uk/europebulletin/france/extreme_right_politics/1995/ak000006.html (accessed January 31, 2009).

Filer, Randall, Daniel Hamermesh, and Albert Rees. 1996. *The Economics of Work and Pay.* New York: HarperCollins.

General Accounting Office. 1988. *Illegal Aliens: Influence of Illegal Workers on the Wages and Working Conditions of Legal Workers.* PEMD-88-13BR. Washington, DC: General Accounting Office.

International Labour Office. 2009. *Total and Economically Active Population, Employment and Unemployment (Population Censuses).* Geneva: International Labour Office. http://laborsta.ilo.org/applv8/data/SSM5/E/ssm5.html (accessed September 20, 2009).

Lemert, Charles C. 2005. *Social Things: An Introduction to the Sociological Life.* New York: Rowman and Littlefield.

Lowenstein, Roger. 2006. "The Immigration Equation." *New York Times Magazine,* July 9, pp. 36–43, 69–71. http://www.nytimes.com/2006/07/09/magazine/09IMM.html (accessed January 31, 2009).

Martin, Philip L. 1996. *Promises to Keep: Collective Bargaining in California Agriculture.* Ames, IA: Iowa State University Press.

Martin, Philip L., and David Martin. 1993. *The Endless Quest: Helping America's Farm Workers.* Boulder, CO: Westview Press.

Martin, Philip L., and Elizabeth Midgley. 2006. "Immigration: Shaping and Reshaping America." *Population Bulletin* 61(4): 3–28.

McCullagh, Declan. 2005. "Gates Wants to Scrap H-1B Visa Restrictions."

ZDNet News and Blogs, April 27. http://news.zdnet.com/2100-3513_ 22-142533.html (accessed January 31, 2009).

Migration News. 1994. "Prop. 187 Approved in California." *Migration News* 0(4). http://migration.ucdavis.edu/mn/more.php?id=492_0_2_0 (accessed January 31, 2009).

———. 2006. "Senate Approves CIRA." *Migration News* 12(3). http://migration.ucdavis.edu/mn/more.php?id=3199_0_2_0.July (accessed June 3, 2009).

———. 2007a. "Senate: Immigration Reform Stalls." *Migration News* 13(3). http://migration.ucdavis.edu/mn/more_entireissue.php?idate=2007_ 07&number=3.July (accessed June 3, 2009).

———. 2007b. "DHS: Border, Interior." *Migration News* 13(2). http://migration.ucdavis.edu/mn/more.php?id=3272_0_2_0 (accessed January 31, 2009).

———. 2008. "China: Migrants, Taiwan." *Migration News* 14(2). http://migration.ucdavis.edu/mn/more.php?id=3353_0_3_0 (accessed June 3, 2009).

Mines, Richard, and Philip L. Martin. 1984. "Immigrant Workers and the California Citrus Industry." *Industrial Relations* 23(1): 139–149.

Passel, Jeff. 2006a. "Size and Characteristics of the Unauthorized Migrant Population in the United States: Estimates Based on the March 2005 Current Population Survey." Research report. Washington, DC: Pew Hispanic Center. http://pewhispanic.org/files/reports/61.pdf (accessed June 26, 2009).

———. 2006b. "Modes of Entry for the Unauthorized Migrant Population." Pew Hispanic Center Fact Sheet no. 19. Washington, DC: Pew Hispanic Center. http://pewhispanic.org/files/factsheets/19.pdf (accessed June 26, 2009).

Portes, Alejandro, ed. 1995. *The Economic Sociology of Immigration.* New York: Russell Sage Foundation.

Portes, Alejandro, and Robert L. Bach. 1985. *Latin Journey: Cuban and Mexican Immigrants in the United States.* Berkeley, CA: University of California Press.

Ruhs, Martin, and Philip L. Martin. 2008. "Numbers vs. Rights: Trade-offs and Guest Worker Programs." *International Migration Review* 42(1): 249–265.

Rural Migration News. n.d. Various issues. http://migration.ucdavis.edu/rmn/index.php (accessed January 31, 2009).

Smith, James P., and Barry Edmonston. 1997. *The New Americans: Economic, Demographic and Fiscal Effects of Immigration.* Washington, DC: National Academies Press.

Teitelbaum, Michael S. 2003. "Do We Need More Scientists?" *Public Interest* no. 153, 40–53.

Torpey, John. 1999. *The Invention of the Passport: Surveillance, Citizenship and the State*. Cambridge: Cambridge University Press.

United Nations Population Division. 1999. *The World at Six Billion*. New York: United Nations.

———. 2006. *International Migration Report 2005*. ST/ESA/SER.A/220. New York: United Nations. http://www.un.org/esa/population/publications/2006Migration_Chart/2006IttMig_chart.htm (accessed January 31, 2009).

United Nations Population Fund. 2007. *State of World Population 2007*. New York: United Nations Population Fund. http://www.unfpa.org/swp/2007/english/introduction.html (accessed January 31, 2009).

U.S. Bureau of Labor Statistics. 2008. *Consumer Expenditure Survey*. Washington, DC: U.S. Bureau of Labor Statistics. http://www.bls.gov/cex/ (accessed January 31, 2009).

U.S. Census Bureau. 2005. *Educational Attainment in the United States: 2005*. Washington, DC: U.S. Census Bureau. http://www.census.gov/population/www/socdemo/education/cps2005.html (accessed June 26, 2009).

U.S. Department of Agriculture. 2008a. *Price Spreads from Farm to Consumer*. Washington, DC: Economic Research Service, U.S. Department of Agriculture. http://www.ers.usda.gov/Data/FarmToConsumer/index htm (accessed June 26, 2009).

———. 2008b. *NASS Farm Labor*. Washington, DC: National Agricultural Statistics Service. http://usda.mannlib.cornell.edu/MannUsda/viewDocumentInfo.do?documentID=1063 (accessed January 31, 2009).

U.S. Department of Homeland Security. 2009. *Immigration Statistics*. Washington, DC: U.S. Department of Homeland Security. http://www.dhs.gov/immigrationstatistics (accessed June 3, 2009).

U.S. Department of Labor. 2008. *Foreign-Born Workers: Labor Force Characteristics in 2007*. Washington, DC: U.S. Department of Labor. http://www.bls.gov/news.release/pdf/forbrn.pdf (accessed January 31, 2009).

World Bank. 2009. *Key Development Data and Statistics*. Washington, DC: World Bank. http://web.worldbank.org/WBSITE/EXTERNAL/DATASTATISTICS/0,,contentMDK:20535285~menuPK:1192694~pagePK:64133150~piPK:64133175~theSitePK:239419,00.html (accessed June 3, 2009).

5

Assessing the Briggs Approach
to Political Refugee Policy

Larry Nackerud
University of Georgia

Vernon Briggs's legacy in the landscape of U.S. immigration policy is secure. His research and writings are extensive, stretching from 1965 to today, and he is recognized as a leading national and international expert in his field. The accolades for his work, the stature of his coauthors, and the never-ending list of scholars who cite his publications, all speak to Briggs's footprint on U.S. immigration policy. This chapter, however, is not about Briggs's wide-ranging work in immigration pol icy; rather, it is focused on a more narrowly defined policy arena about which he was passionate—political refugee and asylee policy. In this chapter I posit that, while Briggs writes and speaks often of political refugee and asylee policy, his work in this area is ripe for extension, and yes, even debate. I am confident that Briggs will encourage and support such work, as nothing signifies Briggs's work more than discourse, debate, and lively discussion.

This confidence is bolstered by my personal experience with Briggs. In the mid 1980s, I studied at Cornell University to pursue an interest in social policy analysis. I sought knowledge about federal social policy formulation, local-level impact, and community-driven efforts to shape or modify those policies. Given this interest, Alan Hahn (my graduate committee chair) recommended I take a seminar in immigration and political refugee policy from "this fellow" over in the School of Industrial and Labor Relations.

As the seminar's first session was about to begin, Briggs shuffled into the classroom with a pile of books and well-worn notes under his arm. He placed the books and notes in front of him on the table and began to speak. I remember initially thinking, "This will be a long semester." Quickly, though, Briggs won me over. I was soon captivated by the breadth and depth of his historical and technical knowledge of immigration as well as of political refugee and asylee policy.

Briggs promoted academic dialogue and civil discourse. He encouraged students to express differing opinions and challenging questions in respectful and informed ways. He provoked an appreciation for the "unending conversation" that is central to the academic dialogue (Bruffee 1997). Critical to Briggs's view of such dialogue was that students should understand that academic work, be it teaching, research, or writing, is merely a conduit to a conversation of persons who are, in important ways, "fundamentally disagreeing" (Bean 2001, p. 18). Anyone who has followed Briggs's career is aware of his extraordinary ability to disagree, to state an opinion contrary to the popular view, and to do so with respect for others. For evidence of this unique ability, one need look no further than his recent public testimony, "Real Immigration Reform: The Path to Credibility," before the Subcommittee on Immigration of the Judiciary Committee of the U.S. House of Representatives (Briggs 2007).

I experienced firsthand Briggs's ability to encourage and support dialogue, even when there was political incongruence. In the classroom and during the years he was on my doctoral committee, it was clear that, although Briggs and I shared an interest in political refugee and asylee policy, our politics were not in complete congruence (on matters including the role of government, the position of humanitarian concerns in policymaking, and our concerns about the economy). I cringed when I heard Briggs say something to the effect that every person admitted to the United Stated should be first judged for her or his capacity to positively contribute to the economy. I would sometimes counter, "Even in the world of political refugee policy?" Not always, but often, Briggs, after a pensive pause, would answer in the affirmative.

His talk of neutrality with respect to political ideology and economic accountability for each U.S. entry decision sometimes struck me as cold. I came to realize, though, that our common interest in societal equity and the well-being of people seeking refuge in another country was merely constructed and expressed differently. Moreover, it was his tolerance of difference that contributed mightily to my oft-confirmed belief in Briggs as the "consummate academic." At the core of such an academic, in my opinion, is a willingness to nurture the expression of a varying belief held by another.

When asked to write this chapter, I first read and reacquainted myself with many of Briggs's works, including books and journal articles. I was struck by the extensive use of three considerations in his writing: economic accountability for each entry decision into the United States, neutrality with respect to political ideology, and societal equity. That threefold emphasis is the point of departure for this chapter: Can these considerations ever become the foundation for decision making in the complex arena of political refugee and asylee policy? This chapter considers that question through a review of the scholarship of Briggs and others.

HISTORY AS THE CONTEXT

Regardless of whether one is attempting to emulate Briggs or seeking to thoughtfully examine his three considerations (economic accountability, political neutrality, and societal equity), there can be only one starting point—history. Briggs, the consummate historian, started nearly each class and written piece with a historical review, particularly past policy developments. In this section, as a means of setting the foundation for a discussion of his three considerations, I present a brief history of U.S. political refugee policy, followed by a synopsis of the current state of affairs in U.S. political refugee policy.

In the historical section of his classic work, *Immigration and American Unionism*, Briggs states that issues surrounding accommodation of political refugees or asylees did not concern U.S. policymakers until the 1930s (Briggs 2001). In fact, prior to the passage of the Immigration Act of 1924, there was little need to be concerned about how the United States might respond to the needs of persons who sought to escape persecution in their homeland. In short, if they could get to the United States, they were generally admitted. The era of entrance upon arrival ended with the Immigration Act of 1924. It was not until after World War II that political refugee accommodation moved to a prominent position within the international community and the United States. In fact, the Displaced Persons Act of 1948, which President Harry Truman first promoted in 1945, was the first-ever piece of U.S. legislation focused solely on political refugee accommodation (Briggs 2003a).

Internationally, the world of political refugee accommodation witnessed a watershed event in 1951: the United Nations Convention Relating to the Status of Political Refugees. The Status provided the now classic definition of a person seeking refugee or asylee status:[1]

> [O]wing to [a] well-founded fear of being persecuted for reasons of race, religion, nationality, membership of a particular social group or political opinion, is outside the country of his nationality and is unable, or owing to such fear, is unwilling to avail himself of the protection of that country; or who, not having a nationality and being outside the country of his former habitual residence as a result of such events, is unable or, owing to such fear is unwilling to return to it. (Office of the United Nations High Commissioner for Human Rights 1951)

Providing a backdrop for the 1951 Convention was passage of the Declaration of Human Rights by the United Nations in 1948. Of the 30 articles expressed in the Declaration of Human Rights, none was more applicable to a discussion of political refugee and asylee policy than Article 14, which indicated that everyone has the right to seek and to enjoy in other countries asylum from persecution (Office of the United Nations High Commissioner for Human Rights 1948).

As the international community embraced a more rights-based and nondiscriminatory conscience for the consideration of the movement of people about the world, the United States countered with the Immigration and Nationality Act of 1952, which continued to employ a discriminatory, national-origins admission system (Briggs 2003a). Persons described as refugees continued to come to the United States in the 1930s, 1940s, and even 1950s; however, they did so at a time when the overall immigration levels were low.

After passage of the Political Refugee Relief Act of 1953, it was the parole authority of the Eisenhower administration that had the most profound impact on political refugee policy. The use of parole authority to bring refugees into the country was first used in 1956 and culminated with the admission of several hundred thousand Indochinese as part of the Indochinese Refugee Act of 1977 (Jeffreys 2007). Interestingly, the use of the parole authority admission process for political refugees continued even after the passage of the Immigration Act of 1965, which specified 17,400 visas for political refugees worldwide (Briggs 2001).

Another document, equal internationally to the impact of the 1951 Convention, was the 1967 United Nations Protocol Relating to the Status of Refugees. This prohibited any nation from returning a person claiming to be a refugee to a country where her or his life or freedom would be threatened. The United States signed onto the Protocol in 1968 (Jeffreys 2007), and this concept of "non-refoulement" took its place in U.S. political refugee and asylee policy deliberations.

In 1978, the U.S. Select Commission on Immigration and Political Refugee Policy (SCRIP) was formed. The commission was charged with bringing some sense to the country's admission policies. While the work of SCRIP was extensive and historically well regarded, it was the refugee-producing conditions in Southeast Asia that hurried the U.S. Congress to passage of the Refugee Act of 1980 (Briggs 2001). This Act established, at least in theory, a geographically and politically neutral adjudication standard for refugee or asylee status (Jeffreys 2007). It did so by removing the previous standard—which involved fleeing Communism or being from the Middle East—and replacing it with the persecution standard expressed in the 1951 U.N. Convention (Nackerud 1993).

The Refugee Act of 1980 essentially removed political refugees and asylees from immigration law by eliminating the refugee category declared earlier in the Immigration Act of 1965. A new system for the admission of political refugees and consideration of asylee status was thus created. Central to the new system was a consultation process between the President and Congress to determine numerical allocations and targeted geographic preferences (Nackerud 1993). The Refugee Act of 1980 was also designed to stop the use of the parole authority to admit large numbers of political refugees without numerical restriction (Briggs 2001). It also brought the United States into greater congruence with the international community, primarily through adoption of the U.N.-sponsored definition of who might be judged a political refugee or asylee (Nackerud 1993).

Briggs highlighted the fact that asylee policy was the least thought-through provision of the Refugee Act of 1980. Asylee status was intended to apply to individual cases and no one foresaw that the United States would become a nation of first instance for massive numbers of persons who, once ashore, would seek political asylum. Within weeks of its passage, that is precisely what happened (Briggs 2001, p. 148). Over the years, particularly large numbers of asylum seekers from Cuba and Haiti would challenge the effectiveness of the 1980 Refugee Act as a policy instrument.

That Act specified the creation of the Office of Refugee Resettlement within the Department of Health and Human Services, which was charged with ensuring that persons admitted as political refugees become self-sufficient and free from long-term dependence on public assistance (Newland, Tanaka, and Barker 2007). The consultative pattern established in the 1980 Refugee Act continues to this day. Before each fiscal year, the President consults with Congress and a worldwide refugee admissions ceiling is established. Allocations for each of the six geographic regions of the world are set (Jeffreys 2007). From 1980 to 2006, 2.3 million political refugees were admitted to the United States. An additional 344,507 individuals were granted asylum from 1990 to 2005. Thirty U.S. metropolitan areas and six states, California, Texas, Florida, New York, Washington, and Illinois, received over 60 percent of all resettled political refugees from 1983 to 2004 (Newland, Tanaka, and Barker 2007).

In 2007, political refugees constituted a mere 10 percent of annual overall immigration flow to the United States, but they were more noticeable as a subpopulation because of their tendency to congregate geographically. Refugees have historically congregated in certain major metropolitan areas, such as New York, Los Angeles, and Chicago, but they are also now doing so in mid-sized cities such as Sioux Falls and Fargo, South Dakota, and Binghamton, New York. For the last seven years, the United States has set its annual political refugee admissions ceiling at 70,000, a 70 percent decline from where it was set when the notion of a numerical limit was first introduced some 28 years ago. Despite this downward trend, the United States continues to resettle more political refugees overall than any other country, although other countries, particularly the Scandinavian social welfare states, resettle higher proportions of political refugees relative to the size of their native populations (Newland, Tanaka, and Barker 2007).

Table 5.1 depicts the numerical history of refugee admissions. Of particular note are the two years following most closely in the wake of the terrorist attacks of September 11, 2001, and their historically low levels of refugee admissions (26,773 and 28,304 in 2002 and 2003, respectively).

Low levels of refugee admissions (relative to those seen before 2002) continued even after 2002 and 2003. Indeed, the total number of political refugees admitted to the United States decreased 23 percent from 2005 (53,738) to 2006 (41,150). Overall, the annual average number of refugee arrivals declined from approximately 100,000 during the 1990s to 50,000 during the 2000–2006 period. This decline is often attributed to changes in security procedures after September 11, 2001, as well as admission requirements resulting from the Patriot Act of 2001 and the Real ID Act of 2005 (Jeffreys 2007). The composition of refugees has also shifted over the years, paralleling evolving humanitarian crises around the world and often more directly reflecting U.S. foreign policy priorities (Newland, Tanaka, and Barker 2007). The political asylee applicant must meet the same definition of persecution set forth in the Refugee Act of 1980. Asylee claims have risen through the years and claims averaged just over 26,000 a year from 2004 to 2006 (Jeffreys 2007).

This history and synopsis dovetails with one of Briggs's main historical points; the initial assignment for policy interpretation and implementation regarding entry of persons into the United States was with the Department of Labor upon its creation in 1913, but the assignment has shifted over time. In 1933, responsibility was transferred to the Department of Justice, and in 2003, it was moved to the Department of Homeland Security (Briggs 2003a). In 2007, responsibility was divided among three bureaus of the Department of Homeland Security: Customs and Border Protection, Citizenship and Immigration Services, and Immigration and Customs Enforcement (General Accounting Office 2004).

Table 5.1 Refugee Arrivals, Fiscal Years 1980 to 2006

Year	Number
1980	207,116
1981	159,252
1982	98,096
1983	61,218
1984	70,393
1985	67,704
1986	62,146
1987	64,528
1988	76,483
1989	107,070
1990	122,066
1991	113,389
1992	115,548
1993	114,181
1994	111,680
1995	98,973
1996	74,791
1997	69,276
1998	76,181
1999	85,076
2000	72,143
2001	68,925
2002	26,773
2003	28,304
2004	52,837
2005	53,738
2006	41,150

NOTE: Data series began following the Refugee Act of 1980. Excludes Amerasian immigrants, except in fiscal years 1989 to 1991.
SOURCE: U.S. Department of State (2007).

THE THREE CONSIDERATIONS

Economic Accountability for Each Entry Decision into the United States

Can economic accountability for each entry decision ever become the foundation for decision making in the complex arena of political refugee and asylee policy? Even though Briggs's work in the use of economic accountability for overall immigrant entry decisions is extensive and strong, I do not believe it is in the best interest of the United States to fully overlay that consideration onto the arena of political refugee and asylee policy. In fact, I believe even some of Briggs's work on economic accountability and political refugee and asylee policy may benefit from a bit of an extension of his ideas.

If a single mantra had to be selected from the legacy of Briggs's work, then the one that most fully embodies his career and impact is the notion of linking immigration decisions and economic accountability. In almost all writings and speaking opportunities, Briggs proffers this idea. In public testimonies as recent as May of 2007, he emphasized the impact on the labor force of any change in entry policy. In Briggs's view, each entrant should be judged for: 1) their ability to bring human capital with them when they enter the country, 2) the probability that an individual entering the country will be an asset to the U.S. economy, and 3) particularly with regard to subpopulations, such as political refugees and asylees, the probability that the individual will not become or remain welfare dependent. Briggs's belief in viable economic accountability is captured in the following quote:

> The United States needs to adopt an immigration policy that is consistent with its rapidly changing labor-market trends. If congruent, immigration policy can provide a valuable tool to national efforts to enhance economic efficiency and to achieve societal equity. If contradictory, immigration policy can present a major barrier to the accomplishment of either or both goals. The luxury of allowing immigration policy to continue to be determined on political criteria (i.e., to placate special interest groups) and to achieve idealistic social dreams (i.e., to pursue diversity simply for its own sake) can ill be afforded. Making immigration policy primarily a human

resource development policy would give immigration policy what it now lacks: economic accountability for most of what it does. (Briggs 2003a, p. 282)

With regard to political refugee and asylee policy, however, Briggs's economic accountability idea is open to debate. In a paper presented in 2003 before the Association for Evolutionary Economics, Briggs contended that "unexpected consequences" of immigration policy have played a significant part in the creation of poverty in the United States since 1965. Listing six of these consequences, Briggs described number five as the "extensive admission of refugees, mostly from third-world nations." Number six on Briggs's list is as follows: "The arrival of many poor persons, also from mostly the third world, who often falsely make claims for political asylum to justify their presence and then abscond before their hearing dates are held or, if they receive a negative ruling, after being ordered to depart" (Briggs 2003b, p. 328).

I believe Briggs overstates the rather complex relationship between the entry of political refugees and asylees and U.S. poverty. For example, the U.S. poverty rate fell from 12.6 percent in 2005 to 12.3 percent in 2006 (U.S. Census Bureau 2007). Considering that the U.S. population had recently surpassed 300 million people, a 12.3 percent poverty rate equates to approximately 36.9 million persons living in poverty. Even if the full allocation of 70,000 political refugees had been filled in 2006, political refugees would still only amount to 0.002 percent of the nation's impoverished persons. In fact, the actual number of political refugees admitted for 2006 was 41,150, and if one assumes that all of these people were living in poverty, then the percentage of the nation's poor attributable to political refugee admissions would represent only 0.0013 percent of the total number of poor persons for that year.

Further, the cumulative total of political refugees admitted from 1980 to 2006 is less than 2.3 million. If every political refugee admitted to the United States during this period lives in poverty (which is clearly not true), they represent only 0.076 percent of the overall U.S. population and less than 1 percent of the nation's poor. Even with the most draconian effort to estimate the impact of the nation's political refugee population, these numbers remain incredibly small. And they remain so even when the relatively small number of asylees is added to the mix.

In 1994, in *Still an Open Door?* Briggs hypothesized that the accommodation of political refugees and asylees would be a challenge to address in an overall immigration system based on economic needs. Then he and coauthor Stephen Moore made a number of recommendations for accomplishing this objective, including the following (Briggs and Moore 1994):

- A method should be instituted to expedite asylee applications and separate the legitimate claims for political asylum from claims by people who simply seek a pretext to enter the country for personal economic gain (the current process, which offers both an affirmative and defensive route to asylum, probably does some of this, see TRAC Immigration [2006]).

- Even though political refugees should represent an exception to the rules of general immigration, restrictions on political refugee levels should still be in place.

- U.S. support is critical for resettlement, repatriation, and maintenance of quality of life standards in the world's refugee camps.

- The U.S. should link its foreign aid and foreign trade policies to adherence to human rights principles in those countries that generate mass numbers of political refugees.

- Once a political refugee is admitted, one less immigrant should be admitted.

Even with these recommendations, Briggs concluded by expressing doubts about the ability to fully accommodate refugees and asylees in an immigration system based on economic accountability, and I agree. Although economic concerns will always play a major role in international affairs, there are certainly instances when foreign policy concerns or the execution of reciprocal humanitarian agreements may rise to greater prominence. In those instances, refugee and asylee accommodation, and the inclusion of a non-economic basis for entrant decision making, may assist in furthering the interests of the United States.

Indeed, one argument against strictly applying the consideration of economic accountability is that political refugees and asylees may have human capital characteristics that are much higher than generally perceived. In *Mass Immigration and the National Interest*, Briggs indicates there have been times when the human capital characteristics of political refugees (including levels of education, years of experience in the formal labor market, and language[s] spoken) have measurably enhanced the characteristics of the entire immigrant population (Briggs 2003a), but that is only part of the story.

I contend that refugees who make it to the United States for resettlement are tremendously different from their less-resilient peers. Those who get here must have the ability to flee their country with virtually nothing, migrate to a host country (most often to a U.N.-sponsored camp), convince a consortium of nongovernmental organization representatives that they qualify as a political refugee, and get accepted for resettlement into the United States. To even undertake such a journey, many refugees have already demonstrated they possess personal qualities that will promote their success in this country, including (but not limited to) risk taking, quick and effective decision making, the ability to convince others and to negotiate difficult bureaucracies, and resilience in the face of overwhelming odds. This is obviously not true of all political refugees, but it is a safe bet to say that many, if not most, political refugees who resettle in this country are likely to do well, particularly when given a chance to do so over time (see Singer and Wilson 2006).

Can—indeed, should—the consideration of "economic accountability for every entrant" serve as a foundation for U.S. political refugee and asylee policy? I do not think so.

Neutrality with Respect to Political Ideology

Briggs has often touted the need for neutrality with respect to political ideology in the development, interpretation, and implementation of immigration and political refugee and asylee policy. Can neutrality with respect to political ideology ever become a strong consideration in political refugee and asylee policy? I believe this is an unachievable goal. And if ever achieved, it would be very difficult to maintain.

Any student of U.S. political and refugee policy would do well to read Briggs's view of how political refugee and asylee policy became politicized in the United States (Briggs 2003a, pp. 136–173). That discussion, in a chapter titled "Unexpected Consequences," leads the reader through the years 1965 to 1994, from President Lyndon Johnson to President Bill Clinton. Briggs carefully outlines the government's increasingly politicized response to crises facing a diverse group of refugee populations, including Cubans, Vietnamese, Haitians, Guatemalans, and Salvadorans. He concludes this section of the book with a heading, "The Continuing Weakness of Asylee Policy" (Briggs 2003a, p. 170).

For the nation to move beyond a highly politicized policy, Briggs stresses that social goals must override political goals (Briggs 2003a). Thus, he argues that social goals, such as compassion, humanitarianism, and a desire to reduce discrimination, should take precedence over political goals, such as enhanced use of family reunification in political refugee and asylee policy. The notion appears to be in congruence with philosopher John Rawls's view of society, which maintains, "In a just society the rights secured by justice are not subject to political bargaining or the calculus of social interests" (Keat and Miller 1974, p. 4). Without politics, however, what would give meaning to "social goals"? It is difficult to accept the suggestion that political aims would or could ever be absent in any policy arena, especially in one that involves the relationship between the United States and the rest of the world.

Is the world really a better place when a superpower like the United States fails to take an ideological stand on the many important policy questions associated with political refugee or asylee policy? The downside risk of not taking a stand is, to quote a popular country song, "If you don't stand for something, you stand for nothing." Since the U.S. Constitution does not spell out an entry policy, immigration and refugee policies are, as Briggs recognizes, "a purely discretionary duty of the U.S. government" (Briggs 2001, p. 5). Within this rather arbitrary discretionary duty, I believe, is the opportunity for the nation to stand for something, which includes adopting a never-wavering position on human rights (as expressed in the U.N.'s Declaration of Human Rights) and opposing totalitarian regimes. My fear is that unless a proactive (rather than a neutral) political ideology is firmly embraced in political refugee and asylee policy, it will always be chaotic and implemented with no enduring purpose except to fuel the bureaucracy of government.

We need to remember that in the case of political refugees and asylees, U.S.-based policymakers are, by default, publicly declaring that another national government cannot, or will not, protect its own citizens. In political asylee cases, policymakers are saying that it is more than reasonable to support the claim of an individual who maintains his or her life or freedom will be threatened if they are returned to their homeland (Jeffreys 2007). Few (if any) national governments wish to be deemed unable or unwilling to protect their citizens.

Perhaps an alternative approach is to slightly change the question to "How might neutrality with respect to political ideology become a meaningful contributor in political refugee and asylee policy?" With that in mind, I offer the following recommendations.

First, eligibility criteria for the status of either a political refugee or a political asylee need to be broadened. As noted earlier in this chapter, the persecution standard in the U.S. Refugee Act of 1980 is linked to an individual's experience and a well-founded fear of persecution. However, much of the international community (as particularly noted in the definition of a refugee by the former Organization of African Unity and now the African Union, and in the Americas, as expressed in the Cartegena Declaration of 1984) sees political refugee and asylee status as more closely associated with group flight. If U.S. refugee and asylee policy is ever to become more neutral with respect to political ideology, then the U.S. standard of persecution should probably be expanded to include considerations such as conditions that caused one to flee home (not just their country), general chaos or violence in the applicant's homeland, and flight as a member of a family or community (not just flight related to race, religion, political opinion, or nationality).

Second, the United States may need to more fully embrace the idea of participating in the development of a regional alliance with the countries of the Americas and the Caribbean. Such an alliance could help achieve a more neutral ideology with respect to hemispheric political refugee and asylee policies. At present, the countries of Latin America have varied definitions and standards in these two policy areas. The U.S. definition, while congruent with the U.N. standard, may need to be tweaked and brought into greater congruence with an overall policy in the Americas (Fischel de Andrade 1998).

Third, the use of U.S. political refugee and asylee policy to achieve "national security" in a post–September 11 world is problematic if the goal is to achieve a more neutral political ideology (Kerwin 2005). A number of policy actions supposedly aimed at helping to achieve national security, including reductions in refugee admissions, the criminal prosecution of asylum seekers, and the blanket detention of Haitians, do little to advance public safety. Indeed, they violate the rights of political refugee and asylee seekers, and they fuel, rather than neutralize, the spread of political ideology (both at home and abroad) (Kerwin 2005, p. 755). Replacing the "fear of persecution" consideration with a more easily applied standard involving "human security" could help reduce the urge to manipulate political ideology from case to case (Afzal 2006).

In short, political refugee and asylee policy cannot and should not be made neutral with respect to political ideology. Like the notion of economic accountability for every entrant, political neutrality cannot serve as the foundation for this policy, though the problems of politicization that Briggs identifies are real, and there may indeed be room for some movement in the general direction of greater neutrality.

Societal Equity

Can the consideration of social equity ever become the foundation for decision making in the complex arena of political refugee and asylee policy? I believe so. And Briggs helps us in that effort. His work is a good starting point, and extension of his ideas on this matter could come easily.

Briggs's scholarship consistently mentions societal equity as an immigration consideration. In the foreword to *Mass Immigration and the National Interest*, for example, he makes the point with a statement from the 1994 U.S. Commission on Immigration Reform: "It is both a right and a responsibility of a democratic society to manage immigration so that it serves the national interest" (Briggs 2003a, p. v). For Briggs, linking public policy to the national interest means serving the greater good and is a powerful expression of societal equity concerns. Thus, he consistently criticizes advocates for any particular group of potential political refugees or asylees for tending to overlook the national interest and focusing too narrowly on the needs of persons in a particular group.

Briggs also highlights societal equity when he emphasizes the plight of members of less-advantaged groups in the United States. In *Chicanos and Rural Poverty*, for example, he stated that if the goal is to create a more "equitable and humane society," then it is necessary in all policy work to keep attention on the impact of policy on disadvantaged subpopulations (Briggs 1973, p. 1). Even a cursory review of Briggs's scholarship reveals a great deal of attention devoted to the link between policy (development, interpretation, and implementation) and its impact on low-wage workers, particularly those who are African Americans, rural residents, or agricultural workers, whom he has often referred to (lamentingly, of course) as "second-class citizens."

Briggs is especially mindful of the often-unintended consequences of public policies and the unequally distributed negative impact of social legislation on unskilled workers. He reminds us that not all low-wage workers experience equally the benefits of the U.S. labor movement's policy achievements, which include minimum-wage protection, unemployment insurance, workers' compensation, and the right to engage in collective bargaining (Briggs 2001).

Briggs often cites the U.N. Declaration of Human Rights as an argument for including societal equity as a fundamental immigration consideration. He emphasizes Article 14, which (as mentioned earlier) includes the right to seek asylum in any country while fleeing persecution, and Article 28, which states that "everyone is entitled to a social and international order in which the rights and freedoms set forth in this Declaration can be fully realized" (Office of the United Nations High Commissioner for Human Rights 1948).

Even though Briggs speaks of social equity as a consideration in political refugee and asylee policy, his work could be more valuable if clarified and extended. What should be the philosophical and conceptual foundation for a consideration of social equity? What guiding principles or criteria should be used when applying the consideration of social equity? Although Briggs does not say so directly, John Rawls's (1971) *A Theory of Justice* appears to have influenced his thinking. If so, he would not be alone; Rawls influenced many academics and advocates whose careers were hitting their stride in the 1970s and whose interests involved matters of social equity. Yet Rawls was a theoretician, and most of what Briggs reached for in his career was application into the world of actual policy and policy decisions. Thus, Briggs and others who extend his work may want to consider the following.

First, the United States needs to return to its position of prominence in the international community of nations that accept political refugees. If societal equity is to be considered more prominently in the U.S. political and refugee policy landscape, then the country's failure to even meet the annual allocation for political refugees must be reversed. A numerical allocation of 70,000 potential political refugees is not an untenable number, especially considering the existence of over 40 million refugees and persons displaced by violence and persecution around the world (Office of the United Nations High Commissioner for Human Rights 2007).

Second, in discussions and negotiations with the international community, the United States has often spoken with a sanctimonious voice and criticized other countries for their political refugee and asylee policies, especially in the event of uneven implementation of those policies (China is just one example). The United States can take a lofty position partly because our borders are far from most refugee-producing countries, but even we have had our problems, especially when dealing with refugees and asylum seekers from Cuba, Haiti, and Central America. If societal equity is to be a more viable consideration in U.S. political refugee and asylee policy, then that policy must reflect our geographic proximity to countries in the Caribbean and Latin America.

At the top of my reform list would be a policy that ensures complete congruence of the treatment of Haitians and Cubans. Haiti has become more peaceful since holding national elections in 2007, and Cuba continues to move closer to an economic system characterized by market exchange. Thus, we can no longer assume that all Haitian nationals are fleeing poverty and thus not generally eligible for political refugee or asylee status and that all claims by Cubans are legitimate. Under three U.S. presidents, this country has suffered incalculable embarrassment in the international community by stressing poverty too strongly as a disqualifying characteristic in the adjudication of Haitian asylee claims. Granted, fleeing poverty need not be the only standard, but when combined with fleeing oppression or violence, it need not summarily disqualify an individual.

Briggs's work can serve as a foundation for enhancing the use of social equity as a consideration in political refugee and asylee policy, but realizing that goal requires an extension of his work in the areas and along the lines described above.

MY TRUE PURPOSE

In responding to the invitation to write this chapter, my officially stated purpose was to write an academic piece on some element of immigration policy using Briggs's work. Thus, I have focused on political refugee and asylee policy and attempted to assess Briggs's use of three major considerations—economic accountability for each entry decision, neutrality with respect to political ideology, and social equity. I hope I have done so in a manner respectful of Briggs's legacy of impressive work.

But my unofficial purpose for writing the chapter is to thank Dr. Briggs. He opened my eyes to the world of immigration in general and to political refugee and asylee policy in particular. He showed me how an interest in federal social-policy formulation, local-level impact, and community-driven efforts to shape those policies all fit perfectly within the dynamic policy arena of political refugee and asylee policy. It was Briggs who suggested I travel to Brownsville, Texas, and Matamoras, Mexico, to collect dissertation data as Central Americans fled country-based violence and streamed through south Texas in the late 1980s. It was Briggs who said go there and witness firsthand the hardscrabble reality of what had previously been only an abstract academic interest. He set me on a lifetime path as an academic. I will be forever grateful.

Note

1. Although individuals seeking political refugee or political asylee status are both seeking sanctuary, have crossed over the international border of their homeland, and must meet the definitional criteria for fleeing a "well-founded fear of persecution," differences do exist. The major differences between the two are in the journey the person undertakes and the site from which the application for either refugee or asylee status is made. Persons seeking refugee status do so most often from within the confines of a U.N. High Commissioner for Refugees (UNHCR) sponsored camp and outside the borders of the country of desired resettlement. Persons seeking political asylee status do so after first leaving their home country and then initially or eventually entering the country within which they wish to remain. Both require a recognition by the United States federal government of a country whose federal government cannot protect its own citizens and represent one of only three areas of designation by which people can enter the United States, the other two being family reunification and labor economics.

References

Afzal, Mehreen. 2006. "'A Violation of His or Her Human Security'—New Grounds for the Recognition of Refugee Status: A Proposal for Reform." *New Issues in Refugee Research*, paper no. 140. Geneva: Policy Development and Evaluation Service, U.N. Office of the High Commissioner for Human Rights.

Bean, John C. 2001. *Engaging Ideas: The Professor's Guide to Integrating Writing, Critical Thinking, and Active Learning in the Classroom*. San Francisco: Jossey-Bass Publishers.

Briggs, Vernon M. Jr. 1973. *Chicanos and Rural Poverty*. Baltimore: Johns Hopkins University Press.

———. 2001. *Immigration and American Unionism*. Ithaca, NY: Cornell University Press.

———. 2003a. *Mass Immigration and the National Interest*. 3rd ed. Armonk, NY: M.E. Sharpe.

———. 2003b. "Immigration and Poverty Reduction: Policy Making on a Squirrel Wheel." *Journal of Economic Issues* 37(2): 232–330.

———. 2007. "Real Immigration Reform: The Path to Credibility." Testimony before the Subcommittee on Immigration of the Judiciary Committee of the U.S. House of Representatives. Ithaca, NY: School of Industrial and Labor Relations, Cornell University. http://digitalcommons.ilr.cornell.edu/briggstestimonies/24 (accessed February 1, 2009).

Briggs, Vernon M. Jr., and Stephen Moore. 1994. *Still an Open Door? U.S. Immigration Policy and the American Economy*. Washington, DC: American University Press.

Bruffee, Kenneth A. 1997. "Collaborative Learning and the 'Conversation of Mankind.'" In *Cross-Talk in Comp Theory: A Reader*, Victor Villanueva Jr., ed. Urbana, IL: National Council of Teachers of English, pp. 393–414.

Fischel de Andrade, Jose H. 1998. "Regional Policy Approaches and Harmonization: A Latin American Perspective." *International Journal of Refugee Law* 10(3): 389–409.

General Accounting Office. 2004. *Homeland Security: Management Challenges Remain in Transforming Immigration Programs*. Washington, DC: General Accounting Office.

Jeffreys, Kelly. 2007. *Refugees and Asylees: 2006*. Washington, DC: Office of Immigration Statistics, Department of Homeland Security.

Keat, Russell, and David Miller. 1974. "Understanding Justice." *Political Theory* 2(1): 3–31.

Kerwin, Donald. 2005. "The Use and Misuse of 'National Security' Rationale in Crafting U.S. Refugee and Immigration Policies." *International Journal of Refugee Law* 17(4): 755–763.

Nackerud, Larry. 1993. *The Central American Refugee Issue in Brownsville, Texas: Seeking Understanding of Public Policy Formulation from within a Community Setting*. San Francisco: Mellen.

Newland, K., H. Tanaka, and L. Barker. 2007. *Bridging Divides: The Role of Ethnic Community-Based Organizations in Political Refugee Integration*. Washington, DC: International Rescue Committee, Migration Policy Institute.

Office of the United Nations High Commissioner for Human Rights. 1948. *The Universal Declaration of Human Rights*. Geneva: United Nations. http://www.unhchr.ch/udhr/ (accessed February 1, 2009).

———. 1951. *Convention Relating to the Status of Refugees*. Adopted on 28 July 1951 by the United Nations Conference of Plenipotentiaries on the Status of Refugees and Stateless Persons. Geneva: United Nations. http://www2.ohchr.org/english/law/refugees.htm (accessed September 20, 2009).

———. 2007. *World Refugee Day: Displacement in the 21st Century. A New Paradigm*. Geneva: United Nations.

Rawls, John. 1971. *A Theory of Justice*. Cambridge, MA: Harvard University Press.

Singer, Audrey, and Jill H. Wilson. 2006. *From "There" to "Here": Refugee Resettlement in Metropolitan America*. Washington, DC: Brookings Institution.

TRAC Immigration. 2006. "The Asylum Process." TRAC Immigration Report no. 159. Syracuse, NY: Transactional Records Access Clearinghouse, Syracuse University. http://trac.syr.edu/immigration/reports/159/ (accessed February 1, 2009).

U.S. Census Bureau. 2007. "Household Income Rises, Poverty Rate Declines, Number of Uninsured Up." News release, August 28. Washington, DC: U.S. Census Bureau. http://www.census.gov/Press-Release/www/releases/archives/income_wealth/010583.html (accessed June 29, 2009).

U.S. Department of State. 2007. *Bureau of Population, Refugees, and Migration.* Washington, DC: U.S. Department of State. http://www.state.gov/g/prm (accessed March 2, 2009).

6

Training and Immigration in the Real World

Ernesto Cortés Jr.
Interfaith Education Fund

Although it has been more than 40 years since I sat in Vernon Briggs's classroom at the University of Texas, his insights into the value of training in the labor market and the role of the public sector are echoed in my work every day. Briggs's economics has always been about moving beyond theory and into the realm of action and practical problem solving.

In this chapter, I describe how I have continued to act and examine issues in the spirit of what I learned in Briggs's classroom, even when our policy conclusions have diverged. I first highlight an initiative to establish labor-market intermediary institutions and then address the subject of immigration.

STRUCTURAL UNEMPLOYMENT AND TRAINING

Not long after I left the University of Texas, I began organizing with the Industrial Areas Foundation (IAF), the nation's largest community organizing network, founded by Saul Alinsky in Chicago in the 1940s. For more than three decades, my colleagues and I have been working, primarily in the Southwestern United States, to build broad-based community organizations with the power to address the responsibilities of both the public and private sectors in a dynamic economy and democratic society.[1] These organizations have won countless victories for their families and communities throughout the years.[2]

IAF leaders in the Southwest consulted with Briggs when we were developing the concept of labor-market intermediaries about two decades ago. His reflections on the nature of structural unemployment, a form of joblessness not responsive to mere changes in aggregate demand, supported our leaders' instincts that a mediating institution could serve as a bridge between workers and employers and be beneficial to both. It is not that fiscal and monetary policies are unimportant, Briggs explained, but changes in the U.S. economy were fundamentally altering the nature of the American labor market.

Today, of course, what Briggs was teaching is accepted as common knowledge as America's economy has moved from the production of goods to the production of services as its driving force. However, his analyses of national and global trends were both insightful and tremendously useful as IAF leaders began to puzzle through the changes they were experiencing in local labor markets in the late 1980s.

One of Briggs's most powerful lessons is reflected in IAF efforts to improve education and training: the success of a democracy and the wealth of a society are based largely on their human capital. In San Antonio, Communities Organized for Public Service (COPS) and the Metro Alliance created Project QUEST, the first high-skill, high-wage job-training program developed by the IAF organizations in the Southwestern United States. Learning from the lessons of Project QUEST, Valley Interfaith leaders organized VIDA (Valley Initiative for Development and Advancement), the Pima County Interfaith Council formed JobPaths, Austin Interfaith leaders created Capital IDEA, and the El Paso Interreligious Sponsoring Organization founded Project ARRIBA. Since 1992, these five independent job-training institutions have trained and placed more than 10,000 participants in jobs that pay an average of nearly $32,000 annually. This is particularly significant considering the average annual wage of program participants before participation was less than $10,000.

The IAF emphasis on human capital will translate into roughly 30 years of increased wages and productivity for each job-training graduate. This benefits not only the individual worker but also his or her family and employer. As the number of graduates increases, local labor markets will reap the still larger community benefits of a well-educated, well-paid workforce with the skills necessary to succeed in the face of structural economic changes.

IMMIGRANT HUMAN CAPITAL

Although I agree with Briggs's views on structural unemployment and the usefulness of labor-market intermediaries, I disagree with his views on the role of immigrant human capital in a dynamic economy. He views a more generous immigration policy as an impediment to raising wages, improving working conditions, and securing employment opportunities for U.S. workers (see, for example, Briggs 1996). In response, I would stress the contributions that immigrant workers make in terms of increasing demand for domestic goods and services, which in turn creates new jobs (Legrain 2006, p. 136).

Immigrants also add to the diversity of communities, which urban-studies expert Richard Florida and demographer Gary Gates identify as an important driver of regional economic growth. In fact, Florida and Gates report that eight of the top 10 U.S. metropolitan areas with the highest percentage of foreign-born residents are among the nation's top 15 high-technology regions (Florida and Gates 2001). According to British economist Philippe Legrain, "Big global cities capture the whole world in one place" (Legrain 2006, p. 119). Surely this is a benefit, given the increasing globalization of our economy.

Briggs criticizes labor unions for supporting more generous immigration policies, stating that it is not in the interest of their members to do so given recent declines in U.S. real wages (Briggs 2001). There is no question that employers have been successful in reducing the real wages of workers, but those declines appear to be due overwhelmingly to changes in technology and the rise of global production, not to immigrants (Head 2007). "Since 1995, when the 'new economy' based on information technology began to take off, workers' incomes have not kept up with productivity, and during the past five years the two have spectacularly diverged," observes Simon Head, author of *The New Ruthless Economy* (Head 2007).[3]

Labor unions should work aggressively to organize all workers, including immigrants. A number of labor organizations, including the Service Employees International Union (SEIU) and the United Food and Commercial Workers International Union (UFCW), have been very successful in organizing immigrant workers and their success has somewhat mitigated the effects of decades of declining union membership. If the estimated 12 million undocumented immigrants in the labor force today were legalized, they would also become potential union members.

Conversely, if those 12 million undocumented workers were somehow miraculously located, detained, and deported, the shock to the economy and its day-to-day functioning would be tremendous. Even assuming that every unemployed person in the United States would be in the right location and have the right skill set and the right frame of mind to replace the deported workers, there would not ordinarily be enough job seekers to fill the gap. In August 2007, for example, the U.S. Bureau of Labor Statistics recognized only 7.1 million unemployed workers as actively seeking employment (U.S. Bureau of Labor Statistics 2007).[4]

Although it is generally agreed that immigrants contribute to the downward pressure on wages of high-school dropouts, at most only 20 percent of the incidence is attributable to the availability of immigrant labor. The remaining 80 percent is directly related to the substitution of capital for labor, advances in technology, and other issues unrelated to immigrants (Goldin and Katz 2008).

Studies also indicate that, although immigrants lower the wages of high-school dropouts by 1 percent, they increase the wages of workers who graduated from high school by as much as 4 percent (Legrain 2006, pp. 142–143). This occurs because immigrants rarely substitute for U.S.-born workers, even when their education and experience levels are similar. Instead, immigrant skills are often complementary to those of native workers. Indeed, this is true both for immigrants with high levels of education and experience (in science and technology occupations, for instance) and for those with low levels of formal education (in occupations such as cooking, caregiving, and gardening) (Legrain 2006, pp. 68–75; Ottaviano and Peri 2006a,b).

Since competition for jobs held by undocumented immigrants largely affects the most poorly educated segment of the native labor market, a closer examination of education policies is in order. One way to address the concern about poorly educated U.S.-born workers would be to ensure that fewer U.S. students drop out of high school, thereby making them eligible for higher skilled jobs that pay better wages. The question of education policy is also central to the immigration debate from another perspective. As baby boomers continue to age, the United States economy is going to lose hundreds of thousands, if not millions, of its most highly skilled workers to retirement over the next two decades. To meet the coming demand for a skilled workforce and continue our pace of economic growth as a nation, it is in the national interest to invest in educating all children, regardless of whether their parents have legal residency papers.

IMMIGRATION, TRADE, AND DEVELOPMENT POLICIES

The debate over immigration and immigration reform in the United States must also be linked to a broader discussion about trade and economic-development policies. To consider immigration in isolation from these policies is not merely impractical, it also denies the role that U.S. policymaking has played in driving up the numbers of people that have come here outside the legal process.

The North American Free Trade Agreement (NAFTA) is an example of a trade policy that has contributed to the growth of worker migration to the United States. As a consequence of NAFTA, Mexico was forced to eliminate its agriculture subsidies to subsistence farmers, destroying what had been in effect an employment and anti-hunger strategy. By purchasing agricultural products at above-market prices, the Mexican government kept farmers working, and its policy of reselling the products at a loss (through government-owned stores) made them affordable to the poorest of the nation's families. NAFTA forced these subsistence farmers into the cities to look for work, which depressed wages in the urban areas at the same time that food prices rose (Stiglitz 2007, pp. 64–66).

It should come as no surprise that these pressures left many poor Mexican nationals with few options beyond seeking work across the border. In the mid 2000s, while Mexico's agricultural subsidies were being removed, the California and Arizona economies were booming. This boom produced a tremendous demand for labor, especially in agriculture, which now had new opportunities to sell products in Mexico, and construction. The United States needed labor; Mexicans needed jobs.[5]

The World Bank's structural adjustment policies created similar pressures in other developing countries (see, for example, Komisar 2000). An insistence on the elimination of subsidies and market protections forced countries to skip the middle steps in developing a strong market economy. The success of the U.S. economy followed some 200 years of infrastructure development, as well as subsidies and protectionism. The World Bank's conditions for aid ignore the role such policies played in the development of strong economies, and they create economic circumstances that lead millions of people to emigrate and even to risk their lives by immigrating illegally to developed nations in an attempt to support their families.

When the European nations decided to link their economies more closely to one another, they deliberately chose a common-market strategy rather than a trade agreement in an attempt to avoid these types of unintended consequences. They recognized the disparities between their various countries and created a huge social-investment fund to build up the infrastructure in poorer countries. They also established common labor standards. While the European Union's policy decisions have by no means completely eliminated economic tensions and immigration challenges, they appear to represent a more practical approach to international trade and development than that pursued by the United States to date.

CIVIL LIBERTIES AND POLICY IMPLEMENTATION

In addition to believing that U.S. immigration policy is hampered by not being sufficiently considered in its wider context, I am concerned that its implementation has at times infringed on the civil liberties of U.S. citizens as well as noncitizens.

For example, I have heard testimony from Hispanic women with strong West Texas accents who were handcuffed in workplace raids, marched to their lockers, and then upon presenting evidence that they were citizens, told that such evidence was meaningless because it could be faked. A request for a female agent was denied, and the male agents proceeded to frisk the women—women who had proof of their citizenship status. The presumption in such cases is clearly one of guilt rather than innocence, in direct violation of the Supreme Court's interpretation of the civil rights and civil liberties guaranteed by the U.S. Constitution.[6]

To be sure, the intention to enforce our current laws may have merit. Yet the possibility of unintended consequences and disastrous implementation only underscores the need to craft our policies in a way that ensures they are executed with good judgment, care, consideration, and thoughtfulness. Otherwise, our incapacity to do so trumps the logic of our policies.[7]

THE BRIGGS TRADITION

Briggs has consistently shown he cares about people, particularly about people of color. With that concern as a guide, he made major practical contributions to problem solving through his work on structural unemployment and training (see, for example, Briggs 1979, 1973; Marshall and Briggs 1967). I have drawn directly on his insights and guidance in my own work relating to labor-market intermediaries and economic issues more generally. It is a testament to his scholarship and integrity that my colleagues and I are still benefiting from what I first began to learn from him more than 40 years ago.

On immigration policy, our views are obviously different. Yet, the pragmatic approach to public policy I learned from Briggs makes me confident that it is fully within our capacity as a nation to address the formidable education, trade, development, and civil rights issues—especially those relating to unintended consequences and practical policy implementation—confronting the nation with respect to immigration.

Notes

1. These organizations include A Mid-Iowa Organizing Strategy (AMOS) in Des Moines; Albuquerque Interfaith; Allied Communities of Tarrant in Fort Worth; Austin Interfaith; Bay Area Organizing Committee in San Francisco; Border Interfaith in El Paso; The Border Organization in Del Rio and Eagle Pass, Texas; Communities Organized for Public Service (COPS) in San Antonio; Communities Organized for Relational Power in Action (COPA) in Watsonville, Salinas, and surrounding California communities; Dallas Area Interfaith; El Paso Interreligious Sponsoring Organization (EPISO); The Jeremiah Group in New Orleans; Marin Organizing Committee (Northern California); The Metro Alliance in San Antonio; North Bay Sponsoring Committee in Sonoma/Napa (Northern California); Northern Arizona Interfaith Council; Northern and Central Louisiana Interfaith; Oklahoma City Sponsoring Committee; Omaha Together One Community (OTOC); One LA—IAF in Los Angeles; Pima County Interfaith Council in Tucson; Sacramento Valley Organizing Community; The Metropolitan Organization (TMO) in Houston; Valley Interfaith in the Lower Rio Grande Valley; Valley Interfaith Project (VIP) in metropolitan Phoenix; the West Texas Organizing Strategy in Lubbock, San Angelo, and surrounding communities; and the Yuma County Interfaith Sponsoring Committee in Yuma, Arizona.
2. For discussions of the work of these organizations, see, for example, Greider (1992), Osterman (2002), Putnam and Feldstein (2003), Rogers (1990), Warren (2001), and Wilson (2001). A list of additional references is available from the author.
3. Head adds that between 1995 and 2006, U.S. worker productivity grew 340 percent more than real wages—and 779 percent more than wages in the last six years (Head 2007).
4. In December 2008, a year after the latest recession began, the U.S. Bureau of Labor Statistics reports there were 11.1 million unemployed workers (U.S. Bureau of Labor Statistics 2009).
5. As this chapter is being prepared for publication, the U.S. economy is in recession. However, when recession gives way to recovery, states on the border will again be a magnet for Mexico's displaced farmers and struggling urban workers.
6. The author heard this testimony at a public hearing sponsored by the UFCW in Omaha, Nebraska, on August 16, 2007 (UFCW 2007). In contrast, according to the U.S. Supreme Court, "The principle that there is a presumption of innocence in favor of the accused is the undoubted law, axiomatic and elementary, and its enforcement lies at the foundation of the administration of our criminal law" (U.S. Supreme Court 1895).
7. A failure of the capacity to implement policy effectively is, of course, not unique to immigration policy. For example, this failure is one of the fundamental flaws in the No Child Left Behind legislation. The internal logic of an educational accountability system has, in implementation, created monstrous requirements and strained the capacities of our nation's teachers and schools (see, for example, Young 2009).

Another example is the U.S. policy in Iraq (see Ignatieff 2007). Attention must be given to ensure that policies work in practice, not just in theory.

References

Briggs, Vernon M. Jr. 1996. "Immigration Policy and the U.S. Economy: An Institutional Perspective." *Journal of Economic Issues* 30(2): 371–389.

———. 1973. *Chicanos and Rural Poverty*. Baltimore: Johns Hopkins Press.

———. 1979. "Special Labor Market Segments." In *Manpower Research and Labor Economics*, Gordon Swanson and Jon Michaelson, eds. Beverly Hills, CA: Sage Publications, pp. 243–276.

———. 2001. *Immigration and American Unionism*. Ithaca, NY: Cornell University Press.

Florida, Richard, and Gary Gates. 2001. *Technology and Tolerance: The Importance of Diversity to High-Technology Growth*. Washington, DC: Brookings Institution.

Goldin, Claudia, and Lawrence Katz. 2008. *The Race between Education and Technology*. Cambridge, MA: Belknap Press.

Greider, William. 1992. *Who Will Tell the People?* New York: Simon and Schuster.

Head, Simon. 2007. "They're Micromanaging Your Every Move." *New York Review of Books* 54(13): 42–44. http://www.nybooks.com/articles/article-preview?article_id=20499 (accessed June 3, 2009).

Ignatieff, Michael. 2007. "Getting Iraq Wrong." *New York Times Magazine*, August 5: 29.

Komisar, Lucy. 2000. "Interview with Joseph Stiglitz." *Progressive* 64(6): 34–38. http://www.progressive.org/0901/intv0600.html (accessed June 3, 2009).

Legrain, Philippe. 2006. *Immigrants: Your Country Needs Them*. Princeton, NJ: Princeton University Press.

Marshall, Ray, and Vernon M. Briggs Jr. 1967. *The Negro and Apprenticeship*. Baltimore: Johns Hopkins Press.

Osterman, Paul. 2002. *Gathering Power: The Future of Progressive Politics in America*. Boston, MA: Beacon Press.

Ottaviano, Gianmarco I.P., and Giovanni Peri. 2006a. "The Economic Value of Cultural Diversity: Evidence from U.S. Cities." *Journal of Economic Geography* 6(1): 9–44.

———. 2006b. "Rethinking the Gains from Immigration: Theory and Evidence from the United States." Revision of NBER Working Paper no. 11672. Cambridge, MA: National Bureau of Economic Research.

Putnam, Robert, and Louis Feldstein. 2003. *Better Together: Restoring the American Community.* New York: Simon and Schuster.

Rogers, Mary Beth. 1990. *Cold Anger: A Story of Faith and Power Politics.* Denton, TX: University of North Texas Press.

Stiglitz, Joseph. 2007. *Making Globalization Work.* New York: W.W. Norton and Company.

UFCW. 2007. "Workers Decry Abusive ICE Misconduct: Hold First National Meeting on ICE Misconduct and Violations of 4th Amendment Rights." News release, August 16. Washington, DC: UFCW. http://www.ufcw.org/press_room/index.cfm?pressReleaseID=343 (accessed June 29, 2009).

U.S. Bureau of Labor Statistics. 2007. "The Employment Situation: August 2007." News release, September 7. Washington, DC: U.S. Department of Labor, Bureau of Labor Statistics. http://www.bls.gov/news.release/archives/empsit_09072007.pdf (accessed June 26, 2009).

————. 2009. "The Employment Situation: December 2008." News release, January 9. Washington, DC: U.S. Department of Labor, Bureau of Labor Statistics. http://www.bls.gov/news.release/archives/empsit_01092009.pdf (accessed June 26, 2009).

U.S. Supreme Court. 1895. *Coffin v. United States.* 156 U.S. 432.

Warren, Mark. 2001. *Dry Bones Rattling: Community Building to Revitalize American Democracy.* Princeton, NJ: Princeton University Press.

Wilson, William Julius. 2001. *The Bridge over the Racial Divide.* Berkeley: University of California Press.

Young, John. 2009. "Standardized Testing Leaves Collateral Damage." *Austin-American Statesman*, February 14, A:15.

7

Immigration Policy and Economic Development

James T. Peach
New Mexico State University

For more than three decades, Vernon M. Briggs Jr. argued that U.S. immigration policy should be determined largely on the basis of the nation's rapidly changing labor-market trends. In Briggs's view, U.S. immigration policy and the needs of the labor market have been mismatched. He has been particularly concerned about a new (fourth) wave of migration with detrimental effects disproportionately felt by unskilled workers and minorities, especially blacks and Hispanics. What is needed, Briggs argues, is an immigration policy that reduces the massive flow of international migration to the United States and matches the characteristics of immigrants with genuine labor force needs.

Briggs's policy conclusions are based on a careful, detailed analysis of immigration law and the often-unintended consequences of changes in immigration law. His analysis is logical, subtle, and compelling. Yet Congress has failed to pass immigration legislation consistent with changing labor-market conditions and needs.

The latest attempt to pass a major immigration reform law in 2007 contained some elements consistent with Briggs's proposals, but it had almost no chance of being passed by a deeply divided Congress. Not surprisingly, there were no major immigration law changes in the 2008 presidential election year, nor did immigration policy play a major role during the presidential campaign. Immigration was simply too controversial for either major party to bring into play. Given the global economic and financial crisis that became more serious in late 2008 and continued into 2009, immigration is not likely to be a high priority on the policy agenda of Congress or the Obama administration. In brief, major U.S. immigration reform may not occur for many years.

The immigration problem is not intractable. The main theme of this chapter is that policies designed to accelerate the process of economic development in migrant-sending nations should be the key element of an overall immigration policy. Certainly, the convoluted, illogical, contradictory, and generally unenforced mess that is now immigration law in the United States is badly in need of reform, and Briggs's suggested labor-market-oriented changes to immigration policy could form a solid foundation for such reform. Changes in the law, however, cannot directly affect the root causes of migration. In contrast, rapid economic development in the sending nations *can* affect the flow of migration.

The development of this thesis is not a critique of Briggs's analysis and does not contradict his major research and policy conclusions. Most of the key ingredients of the argument presented here can be found in Briggs's own works. While his work has focused mainly on the inconsistency between U.S. labor-market needs and immigration policy, he has consistently mentioned the need for economic development and economic-development assistance, particularly to Mexico, as one element in a comprehensive strategy. The proposal developed here represents only a change in emphasis. In brief, U.S. immigration reform will not reduce the flow of international migration to the United States unless major sending regions are more successful in their economic-development efforts.

Two related labor-market issues also need to be addressed briefly. First, whether or not immigration flows are increasing, the United States must address the educational and workforce training needs of its residents in a fashion consistent with rapidly changing economic trends and labor-market conditions. Although the previous sentence is not a direct quote from Briggs's published works, it will surely sound familiar to those who have read them.

Almost every release of data on U.S. educational attainment paints a deteriorating picture, and the No Child Left Behind Act has failed to reverse these trends. Institutions of higher education are struggling with tight budgets and increasing costs, and state and local governments are unlikely to provide the needed resources.

The educational and workforce training problem is national in scope and needs to be addressed at the federal level. The need to do so is obvious. In February 2009, the unemployment rate among those with less than a high-school education was 15.1 percent, whereas the comparable rate for those with a bachelor's degree or higher was 4.2 percent (U.S. Bureau of Labor Statistics 2009). Income levels by education show similar disparities. What the nation does with immigration policy will matter little over the next several decades unless there is a huge effort to provide education and training for all U.S. residents consistent with success in an increasingly high-technology and internationalized economy.

Second, there is no excuse for failing to address the U.S. unemployment problem. The opportunity cost of employing the unemployed is zero.[1] The unemployed are, from an economic perspective, wasted resources who do not add to the nation's output. Little imagination is required to devise policies to eliminate unemployment, and there is more than enough useful work that needs to be done.

It is obvious that macroeconomic stability and relatively strong long-term economic growth during the quarter century from 1982 to 2007 have not been sufficient to ensure employment for all of those who want to work. The current economic crisis brings added urgency to the unemployment problem. In February 2009, the U.S. unemployment rate reached 8.1 percent, and many analysts expect continued labor-market deterioration (U.S. Bureau of Labor Statistics 2009).

In early 2009, 12.5 million people in the United States were unemployed, an additional 5.6 million wanted a job but quit looking for work, and 4.0 million others worked part time but would have preferred to work full time (U.S. Bureau of Labor Statistics 2009). In 2008, the average U.S. worker added about $100,000 to the nation's gross domestic product (GDP) (author calculations based on U.S. Bureau of Economic Analysis 2009). The lost output from 12.5 million unemployed persons is more than a trillion dollars.

Although there are indications that immigration to the United States, particularly from Mexico, has declined during the current economic downturn, it remains a rather odd policy to allow in-migration when there are millions of current U.S. residents without a job. Even stranger is that the nation tolerates domestic unemployment on a large scale even though there are policy options available to eliminate all or nearly all of it.

There are several powerful arguments for placing economic development, education, workforce training, and unemployment higher on the policy priority list than immigration reform. First, as indicated above, the U.S. political process is not likely to soon produce immigration reform or allocate immigration enforcement resources along the lines suggested by Briggs. Second, the politics of immigration reform will be easier to address once U.S. unemployment is reduced to zero (or almost zero), the educational and training needs of the current and future labor force are adequately addressed, and migrant-sending nations are progressing rapidly. Third, economic development issues, unemployment, and education issues need to be addressed whether or not the nation grapples with the immigration issue. Fourth, the immigration issue is far more complex and contentious than the other three issues. Unfortunately, there is little reason for optimism that the nation will seriously address any of these issues, including immigration reform.

AUTHOR BIASES

Gunnar Myrdal, a Nobel Laureate in economics, argued forcefully that there is no such thing as a value-free social science (Myrdal 1968). Myrdal argued the best we can do is be as aware of our value judgments and biases as possible and state them explicitly. Not doing so leads to a false sense of scientific objectivity.

With that in mind, I first confess that I took three classes in labor economics from Briggs when I was an undergraduate majoring in mathematics at the University of Texas at Austin in the 1960s. I have respected him and his work very highly for more than four decades. I am honored to have the opportunity to contribute a chapter to this volume. I am equally honored that after more than four decades he remains a valued friend and colleague.

Second, I have always shared Briggs's concern over the plight of the poor. His concern for the underprivileged is genuine, and whether he is addressing immigration or other structural imbalances in the economy, that value judgment or bias is apparent.

Third, in 1974 (or possibly early 1975), I was extraordinarily privileged to listen to a great debate on immigration policy between Briggs and his University of Texas colleague Wendell C. Gordon at the supper seminar series sponsored by the university's Department of Economics. The supper seminar series was always a well-attended and intellectually stimulating event. The Briggs–Gordon debate on immigration was the best of them all. Briggs presented the case for a more restrictive border policy, while Gordon presented the case for a more open border. Both participants' remarks were later published in the *Social Science Journal* (Briggs 1975; Gordon 1975). Better short statements of the two opposing sides of the immigration debate are hard to find, and I still have my students read those articles. Today, I have the same mixed feelings about the immigration issue that I had more than 30 years ago during this great debate. As Briggs has maintained, the labor-market consequences of relatively unconstrained immigration are felt disproportionately by the unskilled and poor. At the same time, borders and nationalism broadly defined are impediments to the process of economic development. Sorting out the issues about the costs and benefits of migration empirically is an almost impossible task.

Finally, both Briggs and I are long-standing members and past-presidents of the Association for Evolutionary Economics. We share a common intellectual heritage dating back to the works of Thorstein Veblen, John R. Commons, and Clarence E. Ayres. The institutional or evolutionary tradition places great emphasis on technological and institutional change as major determinants of the way economies evolve. Among institutional economists, there is no automatic assumption that markets will cure all economic problems. Yet institutionalists, like mainstream economists, have expressed very different and sometimes conflicting views on immigration. Veblen regarded borders and restrictions on immigration as significant obstacles to the efficient functioning of the industrial system. Commons thought that restrictions on immigration were needed. A brief attempt to examine and reconcile these views is presented in Peach (2007).

CONTRASTING BRIGGS'S PERSPECTIVE WITH SOME FALSE ISSUES

Briggs's view toward immigration is that the size of the migration flow to the United States and the characteristics of those who migrate here should complement, rather than disrupt, the functioning of the U.S. labor market. Briggs argues that U.S. immigration issues could, for the most part, be ignored during the 1950s and early 1960s when migration flows were relatively small. Conversely, he argues that the increased migration flows that occurred during the last quarter century can no longer be ignored (Briggs 1984, 1992, 2003).

Briggs's perspective does not imply some numerically precise optimal level of immigration in a dynamic, modern economy. There simply can be no such optimal or desirable migration rate. As a practical matter, Briggs argues that the appropriate number of migrants in any given year should be determined administratively on the basis of labor-market conditions (fewer migrants should be admitted when unemployment rates are high, for example).

A zero migration or zero net-migration policy, promoted by some politicians and commentators, is not the position advocated by Briggs. Zero migration and zero net-migration are very different concepts, but both are absurd notions in an increasingly internationalized or global economic system. Zero migration presumably means no migration—either into or out of a nation. Zero net-migration means that the number of immigrants would exactly equal the number of emigrants, a highly unlikely occurrence. Neither policy could be demographically neutral in the sense of not affecting population size (Bouvier et al. 1995). Zero net-migration is not likely to be demographically neutral because the age and fertility patterns of immigrants and emigrants are likely to be different. Zero migration cannot be demographically neutral because prohibiting all migration would also change a society's fertility and mortality rates.

There are other reasons to reject any notion of zero U.S. migration. For example, such a policy would be virtually impossible to enforce in a democratic society. Further, the aging of the U.S. population and fertility rates near or perhaps even below replacement levels are hard to ignore. Without some level of net in-migration, the prospect of a shrink-ing U.S. labor force is very real. The United Nations reports that more than 40 percent of the world's population already lives in nations with a fertility rate that is below replacement level and that this figure is likely to increase in coming decades (United Nations 2006).

Economists and policymakers have not yet determined how to deal with issues of economic growth or the provision of goods and services in an economy with a declining labor force. In a very meaningful sense, some migration will be essential to keep the U.S. economy growing and to maintain or increase per-capita income over the next decades. Moreover, the Social Security issue complicates the immigration is-sue considerably. With an aging population and population growth due to natural increase slowing down, migration is particularly needed to fund future Social Security obligations. In short, zero migration simply won't work.

The U.S. immigration debate often focuses on numeric estimates of the stock or flow of (legal and illegal) immigrants. Are the num-bers increasing or decreasing? Where are the migrants from? What are their characteristics? These are important and meaningful questions in a policy context. Yet there are no precise numeric answers to many of these questions, and this is particularly the case with regard to estimates of illegal migrants. Despite the best efforts of demographers and econo-mists, estimates of the stock and flow of illegal migration to the United States are undoubtedly wrong and contribute little to a resolution of the immigration debate. Over the last decade or two, the U.S. Census Bureau has amply documented an increase in the number and propor-tion of the foreign-born U.S. population. The trends in the foreign-born population of the United States could not have occurred without sig-nificant in-migration. In a policy context, the Census estimates of the foreign-born population provide enough information to formulate im-migration policy (for example, see Briggs 2003).

Congress and the President, however, address most policy issues without "adequate" data on the nature of the problem or the poten-tial impact of proposed solutions. As Briggs (1984, p. 10) points out, "Obviously, reliable data are needed, but policy formulation and the se-lection of topics for social science inquiry cannot depend on the quality of available data." Fiscal and monetary policies designed to stimulate the economy are adopted without adequate data indicating the magnitude of the problem. For example, no one really knows, or can possibly know, whether the current stimulus package (The American Recovery and Reinvestment Act of 2009) is too large or too small. Energy policy, Social Security policy, environmental policy, and countless other policies are also changed without adequate data.

Another false issue that clouds the immigration debate is ideology. Immigration is not a liberal–conservative or left–right issue. The immigration views of conservatives and liberals, Democrats and Republicans, and corporate executives and labor union leaders do not fall into neat and consistent categories. After all, immigration legislation is often the work of both liberals and conservatives and Republicans and Democrats. The Immigration Reform and Control Act of 1986 (IRCA) was commonly referred to as the Simpson–Rodino bill. Alan Simpson was a conservative Republican senator from Wyoming, whereas Peter Rodino was a more liberal Democratic U.S. representative from New Jersey.

The logic of market-oriented mainstream economics is that any barrier to the mobility of resources or trade in goods and services inhibits the efficient functioning of the economy. But not everyone who thinks that "markets work best" will also favor reducing restrictions on migration. Briggs has often discussed both the neoclassical economists' lack of appropriate theoretical models of immigration and the false issue of ideology (see, for example, Briggs 1984, 1996, 2003). Immigration issues do indeed make for strange bedfellows.

THE CASE FOR ECONOMIC DEVELOPMENT AS IMMIGRATION POLICY

An effective, perhaps the most effective, form of immigration policy is to promote economic development in migrant-sending nations. An important corollary to this thesis is that immigration-law reform—no matter how well intentioned or well designed and regardless of the seriousness of efforts aimed at greater enforcement—will not substantially reduce the flow of in-migration to the United States. International migration is, after all, an international issue and not one that can be adequately addressed by domestic policy alone.

Enforcement of U.S. immigration laws has been about as effective as the enforcement of prohibition in the 1920s and early 1930s and perhaps less effective than the so-called war on drugs. Enforcement is inherently difficult and there have been a number of major changes to U.S. immigration law in the last 20 or more years.[2] The IRCA legislation of 1986 is probably the most widely known of these changes because it 1) made hiring immigrants without proper documentation illegal and 2) provided for amnesty, under certain conditions, for those who were already in the country illegally. IRCA, for the first time, made employers potential targets of enforcement operations. Enforcement of the employment provisions of IRCA has been lax and has apparently had little effect on the flow of undocumented immigrants to the United States (for example, Abraham and Hamilton 2006).

After the events of September 11, 2001, immigration and customs enforcement were consolidated in a single agency, Immigration, Customs and Enforcement (ICE), within the Department of Homeland Security, and enforcement budgets were substantially increased. Between fiscal year 2005 and fiscal year 2009, the ICE budget increased from $3.6 billion to $5.9 billion, an increase of 63 percent in a four-year period (U.S. Immigration and Customs Enforcement 2009). "Operation Jump Start" even brought National Guard troops to the U.S.–Mexico border in 2006 to assist in the enforcement effort, although those troops were reassigned in 2008.[3]

In addition to revisions in immigration law and increased resources for enforcement, there has been considerable controversy over the construction of a fence along the U.S.–Mexico border. Cost estimates of a border fence along the entire border vary considerably—from $47 billion to $59 billion, not including maintenance, surveillance, or enforcement costs. Environmentalists, border residents, and border governors have been less than enthusiastic about the construction of the border fence. Governor Rick Perry (a Republican) of Texas and Governor Janet Napolitano (a Democrat, appointed as Secretary of the Department of Homeland Security in early 2009) of Arizona both oppose the fence for a number of reasons, each using a similar phrase to describe its likely effectiveness: "Show me a 20 foot fence and I will show you a 21 foot ladder."[4]

By most accounts (for example, Camarota 2007), migration flows to the United States were at record levels in the early 2000s despite changes in immigration law, greater expenditures on enforcement, and the construction of fences. If reducing the flow of in-migration to the United States is a desirable goal, it is reasonable to ask whether there is a more cost-effective mechanism for getting the job done.

Investing in the economic development of migrant-sending nations, particularly Mexico, could be a more effective use of scarce resources and provide other benefits as well. This economic-development suggestion is not an argument against meaningful revision of the convoluted and largely unenforced U.S. immigration laws. Indeed, if implemented, the economic-development policy as immigration policy idea could pave the way for successful implementation of immigration law based on U.S. labor-market needs as suggested by Briggs.

The argument presented here is in the context of migration from Mexico to the United States—the issue that initially engaged Briggs's interest and subsequent work on immigration policy (Briggs 1975).[5] Briggs, himself, did not ignore economic development as part of an overall strategy to reduce migration flows. In the 1970s, Briggs (1975, p. 483) stated: "With respect to the special problems associated with illegal entry from neighboring Mexico, the United States should make overtures to Mexico concerning how efforts could be made to develop the economy of Mexico's northern states." He also argued that the United States "should carefully reassess its trade and tariff policies as they pertain to Mexico" (Briggs 1975, p. 483).

Briggs continues to maintain that economic-development assistance to sending nations should be part of the overall policy mix: "More attention should also be given by national policies to addressing the push factors in the major source countries. More economic assistance should be made available and tailored to the particular factors in any country that cause so many of its citizens to leave their homeland" (Briggs 2003, p. 280).

If there is a difference between Briggs's views on the role of economic development as migration policy and my own, it is a matter of emphasis. Briggs places reform of immigration law and increased enforcement as the highest priorities, while the suggestion here is that mutually agreed upon development assistance would be more effective in reducing migration flows than immigration reform or enforcement.

What do we know about Mexican immigrants to the United States? Most of those born in Mexico and residing in the United States are not U.S. citizens (78.5 percent). More than a quarter (27.0 percent or roughly 3.1 million) of these foreign-born noncitizens entered the United States between 2000 and 2006, even though migration from Mexico to the United States may have slowed down for a year or two after the terrorist attacks of September 2001 (U.S. Census Bureau 2007).[6]

Why do these immigrants come to the United States? Migration (domestic and international) occurs for many reasons. Migrants are motivated to relocate for personal reasons such as family reunification, to seek political asylum (to flee real or imagined political persecution), and to satisfy inherent restlessness. Despite this wide range of reasons, economic motives for migration are amply supported by economic theory (Massey et al. 1994; Todaro 1969) and numerous empirical studies (see, for example, Greenwood and McDowell 1991; Passel 1990; Stark and Taylor 1989). In the case of Mexico and the United States, there is strong evidence that large U.S.–Mexico income disparities contribute significantly to U.S. migration from Mexico (see, for example, Díez-Cañedo Ruiz 1984; Passel 2006). That is why policies designed to reduce those income differentials could go a long way toward reducing migration flows between the two nations.

Economic growth theory generally suggests that income differences among nations and regions should disappear over the long run. To the extent that migration is motivated by economic concerns, income convergence should reduce migration to the United States in the long run. But, given the historical record and current policies, it will be a very long time before U.S.–Mexico income convergence occurs. According to World Bank data, U.S. GDP per person ($43,984) was 5.5 times that of Mexico ($8,051; World Bank 2008).[7] If Mexico's GDP per person were to grow at 2 percent per year and U.S. GDP per person did not grow at all, income convergence between the two nations (as measured by GDP per person) would not occur until about 2091. We can be reasonably confident that this is too long to have an effect on early twenty-first-century immigration flows or policy.

The 2 percent per year growth rate used in this example is not entirely arbitrary. GDP per person in the United States has grown at about 2 percent per year for more than a century. If U.S. GDP per person continues to grow, then either a much higher growth rate in Mexico or a much longer time (perhaps centuries) will be required to achieve income convergence between the two nations.

The preferred solution, of course, is faster growth in Mexico and not slower U.S. growth. Rapid economic growth in Mexico is possible. The historical record suggests that the Mexican economy grew at very high rates from the 1940s to the early 1980s, a period commonly referred to as *el milagro* (the miracle). The rapid growth of the Mexican economy during the miracle years was associated with rapid urbanization and even more rapid industrial growth.

Neither market forces nor current policies will reduce U.S.–Mexico income differentials enough to affect the contemporary debate over U.S. immigration policy. The most optimistic projections of the effects of the North American Free Trade Agreement (NAFTA) on economic growth in Mexico and the United States do not suggest that bi-national income convergence is just around the corner. A 2003 Congressional Budget Office Study (2003, p. xiv) concluded that "NAFTA has increased U.S. GDP but by a very small amount—probably no more than a few billion dollars" and that the effects on Mexico were likely to be roughly the same size.

If economic growth in Mexico is important to the United States, it is difficult to tell. Other than trade policy and mild praise from U.S. officials for Mexico's attempts to restrain the growth of its money supply and balance its federal budget, the United States has done little to promote economic growth in Mexico. Worse, it is difficult to claim that praise, restraining money supply growth, or balancing budgets contributes much to growth at all. An argument can be made that the United States has no right to interfere in the internal affairs of its neighbor to the south, despite a long record of doing so, but interference is not what I am suggesting.

A rapidly growing U.S. economy, operating at or near full capacity, is critical to Mexico's economic growth. Thus, investment in education and worker training and an attack on the *U.S.* unemployment problem are essential to the long-term growth of the *Mexican* economy. The two economies are interdependent and have been for some time (Musgrave 1985). Interaction between the two countries is obvious in trade relations, investment patterns, labor-market activities, business cycles, and in the environmental arena. U.S.–Mexico interaction is asymmetric: policies and activities in the United States have much more of an effect in Mexico than the reverse.

Trade is a particularly important part of any economic growth scenario in Mexico. Mexican exports constitute nearly a third of its GDP and now, as a century ago, nearly 90 percent of Mexico's exports are destined for U.S. markets. Trade relations between the U.S. and Mexico reinforce the notion that a growing U.S. economy is important for Mexico's economic development. In the current (2008–2009) U.S. economic downturn, Mexico's exports have plummeted. Between January 2008 and January 2009, Mexico's exports declined by 30 percent (INEGI 2009). In previous U.S. downturns, particularly in 1981–1982, Mexico's exports also decreased.

During the debate over NAFTA in the early 1990s, it was frequently argued that NAFTA would promote prosperity in Mexico and reduce Mexican migration to the United States. This was a false assertion, and there is little evidence that NAFTA has reduced U.S. immigration flows (Passel 2006; Scott, Sala, and Campbell 2006). In fact, in the year NAFTA took effect (1994), Mexico experienced its worst economic crisis since the Great Depression. The United States had little choice except to put together a $50 billion financial rescue package for Mexico, the third U.S. attempt to bolster the Mexican economy since the early 1980s (Peach 1995). Mexico willingly accepted the severe restrictions on its own domestic fiscal and monetary policy that came along with the various rescue plans. It is not impossible to influence Mexico's policy stance and development strategies from north of the border, and the current economic crisis (2008–2009) may provide yet another opportunity to do so. The key question is whether this will be done in a constructive manner.

More meaningful economic-development policies toward Mexico are possible. A modern version of the Marshall Plan, involving large-scale investments by the three NAFTA partners, is another possibility. Such a plan could be easily designed with an emphasis on education, transportation, and energy infrastructure needed to make NAFTA work more effectively. The need for coordinated education, energy, and transportation policies in the three nations has become apparent since NAFTA has been implemented, and such investments could stimulate economic growth in all three nations without threatening national sovereignty.

Another possibility is for the United States to provide several billion dollars in scholarships for Mexican students to study at U.S. universities, perhaps with the condition that they must return home after completion of their studies. This could benefit both U.S. institutions of higher education and the Mexican economy. In fact, both nations already profit from a sizeable Mexican program to subsidize the education of its residents in the United States.

Many other economic-development programs could be devised with just a little imagination and could be paid for with some or all of the billions of dollars the United States already spends on various immigration enforcement activities along its southern border. The need to devise such programs is reinforced by the current global economic crisis. There are many signs that the Mexican economy is again in serious trouble. For example, Mexico's real GDP decreased 8.2 percent between the first quarter of 2008 and the first quarter of 2009, and Mexico's exports decreased 35.6 percent between April 2008 and April 2009 (INEGI 2009). Another Mexican economic crisis would almost certainly increase the flow of migrants from Mexico to the United States, even if the U.S. economy is performing poorly. I suggest we adopt policies that will address both the immediate economic crisis, the long-term development needs of the United States and Mexico, and alter migration flows between the two nations. It is possible to do it all—reform immigration along the lines suggested by Briggs, improve enforcement, and promote economic development in Mexico. But, if we must choose between them, my choice is to emphasize economic development as the highest priority.

Notes

1. I believe that I learned "the opportunity cost of employing the unemployed is zero" from a course taught by Briggs, but memory is a frequently unreliable source.
2. No one does a better job of summarizing and explaining the evolution and subtleties of U.S. immigration law than Briggs (1984, 2003).
3. As this chapter is being written, the Obama administration is also considering deploying troops and law enforcement agents to the border to prevent Mexican drug-cartel violence from spreading into the United States.
4. Border fences produce other forms of controversy and even amusement. In 2007, the Golden State Fence Company, hired to build portions of the border fence near San Diego, entered a guilty plea to charges that it hired illegal immigrants (as many as 250 of its 750 workers) to work on the fence (Horsley 2007).
5. Partly because the United States and Mexico share a common border, migration from Mexico to the United States generally receives the most attention in the media, and this particular migration flow is often discussed in emotional terms. Of course, Mexico is not the sole source of U.S. immigration. The American Community Survey for 2006 (U.S. Census Bureau 2007) indicates that there were 37.5 million foreign-born persons in the United States and that just 11.5 million (30.7 percent) of those were born in Mexico.
6. The American Community Survey estimates of the foreign-born population and the number and percentage of the foreign born who were born in Mexico are very similar to estimates from the Current Population Survey (CPS). See Camarota (2007) for an extended discussion of the CPS data.
7. Using GDP per person may not be the best comparison. The differences in personal income per person in the two nations may be much larger because exports account for a much larger share of GDP in Mexico than in the United States.

References

Abraham, Spencer, and Lee H. Hamilton. 2006. *Immigration and America's Future: A New Chapter; Report of the Independent Task Force on Immigration and America's Future*. Washington, DC: Migration Policy Institute. http://www.migrationpolicy.org/pubs/2006.php (accessed June 10, 2009).

Bouvier, Leon, and Thomas J. Espenshade. 1989. "The Stable Population Model, Migration, and Complementarity." *Population Research and Policy Review* 8(2): 165–179.

Bouvier, Leon F., Dudley L. Poston Jr., and Nanbin Benjamin Zhai. 1995. "Zero Net Migration: What Does It Really Mean?" Washington, DC: Center for Immigration Studies. http://www.cis.org/articles/1995/back1995.html (accessed June 11, 2009).

Briggs, Vernon M. Jr. 1975. "Illegal Aliens: The Need for a More Restrictive Border Policy." *Social Science Quarterly* 56(2): 477–484.

———. 1984. *Immigration Policy and the American Labor Force*. Baltimore: Johns Hopkins University Press.

———. 1992. *Mass Immigration and the National Interest*. Armonk, NY: M.E. Sharpe.

———. 1996. "Immigration Policy and the U.S. Economy." *Journal of Economic Issues* 30(2): 371–390.

———. 2003. *Mass Immigration and the National Interest: Policy Directions for the New Century*. 3d ed. Armonk, NY: M.E. Sharpe.

Camarota, Steven A. 2007. "Immigrants in the United States, 2007: A Profile of America's Foreign-Born Population." *Backgrounder* (November): 1–43. Washington, DC: Center for Immigration Studies. http://www.cis.org/ articles/2007/back1007.pdf (accessed March 22, 2009).

Congressional Budget Office. 2003. *The Effects of NAFTA on U.S.-Mexican Trade and GDP*. Washington, DC: Congressional Budget Office.

Díez-Cañedo Ruiz, Juan. 1984. *La Migración Indocumentada de México a Los Estados Unidos: Un Nuevo Enfoque*. México, D.F.: Fondo de Cultura Económica.

Gordon, Wendell C. 1975. "A Case for a Less Restrictive Border Policy." *Social Science Quarterly* 56(2): 485–491.

Greenwood, Michael J., and John M. McDowell. 1991. "Differential Economic Opportunity, Transferability of Skills, and Immigration to the United States and Canada." *Review of Economics and Statistics* 73(4): 612–623.

Horsley, Scott. 2007. "An Ironic Turn of Events for Golden State Fence." National Public Radio transcript, March 28. http://www.npr.org/templates/ story/story.php?storyId=9177041 (accessed March 22, 2009).

INEGI (Instituto Nacional de Estadistica y Geografia). 2009. Aguascalientes, Mexico. http://www.inegi.org.mx (accessed June 10, 2009).

Massey, Douglas S., Joaquin Arango, Graeme Hugo, Ali Kouaouci, Adela Pellegrino, and J. Edward Taylor. 1994. "An Evaluation of International Migration Theory: The North American Case." *Population and Development Review* 20(4): 699–751.

Musgrave, Peggy B. 1985. *Mexico and the United States: Studies in Economic Interaction*. Boulder, CO: Westview Press.

Myrdal, Gunnar. 1968. *Asian Drama: An Inquiry into the Poverty of Nations*. Vol. 1. New York: Random House.

Passel, Jeffrey S. 1990. "The Social and Economic Origins of Immigration." *Annals of the American Academy of Political and Social Science* 510(1): 60–72.

———. 2006. "The Size and Characteristics of the Unauthorized Migrant Population in the U.S.: Estimates Based on the March 2005 Current Population Survey." Pew Hispanic Center Research Report no. 61. http://pewhispanic .org/files/reports/61.pdf (accessed March 22, 2009).

Peach, James T. 1995. "NAFTA and Mexico's Current Economic Crisis: Short Run vs. Long Run Perspectives." *The Social Science Journal* 34(4): 375–388.

———. 2007. "Institutionalist Perspectives on Immigration Policy." *Journal of Economic Issues* 41(2): 369–374.

Scott, Robert E., Carlos Sala, and Bruce Campbell. 2006. "Revisiting NAFTA: Still Not Working for North America's Workers." EPI Economic Briefing Paper no. 173. Washington, DC: Economic Policy Institute. http://www.epi .org/publications/entry/bp173/ (accessed 10 June 2009).

Stark, Oded, and Edward Taylor. 1989. "Relative Deprivation and International Migration." *Demography* 26(1): 1–14.

Todaro, Michael P. 1969. "A Model of Labor Migration and Urban Unemployment in Less Developed Countries." *American Economic Review* 59(1): 138–148.

United Nations. 2006. *World Population Prospects: 2006.* Department of Economic and Social Affairs, Population Division. New York: United Nations.

U.S. Bureau of Economic Analysis. 2009. "National Economic Accounts." Washington, DC: U.S. Department of Commerce. http://www.bea.gov/ national/index.htm#gdp (accessed June 10, 2009).

U.S. Bureau of Labor Statistics. 2009. "Employment Situation: February 2009." News release, March 6. Washington, DC: U.S. Department of Labor, Bureau of Labor Statistics. http://www.bls.gov/news.release/archives/ empsit_03062009.pdf (accessed March 22, 2008).

U.S. Census Bureau. 2007. *American Community Survey, 2006.* Washington, DC: U.S. Census Bureau. http://www.census.gov/acs/www/Products/ users_guide/2006/index.htm (accessed June 26, 2009).

U.S. Immigration and Customs Enforcement. 2009 *Immigration and Customs Enforcement Budget Fact Sheet.* Washington, DC: U.S. Department of Homeland Security. http://www.ice.gov/pi/news/factsheets/index.htm (accessed March 22, 2009).

World Bank. 2008. *World Development Indicators.* Washington, DC: World Bank. http://www.worldbank.org/data/wdi2008/index.html (accessed March 22, 2009).

8

Employment and Wage Prospects of Black, White, and Hispanic Women

Marta Tienda
Princeton University

V. Joseph Hotz
Duke University

Avner Ahituv
Kibbutz Ramat Yohanan

Michelle Bellessa Frost
Formerly of Princeton University

It was fall 1972 in Austin, Texas. Vernon Briggs was assigned to teach principles of economics—the introductory course for freshmen—and the lead author of this chapter was a first-year graduate student in transition from humanities to social science. However, without a single economics course under her belt, auditing the introductory course seemed prudent. What she never expected was positive lifetime returns from that decision.

In one lecture, Briggs dared to assert that immigrants aggravated rural poverty by depressing wages and displacing Chicanos, but he did so on the basis of detailed knowledge of rural labor markets. He had just finished *Chicanos and Rural Poverty* (Briggs 1973) and understood all too well the dynamics of labor-market competition. He also recognized that employment policy requires not only tight coordination with immigration policy but also appropriate human capital investments in domestic workers, preferably via well-functioning educational institutions. This chapter is a testament to Briggs's concerns and influence.

THE ISSUES

Black, Hispanic, and white women differ in the amount of school they complete, in the timing and character of their family formation, and in their labor-force behavior. White women average the highest level of education while Hispanics complete the fewest years of schooling, with blacks somewhere in between. Decisions about educational investments and work experience during the early life course have profound impacts on later career paths and wage prospects. Although returns on education and work experience have been examined in previous research, most studies have focused on men, whose post-school labor-force activity is virtually universal (Ahituv, Tienda, and Hotz 2000; Hotz et al. 2002; Keane and Wolpin 1997). Because their family formation decisions are highly influential in determining their employment behavior, the situation for women is more complex (Ahituv and Tienda 2004).

Understanding how fertility influences employment decisions during the early life course is complicated because the timing of births influences both school continuation and labor-force decisions at a given age. Younger women's labor-force participation has been increasing over the past century, especially since 1950 (Spain and Bianchi 1996). Compared with men, women continue to experience greater and more frequent interruptions in their career trajectories (Alon, Donahoe, and Tienda 2001). In turn, their family formation choices affect both educational attainment and the acquisition of valuable work experience during the early life course. Finally, fertility decisions are thought to be influenced by women's educational and work career opportunities, giving rise to a potentially important source of endogeneity between the fertility, schooling, and employment decisions of women.

Additionally, women are not a homogeneous group. African-American and Hispanic women earn, on average, lower wages than white women and are less likely to find a job when searching for paid work (Browne 1999). Furthermore, not only decisions surrounding investments in education and work experience, but also choices of family formation differ among racial and ethnic groups. Black women are more likely than either white or Hispanic women to bear a child out of wedlock, yet they complete more years of education than Hispanic women (Ahituv and Tienda 2004; Stier and Tienda 2001). Therefore, it is necessary to consider jointly the interrelationship between fertility, schooling, and employment decisions to appreciate whether minority and nonminority women respond similarly to changing economic opportunities.

From the late 1970s to the present, labor-market conditions became more geographically heterogenous across the United States, implying changing regional incentives to either enter the workforce or remain in school. Tight, dynamic markets may propel young women into the labor force, thereby allowing them to accumulate work experience. However, if this work experience comes at the expense of pursuing additional schooling, participating in the labor force early in one's career may be deleterious in the long run. Due to the geographic and residential separation of racial and ethnic groups in the United States, as well as the geographic differences in amount of industrial restructuring across the country, local labor-market conditions could lead to differing outcomes for black, white, and Hispanic women (Bound and Dresser 1999; Browne 1999).

This chapter addresses several questions about young women's employment and wage prospects in the context of the school-to-work transition. First, how do young women's human capital investment and family formation decisions vary along racial and ethnic lines? Second, what implications do these differences have for labor-force behavior? Third, how does the acquisition of early work experience differ among black, white, and Hispanic women, and are the returns on early experience significant predictors of adult wage inequality? Finally, how sensitive are young women's labor-force decisions to local market conditions?

The next section describes the National Longitudinal Survey of Youth (NLSY) and defines key variables used in the empirical analysis. Following a statistical portrait of the work and schooling experiences for a cohort of young women from ages 17 through 28, we elaborate an econometric specification to estimate the effects of local labor-market conditions, human capital, and fertility on young women's employment behavior and wages and present empirical results. The conclusion highlights key findings and suggests directions for further research.

DATA

The data for our analysis is drawn from the NLSY, a nationally representative sample of U.S. youth between the ages of 13 and 20 as of January 1, 1978. The original sample consisted of a national probability sample of 6,111 men and women in this age range, plus 5,296 individuals from randomly selected oversamples of black, Hispanic, and economically disadvantaged white youth. Beginning in 1979, in-person interviews were conducted annually, and by 1993, the last year we analyze, just over 10 percent of the original sample had been lost to attrition. The detailed life histories specify dates and type of employment, hours of work, wage rates, dates of school enrollment, and dates of childbirth by age, which permit us to record simultaneous activities at specific ages.

Empirical analyses use data for women drawn from the national probability sample and the black and Hispanic oversamples for the 1979–1993 period. We also restrict our analysis to respondents aged 13–16 in 1978 (28–31 in 1993). Except for youth who participate in informal, remunerated jobs prior to the legal age for work (i.e., 14), this sample selection criterion yields the most complete information possible on the entire process of early employment experiences, school departure, and labor-market entry. With these data restrictions, our analysis sample consists of 2,477 young women, including 1,204 whites, 762 blacks, and 511 Hispanics.

Labor-Market Status

Using the detailed work and school histories, we construct a year-by-year classification of women's primary activity.[1] Starting from age 13, each respondent was coded as participating in one of the following four mutually exclusive activities: 1) enrolled in school, 2) part-time work only, 3) full-time work, and 4) homemaker.

For women who had not worked full time, we examined school attendance and employment during the calendar year to see if their dominant activity was school (state 1) or part-time work (state 2). The homemaker activity state (4) also includes a tiny share of childless women who were not working or attending school. This coding exercise produced a person-year file with 15 observations per respondent. Wage rates are available for jobs associated with the first three states. Because we consider whether school is the dominant state, we do not estimate a wage equation for state 1.

Human Capital Measures

We derive indicators of human capital as measured by educational attainment and work experience, measured from a life cycle perspective. Because youth accumulate educational experience over their early life course (Hotz and Tienda 2002; Tienda and Ahituv 1996), we constructed a measure of the years of school attended at each age. We also chart age-specific educational attainment using the school history module to ascertain whether the highest level is less than high school, high-school graduation (or GED), or a bachelor's degree as of each age. With respect to work experience, we use the detailed work history data to construct measures of the number of weeks worked full time and part time at each age. Finally, we include scores on the Armed Forces Qualification Test (AFQT) in our analyses to control for individual differences in labor-market aptitude.

Family Background, Personal Characteristics, and Fertility

Using 1979 baseline NLSY interviews, we follow Caspi et al. (1998) in constructing several family and personal background variables related to young women's labor-market outcomes. These include the income of respondents' parents in 1978, maternal educational attainment, total number of siblings in 1979, and whether or not the respondent lived in a female-headed household at the age of 14.[2] Personal characteristics include race/ethnicity, age, husband's income, urban residence, age of menarche, and whether the respondent was born in a foreign country. From the birth histories available in the NLSY, we construct a measure of cumulative fertility by age, which essentially denotes the number of children ever born at each age.

Labor-Market Conditions

To assess the effects of labor-market conditions on the employment prospects and wages of young female workers, we used county-level data on employment and average earnings distributed by the Bureau of Economic Analysis (BEA) of the U.S. Department of Commerce to construct two time-varying measures of local labor-market conditions: the county average income per worker (expressed in constant 1982 dollars) and the county annual percentage rate of growth in total employment. These time-varying indicators of labor-market conditions were appended to respondents' geo-coded records.

EARLY WORK AND FAMILY EXPERIENCES OF YOUNG WOMEN

Attaining full-time employment represents a successful culmination of the transition from school to work. Ahituv, Tienda, and Hotz (2000) show that there are multiple pathways from school to work that roughly correspond to race and ethnic groups. Table 8.1, which depicts the age-specific allocation of women into the four mutually exclusive activity states, reveals clear racial and ethnic differences in the transition from school to work. At age 17, enrollment in school is the modal activity for all demographic groups, although by that age, almost 30 percent of Hispanic women have left school compared to 21 percent of whites and 16 percent of blacks. Overall, black and white women are more similar to each other in their school-leaving patterns. However, black women are more similar to Hispanic than white women in their full-time age-employment profiles at later ages because, like their male counterparts, they experience delays in the initial entry into the labor market. Thus, by age 24, when most women have finished school, nearly half of Hispanic and black women have become full-time workers, compared with 60 percent of white women. By age 28, 61 percent of white women held a full-time job compared to 53 percent of Hispanic and black women. Although, between the ages of 17 and 28, the share of Hispanic women who were homemakers doubled, while that of black women more than

Table 8.1 Pathways from School to Work: Age-Specific Distribution of Hispanic, Black, and White Women by Four Activity States (%)

Age	Hispanic (N=5,724)[a]				Black (N=8,679)				White (N=13,723)			
	School enrollment	Part-time work	Full-time work	Home-makers	School enrollment	Part-time work	Full-time work	Home-makers	School enrollment	Part-time work	Full-time work	Home-makers
17	70.1	13.2	6.0	10.6	84.2	4.7	2.8	8.3	78.8	10.1	7.1	4.0
18	44.0	28.7	14.5	12.8	56.2	18.0	7.4	18.5	46.3	27.5	19.0	7.2
19	24.3	32.9	23.9	18.9	34.3	27.5	13.6	24.6	32.7	27.7	30.9	8.8
20	17.0	31.4	34.4	17.2	24.4	30.5	19.2	25.9	27.4	27.3	37.6	7.7
21	14.2	30.1	34.2	21.4	16.5	27.7	28.0	27.3	24.4	24.1	41.0	10.5
22	10.0	27.4	41.0	21.6	11.4	32.1	33.7	22.9	12.3	27.0	49.3	11.5
23	6.4	28.8	42.3	22.5	6.8	30.3	39.8	23.1	7.1	25.3	57.3	10.3
24	3.9	24.7	47.6	23.8	4.2	25.9	48.3	21.7	4.8	23.2	61.6	10.5
25	3.9	26.9	50.5	18.7	3.5	25.3	50.2	20.5	3.9	22.3	63.2	10.6
26	4.4	21.7	53.4	20.6	3.2	24.4	53.8	18.7	3.6	24.3	60.4	11.8
27	4.3	23.6	51.3	20.9	2.7	24.9	54.2	18.1	3.2	24.7	61.0	11.2
28	4.7	21.7	53.2	20.4	3.5	23.7	53.2	19.7	2.9	22.7	60.9	13.5

NOTE: Some segments may not total 100 due to rounding.

[a] N's reported are in units of person years. The person year file was created from a sample including 1,204 white, 762 black, and 511 Hispanic women.

SOURCE: NLSY.

doubled, and that of white women almost quadrupled, only 13 percent of white women were full-time homemakers at age 28 compared to about 20 percent of black and Hispanic women.

As has been observed for young men (Ahituv, Tienda, and Hotz 2000), Hispanic women enter the labor force on a part-time basis at younger ages than either white or black women. White and Hispanic women are about equally likely to work full time at age 17. That only about half as many black women work full time at this age reveals their greater difficulty securing employment during adolescence. By age 19, when the majority of young women have left school, about one-third of white women and one-quarter of Hispanic women work full time as compared to only 14 percent of black women. The Hispanic–black gap in full-time employment arises partly because larger shares of black women remain enrolled in school up to age 20, whereas Hispanic women withdraw from school at a significantly faster rate. However, this does not explain the large race gap in the timing of the entry into full-time employment because even larger shares of white women pro-long schooling as compared to blacks. The white advantage in full-time employment that emerges at age 17 persists throughout the early life course: it widens through late adolescence and early adulthood, im-plying acquisition of more labor-market experience. After age 25, the white–minority gap narrows, hovering around 7 percentage points.

At least four reasons can be proffered to account for racial and eth-nic differences in the timing of entry to full-time employment. The first is that, similar to young men (Ahituv, Tienda, and Hotz 2000), black, white, and Hispanic women pursue distinct investment profiles in the transition from school to work. In other words, young women's human capital investment decisions in education and early work experience have direct and lasting consequences for their full-time employment prospects and the wages they can command as young adults. Second, racial and ethnic differences in the timing of births and marriage may contribute to the observed differences in full-time employment. A third reason is Hispanics enjoyed more favorable labor-market conditions than either blacks or whites because they disproportionately live in the sunbelt and were relatively shielded from the industrial decline that di-minished job opportunities in the rustbelt states during the late 1970s and throughout the 1980s. A fourth explanation for these differences is that black women experience more intense labor-market discrimination than Hispanics.

Human Capital Investment

Figure 8.1 addresses the first reason by plotting the age-specific educational attainment of young women. These trends are based on all young women in the sample, regardless of when or if they attained full-time employment prior to age 27. The well-documented differences are clearly evident: namely, whites attain the highest level of education at all ages, Hispanics the lowest level, and blacks an intermediate level. This finding is consistent with the activity state distributions reported in Table 8.1, which show that Hispanics have the fastest rates of school departure while whites exit school at much slower rates.

Educational differentials widen appreciably after age 18 owing to differences in the likelihood of college attendance by minority and

Figure 8.1 Age-Specific Educational Attainment by Race and Hispanic Origin

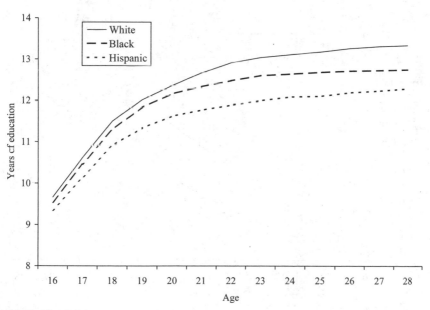

SOURCE: NLYS.

nonminority groups, coupled with low rates of high-school completion among Hispanic women. By the ages of 24–25, white women averaged almost one more year of school than Hispanics and approximately a half year more than blacks. Owing to the greater propensity of white women to pursue post-graduate training, the race gap in education increased slightly by age 27. Group differences in the acquisition of labor-market experience throughout the early life course could also contribute to rising educational inequities by age if this form of human capital acquisition comes at the expense of additional schooling.

As suggested by the data in Table 8.1, black, white, and Hispanic women accumulate unequal amounts of part-time and full-time work experience in their transition from school to work because of differences in the timing of labor-force entry (Hotz and Tienda 2002). Figure 8.2 summarizes racial and ethnic differences in accumulated work experience for young women aged 17–28. In contrast to the trends in

Figure 8.2 Age-Specific Work Experience by Race and Hispanic Origin

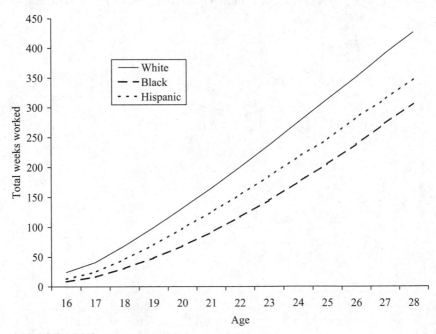

SOURCE: NLYS.

educational attainment, which showed Hispanic women to be most disadvantaged, during the 1980s, Latinas acquired more work experience than their black counterparts but less than whites. In fact, despite their higher levels of education at each age, the work experience curve for blacks is below those of Hispanic and white women throughout the age range considered. Moreover, the ethno-racial experience gaps increased over time. At age 18, white women averaged 0.7 years more work experience than their black age counterparts and 0.4 years more than Hispanics. By age 22, the comparable differentials were 1.6 and 0.9 years for blacks and Hispanics, respectively. And, by the end of the observation period, white women averaged 2.3 years more work experience than blacks and 1.5 years more than Hispanics.

On balance, women's transition from school to work roughly parallels that of young men inasmuch as there appear to be three general profiles (Ahituv, Tienda, and Hotz 2000). The experience of whites is characterized by prolonged schooling and early entry into the workforce, which eventuates in higher stocks of human capital in the form of *both* work experience and schooling. Hispanic women's age-specific full-time labor-force participation rates trail those of whites at every age, but they acquire more labor-force experience than black women. Black women's modal pathway from school to work involves delayed labor-market entry, coupled with prolonged schooling. If the returns on education are greater than the returns on work experience, Hispanic women should be most economically disadvantaged as young adults because they achieve the lowest educational levels. This scenario is likely because returns on education rose appreciably during the 1980s and early 1990s (Danziger and Gottschalk 1993).

Young Women's Family Formation

A second reason for the unequal labor-force experiences of black, white, and Hispanic women is their different patterns of family formation. Group differences in the timing and number of births directly influence women's labor-force behavior, but fertility also is influenced by employment activity and educational attainment (Ahituv and Tienda 2004). Figure 8.3 portrays the cumulative proportions of women married at specific ages for black, white, and Hispanic women, and Figure

Figure 8.3 Age-Specific Cumulative Proportion Ever Married by Race and Ethnicity

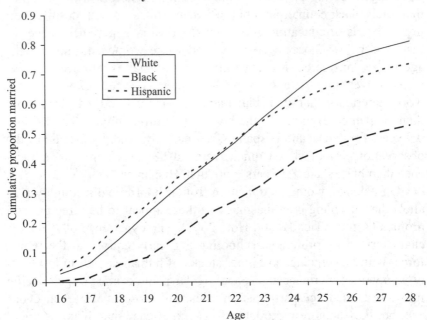

SOURCE: NLYS.

8.4 depicts the cumulative proportions of women from each group with at least one child at specific ages. A striking difference in marriage behavior is that black women are appreciably less likely to marry at any age than either whites or Hispanics. Another noteworthy difference in family formation is that Hispanic women enter marriage at a faster pace than either blacks or whites until about age 22, when the white and Hispanic marriage rates converge. Marriage behavior influences women's labor-force activity in two ways. First, it enables them to remain at home if their spouses' income is sufficient to meet needs and preferences. Second, marriage generally makes childbearing more likely, other things being equal.

Figure 8.4, which displays the cumulative proportion of women with at least one child by age, shows large differences in childbearing patterns. Although childbearing at age 16 is typically uncommon, black

Figure 8.4 Age-Specific Cumulative Proportion with Child, by Race and Ethnicity

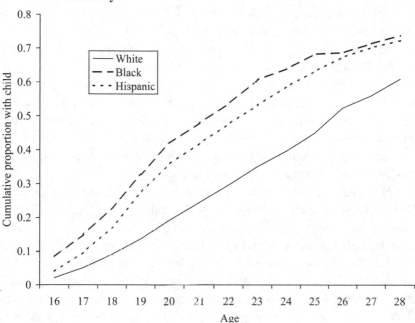

SOURCE: NLYS.

girls are twice as likely as Hispanics and four times as likely as whites to have their first child at this age. During the teen years, childbearing among Hispanics rises steeply so that, by age 20, 36 percent of Hispanic women have borne at least one child compared to 40 percent of black women and only 19 percent of white women. The black and Hispanic cumulative fertility curves remain above that of white women throughout the life course, despite the fact that the proportion of black married women remains lower throughout. Thus, white women's high rates of labor-force participation as young adults also reflect their lesser family constraints relative to minority women coupled with higher stocks of work experience they accumulate as a result. By age 27, only 56 percent of white women had given birth to at least one child as compared to 70 percent of black and Hispanic women.

Local Labor Markets and Young Women's Employment

Young women's decisions about whether to prolong or leave school, enter the labor force, or start a family also depend on labor-market opportunities, which evolved rapidly during the 1980s and 1990s. Between 1979 and 1993, there were two recessions, including a rather severe one during the early 1980s and another during the early 1990s. Unemployment reached 21 percent for young women between 1982 and 1983 and nearly 10 percent for young men (Donahoe and Tienda 2000). Throughout the 1980s and early 1990s, when our cohort had largely completed the transition from school to work, female unemployment rates remained in the double digits.

However, the national trends obscure regional variation in local labor markets, which is germane to our hypothesis that local conditions may be partly responsible for the high employment rates of Hispanics, despite their low educational attainment. During the recession of the early 1980s and until around 1985, when our cohorts were between the ages of 20 and 23, on average, Hispanic youth resided in more dynamic labor markets as compared to black and white youth. This reflects the fact that Hispanics disproportionately resided in California, where labor-market conditions between 1975 and 1987 were consistently more favorable as compared with other regions. Young blacks resided in counties with average labor incomes and employment growth rates significantly below those of counties where white and Hispanic youth resided. After 1985, however, white women enjoyed more favorable labor-market conditions, on average, than either black or Hispanic women.

If local labor-market conditions influence young women's timing of full-time employment and their schooling decisions, they also could contribute to unequal levels of experience for whites, blacks, and Hispanics. In the following section, we address whether and by how much the employment and wage returns on education and experience differ, whether young women's labor-force decisions are sensitive to local labor-market conditions, and whether returns on education and work experience are uniform for minority and nonminority women.

ECONOMETRIC SPECIFICATION

To examine the effects of the factors influencing the employment, education, and fertility choices of young adult women over their life cycle and the effects of these decisions on young women's wages, we employ the same econometric framework used in Hotz et al. (2002) and in Ahituv and Tienda (2004).[3] In essence, we employ an econometric specification that models the school, work, and homemaking activity choices using a discrete-choice multinomial probit model in which the activity-specific and age-specific utility functions depend upon the years of schooling and work experiences accumulated by a given age, a woman's accumulated fertility, the local labor-market conditions prevailing at that age, and family background characteristics, as well as indicators of race and ethnicity. We also specify a fertility equation as of each age, which also depends on these same factors. Finally, we specify a Mincerian wage equation, in which the (log of) wages of women who work depend on our human capital and labor-market condition variables, as well as race, to estimate the returns on wages of these factors and to determine the remaining differences in wages by race and ethnicity.

A key feature of our econometric analysis is to account for the endogeneity of these various choices when estimating their influences on life cycle employment, schooling, fertility, and wage outcomes of women. To account for this endogeneity, we augment the basic estimating equations with a factor-analytic error structure, in which a common factor, with choice-specific factor loadings, econometrically "links" these various choices together, where the distribution of this common factor is approximated by a discrete distribution function, with finite numbers of points of support.[4] In what follows, we present estimates for a specification of the model that does not include this factor structure (the "without heterogeneity" specification) and one that includes this factor structure to account for endogeneity (the "with heterogeneity" specification).

EMPIRICAL RESULTS

Table 8.2 presents descriptive statistics for several measures of family background, including family income and mother's years of schooling. Minority women are more likely than whites to come from economically disadvantaged homes. The average family income of Hispanics was about $13,000 below that of whites and roughly $3,000 higher than that of blacks. If black women represent the most economically disadvantaged family backgrounds, Hispanic women come from the most educationally disadvantaged backgrounds. Mothers of Hispanic women averaged 7.5 years of graded schooling, compared to 10 and 11.5 for blacks and whites, respectively. Also, black women were three times as likely as whites and about twice as likely as Hispanics to have been reared in a mother-only family. Several studies show that differences in financial resources, parental education, and family stability affect various outcomes of young women, including educational attainment (Kane 1994), the likelihood of working during adolescence (Ahituv, Tienda, and Hotz 2000), and the odds of becoming an adolescent mother (McLanahan and Sandefur 1994).

Table 8.2 also reports young women's educational attainment, mean AFQT scores, and work experience. We include the AFQT score as a control in all statistical models and interpret it as pre-market aptitude for market-relevant skills (Neal and Johnson 1996). As presaged by Figure 8.2, white women acquire considerably more work experience than minority women by age 28 (28 percent more than black women and 19 percent more than Hispanics). Not only are white women more likely than their minority counterparts to be married after age 22 (Figure 8.3), but they also enjoy the benefit of higher spousal earnings. The latter could depress their labor supply, particularly during the prime reproductive years because they can afford to become homemakers.

Finally, there is evidence that Hispanic women lived in more dynamic labor markets than blacks, but not necessarily white women, as indicated by the average annual employment growth rate of their county of residence. However, mean per-worker incomes of labor markets where Hispanic women resided were actually lower, on average, than mean incomes where blacks and whites resided. Therefore, the effect of

Table 8.2 Proportions and Means (Standard Deviations) of Endogenous and Independent Variables at Age 28 by Race and Hispanic Origin

	Hispanic	Black	White
Endogenous variables			
Number of births	1.56	1.63	1.10
	(1.40)	(1.41)	(1.10)
Hourly pay ($)	6.85	5.73	7.17
	(4.72)	(3.98)	(4.91)
Independent variables			
Human capital and scholastic achievement			
Education (years)	12.29	12.75	13.34
	(2.32)	(2.02)	(2.35)
Work experience (weeks)	347.10	305.71	426.27
	(186.95)	(174.42)	(158.53)
AFQT Score	57.96	51.34	75.59
	(18.89)	(17.10)	(17.57)
Family background (1979)			
Number of siblings	4.26	4.53	2.97
	(2.79)	(3.01)	(1.92)
Family income ($)	18,532	15,571	31,007
	(13,007)	(13,725)	(17,734)
Mother's education (years)	7.52	9.94	11.40
	(4.21)	(3.69)	(3.34)
% Mother-only family	20.0	37.4	11.0
Personal characteristics			
Age of menarche	12.29	12.70	12.75
	(2.40)	(2.16)	(2.06)
Husband's income	28,671	23,413	31,611
	(38,419)	(18,567)	(38,623)
% Ever birth	72.34	73.84	60.92
% Foreign born	20.21	2.60	2.70
Labor-market conditions			
Employment growth	0.704	0.444	1.062
	(2.849)	(2.557)	(2.433)
Per-worker income ($)	13,736	14,064	14,264
	(3,891)	(3,323)	(3,184)

SOURCE: NLSY.

labor-market conditions on young women's employment and wages is not obvious and requires empirical evidence, to which we now turn.

Tables 8.3, 8.4, and 8.5 report two sets of estimates for the coefficients—and factor loadings for the models that control for heterogeneity using the factor-analytic error specification—for the utility functions associated with three of the four activity states (the "school only" state serves as a reference category), for the state valuation equation, and for the (log) wage functions. Also presented are estimates for the locations and points of support associated with the person-specific, common random factor. In assessing the appropriateness of the two sets of estimates, one can consider the relative explanatory power of the model with and without controls for unobserved heterogeneity using a likelihood ratio test. Based on this test, the improvement in the fit of the model is highly significant when the common factor structure is added to the model without heterogeneity.

With the exception of full-time work in the wage functions and part-time work in both the state valuation and wage functions, the factor loadings are all significantly different from zero for the model with heterogeneity.[5] Although we discuss the results from both models below, the data strongly suggest that controlling for person-specific unobserved heterogeneity is necessary to obtain consistent parameter estimates in the fertility and wage equations and the state-specific valuation functions that characterize the employment and family formation behaviors of young women during the 1980s and early 1990s.

Minority Group Status

Coefficients for minority group status are negative for all activity state choices, implying that black and Hispanic women are more likely than whites to remain enrolled in school as compared with working full or part time or becoming full-time homemakers (Table 8.3). This is consistent with results of Ahituv and Tienda (2004), who find that minority women prolong schooling relative to white women with similar background characteristics. These results are unaltered by the inclusion of controls for unobserved heterogeneity, except that the point estimates change slightly. Note that all values of the factor loadings for the various activities are positive and significant for full-time work activity, negative and significant for homemaking, and not significant for part-time employment.[6] Although the point estimates on the family background and AFQT scores are similar whether or not unobserved heterogeneity is taken into account, this is not so for endogenous variables (e.g., wages and number of children).

Table 8.3 shows that only one endogenous variable—number of children—behaves as expected once unobscrved heterogeneity is taken into account. Specifically, a higher number of children increases the likelihood of homemaking and lowers the likelihood of full-time employment relative to school enrollment. Higher fertility also increases the odds of part-time work relative to exclusive educational activity.

Racial and ethnic effects on family formation reveal a more complex pattern in that black women with children are more likely to remain in school, to work full or part time, or to become full-time homemakers relative to white women with similar characteristics (Table 8.4). These results are consistent with those of other studies (Browne 1999). However, the point estimates for employment activity are greatly attenuated once unobserved heterogeneity is taken into account, suggesting that black mothers who work differ from their nonworking counterparts in unmeasured ways that are systematically corrclated with the decision to work. Hispanic women with children are less likely than white mothers to remain enrolled in school, but they are as likely either to join the labor force or become full-time homemakers. Hispanic mothers are slightly more likely than white mothers to work full time, but this result is on the margin of statistical significance, and therefore tentative.

Finally, results show trivial race effects on both full- and part-time wages irrespective of whether unobserved heterogeneity is taken into account (Table 8.5). Hispanic women, however, earn 7 to 12 percent more than their statistically comparable white counterparts. Note that this effect holds with and without controlling for unobserved heterogeneity. We note that this result differs from those of cross-section analyses (Duncan, Hotz, and Trejo 2006), where one finds that Hispanic women either have *lower* or the same wages after controlling for observable factors. Such studies seldom adequately represent the accumulation of human capital and selection into various work activity states over the life course as is possible with the longitudinal data available in the NLSY.

Table 8.3 Estimates of Activity States

	Without heterogeneity			With heterogeneity		
	Part-time work	Full-time work	Homemaker	Part-time work	Full-time work	Homemaker
Activity-specific factor loading	0.0000 (0.4958)			0.0152 (0.0668)	0.4566*** (0.0584)	−0.2928*** (0.0718)
Intercept		−7.7339*** (0.5026)	−4.7478*** (0.5917)	0.0000 (0.5110)	−8.3800*** (0.5073)	−4.3343*** (0.6388)
Endogenous variables						
Number children	0.1881*** (0.0331)	0.0559* (0.0311)	0.3422*** (0.0355)	0.1840*** (0.0435)	−0.1821*** (0.0392)	0.4215*** (0.0448)
Minority status						
Black	−0.2522*** (0.0295)	−0.1303*** (0.0277)	−0.2727*** (0.0286)	−0.2545*** (0.0290)	−0.1514*** (0.0274)	−0.2681*** (0.0280)
Hispanic	−0.1905*** (0.0299)	0.0844** (0.0270)	−0.2282*** (0.0294)	−0.1911*** (0.0295)	−0.0975*** (0.0266)	−0.2213*** (0.0289)
Human capital and scholastic achievement						
Years of schooling attended	0.0561*** (0.0097)	0.0933*** (0.0089)	−0.0500*** (0.0096)	0.0560*** (0.0094)	0.0870*** (0.0087)	−0.0443*** (0.0091)
Years PT work	0.5727*** (0.0179)	0.4740*** (0.0169)	0.3176*** (0.0168)	0.5732*** (0.0180)	0.4713*** (0.0171)	0.3189*** (0.0170)
Exp previous year						
PT years last year squared	−0.0589*** (0.0023)	−0.0490*** (0.0025)	−0.0452*** (0.0027)	−0.0590*** (0.0023)	−0.0486*** (0.0025)	−0.0453*** (0.0027)

	(1)	(2)	(3)	(4)	(5)	(6)
Years FT work	0.1841***	0.5438***	-0.0419**	0.1836***	0.5472***	-0.0420**
Exp previous year	(0.0162)	(0.0155)	(0.0027)	(0.0162)	(0.0156)	(0.0166)
	-0.0127***	-0.0351***	-0.0003	-0.0130***	-0.0353***	-0.0006
FT years last year squared	(0.0023)	(0.0022)	(0.0026)	(0.0023)	(0.0022)	(0.0027)
	-0.0121***	-0.0072***	-0.0179***	-0.0120***	-0.0069***	-0.0181***
AFQT score	(0.0007)	(0.0007)	(0.0007)	(0.0007)	(0.0007)	(0.0007)
Family background (1979)						
	-0.0028***	-0.0007	-0.0050***	-0.0028***	-0.0007	-0.0052***
Family income	(0.0008)	(0.0007)	(0.0007)	(0.0008)	(0.0007)	(0.0007)
	-0.0231***	-0.0207***	-0.0297***	-0.0229***	-0.0215***	-0.0294***
Mother education	(0.0039)	(0.0037)	(0.0036)	(0.0038)	(0.0037)	(0.0036)
	0.0000	-0.0623**	0.0362*	0.0000	-0.0195	0.0412*
Mother-only family	(0.0265)	(0.0294)	(0.0236)	(0.0262)	(0.0245)	(0.0233)
Personal characteristics						
	-0.0037***	-0.0087***	0.0012	-0.0037***	-0.0084***	0.0012
Husband's income	(0.0007)	(0.0007)	(0.0010)	(0.0007)	(0.0007)	(0.0010)
	0.0000	0.0000	0.0000	0.0000	0.0000	0.0000
Foreign born	(0.0380)	(0.0359)	(0.0371)	(0.0380)	(0.0358)	(0.0369)
	0.0632	0.6479***	0.5480***	0.0616	0.6883***	0.5234***
Age	(0.0465)	(0.0463)	(0.0543)	(0.0472)	(0.0462)	(0.0569)
	-0.0017*	-0.0140***	-0.0100***	-0.0016*	-0.0145***	0.0097***
AgeSq	(0.0010)	(0.0010)	(0.0012)	(0.0010)	(0.0010)	(0.0012)
	0.0000	0.0116	-0.0147	0.0000	0.0153	0.0207
Age78_13	(0.0293)	(0.0273)	(0.0281)	(0.0292)	(0.0274)	(0.0286)

Table 8.3 (continued)

	Without heterogeneity			With heterogeneity		
	Part-time work	Full-time work	Homemaker	Part-time work	Full-time work	Homemaker
Age78_14	−0.0149	−0.0170	0.0239	−0.0143	−0.0174	0.0200
	(0.0263)	(0.0255)	(0.0244)	(0.0262)	(0.0254)	(0.0244)
Age78_15	0.0000	−0.0397*	0.0144	0.0000	−0.0343	0.0018
	(0.0257)	(0.0235)	(0.0239)	(0.0256)	(0.0233)	(0.0242)
Labor-market conditions						
Emp. growth	0.0000	0.0000	0.0000	0.0000	0.0000	0.0000
	(0.3317)	(0.3258)	(0.3440)	(0.3315)	(0.3258)	(0.3433)
Per-worker income	0.0062*	0.0151***	−0.0095**	0.0064*	0.0156***	−0.0098**
	(0.0034)	(0.0030)	(0.0032)	(0.0034)	(0.0029)	(0.0032)

NOTE: Standard errors are in parentheses. Included in the estimates (but not reported) are flags indicating missing values for mother's education, family income, and AFQT score. The variable "number of children" is unique to the activity states equation. Age78_13 refers to being age 13 in 1978; Age78_14 to being age 14 in 1978; and Age78_15 to being age 15 in 1978. $*P < 0.10$, $**P < 0.05$, $***P < 0.01$.

We find that the number of children depresses women's full-time employment activity (Table 8.3), which is consistent with one's expectation that childbearing reduces women's labor supply, at least when the children are young. Having more children increases the odds that women work part time relative to exclusive scholastic activity, but it raises even more the likelihood that they become full-time homemakers. Interestingly, the expected negative effect of fertility on the odds of full-time employment only emerges after accounting for unobserved, person-specific factors that influence both family formation and employment decisions.

Human Capital Effects

The distinct pathways from school to work pursued by young women have direct implications for their age-specific and ultimate educational attainment and acquired work experience. Human capital results are consistent with prior studies (Hotz et al. 2002) showing that higher levels of education raise the odds of working full time, and to a lesser extent part time, relative to remaining enrolled in school (Table 8.3). Conversely, higher levels of education lower the likelihood that women will become full-time homemakers relative to prolonging their schooling further. These effects are robust to the inclusion of person-specific, unobserved factors. Also, higher levels of educational attainment are associated with lower fertility, but the magnitude of this effect is attenuated substantially for women who work part or full time once controls for unobserved heterogeneity are introduced (Table 8.4). Substantively, this implies that educated mothers who work differ systematically from educated mothers who do not work in ways that are unmeasured by covariates included in the empirical model.

For (log) wages, each year of education completed is associated with a 2.8 to 3.1 percent return (Table 8.5), which is consistent with results of cross-section analyses of female wages (Browne 1999; Duncan, Hotz, and Trejo 2006). Moreover, the point estimates are robust to specifications that include and exclude controls for unobserved heterogeneity. Returns on part-time wages were slightly lower than returns on full-time wages, which is another widely replicated empirical result. Completion of high school or its GED equivalent produced no addi-

Table 8.4 Estimates of Birth Outcomes

	Without heterogeneity				With heterogeneity			
	School	Part-time work	Full-time work	Homemaking	School	Part-time work	Full-time work	Homemaking
Activity-specific factor loading					0.6807*** (0.0140)	1.971*** (0.0176)	2.099*** (0.0108)	2.309*** (0.0232)
Intercept	−0.4730** (0.2334)	−3.118*** (0.7042)	−0.3170 (0.5984)	−6.549*** (1.0349)	−1.076*** (0.2153)	−3.777*** (0.3764)	−1.751*** (0.2393)	−8.255*** (0.5319)
Minority status								
Black	0.0829*** (0.0122)	0.2630*** (0.0224)	0.3067*** (0.0104)	0.2696*** (0.0288)	0.0324** (0.0118)	0.0686*** (0.0183)	0.0428*** (0.0093)	0.2129*** (0.0249)
Hispanic	−0.0180 (0.0139)	0.1000*** (0.0233)	0.1284*** (0.0115)	0.1438*** (0.0288)	−0.0343** (0.0118)	−0.0054 (0.0202)	0.0194* (0.0100)	0.0061 (0.0269)
Human capital and scholastic achievement								
Years of schooling attended	−0.1439*** (0.0030)	−0.1820*** (0.0048)	−0.1324*** (0.0027)	−0.1891*** (0.0057)	−0.1287*** (0.0029)	−0.1106*** (0.0040)	−0.0629*** (0.0022)	−0.1172*** (0.0052)
AFQT score	0.0004 (0.0003)	0.0019*** (0.0005)	−0.0010*** (0.0003)	0.0045*** (0.0007)	0.0014*** (0.0003)	0.0009** (0.0004)	−0.0004* (0.0002)	0.0025*** (0.0006)
Family background (1979)								
Number siblings	0.0063*** (0.0016)	0.0084** (0.0025)	0.0197*** (0.0016)	0.0070** (0.0031)	0.0015 (0.0016)	0.0000 (0.0021)	0.0096*** (0.0014)	0.0012 (0.0030)
Family income	−0.0009** (0.0003)	0.0000 (0.0006)	−0.0016*** (0.0003)	−0.0038*** (0.0010)	−0.0006* (0.0003)	0.0001 (0.0005)	−0.0013*** (0.0002)	0.0009 (0.0009)
Mother education	−0.0050** (0.0017)	−0.0093** (0.0030)	−0.0004 (0.0015)	−0.0069** (0.0031)	−0.0041** (0.0016)	−0.0085** (0.0026)	−0.0059*** (0.0014)	−0.0094*** (0.0028)

Table 8.4 (continued)

Mother-only family	−0.0093	−0.0650***	−0.0016***	0.0169	−0.0225**	−0.0006	−0.0366*
	(0.0104)	(0.0176)	(0.0003)	(0.0214)	(0.0102)	(0.0083)	(0.0188)
Personal characteristics							
Age of menarche	−0.0031	−0.0172***	0.0115***	−0.0753***	−0.0067**	−0.0055***	−0.0376***
	(0.0025)	(0.0044)	(0.0024)	(0.0066)	(0.0025)	(0.0020)	(0.0055)
Foreign born	−0.1124***	−0.2833***	−0.1945***	−0.0818**	−0.1213***	−0.1562***	0.0268
	(0.0186)	(0.0428)	(0.0138)	(0.0378)	(0.0175)	(0.0169)	(0.0333)
Age	0.0907***	0.4004***	0.1049**	0.7449***	0.1238***	0.1427***	0.6833***
	(0.0212)	(0.0600)	(0.0492)	(0.0891)	(0.0195)	(0.0199)	(0.0458)
AgeSq	0.0017***	−0.0047***	0.0003	0.0119***	0.0007*	−0.0008*	−0.0101***
	(0.0005)	(0.0013)	(0.0010)	(0.0019)	(0.0004)	(0.0004)	(0.0010)
Age78_13	0.0453***	−0.0021	0.0056	0.1859***	0.0473***	−0.0122	0.2249***
	(0.0126)	(0.0222)	(0.0117)	(0.0283)	(0.0129)	(0.0101)	(0.0261)
Age78_14	0.0180*	0.0241	−0.0024	0.1694***	0.0157*	−0.0238**	0.1874***
	(0.0110)	(0.0198)	(0.0097)	(0.0232)	(0.0105)	(0.0084)	(0.0212)
Age78_15	0.0113	−0.0093	−0.0010	0.0779**	0.0141	0.0046	0.1998***
	(0.0106)	(0.0202)	(0.0097)	(0.0248)	(0.0102)	(0.0082)	(0.0205)
Urban	0.0002	−0.0334*	−0.0303***	−0.1153***	0.0238**	−0.0190**	0.0779***
	(0.0137)	(0.0206)	(0.0110)	(0.0253)	(0.0118)	(0.0092)	(0.0214)
Labor-market conditions							
Per-worker income	0.0043**	−0.0215***	−0.0214***	0.0127***	0.0040**	−0.0077***	0.0008
	(0.0016)	(0.0030)	(0.0014)	(0.0032)	(0.0015)	(0.0023)	(0.0027)

NOTE: Standard errors are in parentheses. Included in the estimates (but not reported) are flags indicating missing values for mother's education, family income, and AFQT score. The variables "age of menarche," "number of siblings," and "urban" are unique to the birth equation. $*P < 0.10$, $**P < 0.05$, $***P < 0.01$.

Table 8.5 Estimates of Hourly Wage Rates

| | Without heterogeneity | | With heterogeneity | |
	Part-time work	Full-time work	Part-time work	Full-time work
Activity-specific factor loading			−0.0148	0.0094
			(0.0141)	(0.0079)
Intercept	0.6204**	−0.8053***	0.6317**	−0.8147***
	(0.2729)	(0.2104)	(0.2735)	(0.2139)
Minority status				
Black	−0.0208*	−0.0021	−0.0192	−0.0032
	(0.0135)	(0.0059)	(0.0135)	(0.0059)
Hispanic	0.0755***	0.1155***	0.0762***	0.1149***
	(0.0134)	(0.0067)	(0.0134)	(0.0067)
Human capital and scholastic achievement				
Years of schooling attended	0.0277***	0.0304***	0.0272***	0.0306***
	(0.0040)	(0.0019)	(0.0040)	(0.0020)
High school or GED	−0.0054	0.0052	−0.0054	0.0050
	(0.0099)	(0.0056)	(0.0099)	(0.0056)
Bachelor's degree or more	0.2182***	0.1348***	0.2173***	0.1350***
	(0.0225)	(0.0081)	(0.0225)	(0.0081)
Years PT work exp previous year	−0.0165*	0.0022	−0.0161*	0.0020
	(0.0091)	(0.0039)	(0.0091)	(0.0040)
PT years last year squared	0.0018*	−0.0036***	0.0017*	−0.0036***
	(0.0011)	(0.0007)	(0.0011)	(0.0007)
Years FT work exp previous year	0.0474***	0.0510***	0.0471***	0.0512***
	(0.0068)	(0.0043)	(0.0069)	(0.0043)
FT years last year squared	−0.0017*	−0.0023***	−0.0017*	−0.0023***
	(0.0009)	(0.0005)	(0.0009)	(0.0005)
AFQT score	0.0019***	0.0034**	0.0013***	0.0034***
	(0.0003)	(0.0002)	(0.0003)	(0.0002)
Family background (1979)				
Family income	0.0013**	0.0012***	0.0013**	0.0012***
	(0.0004)	(0.0002)	(0.0004)	(0.0002)
Mother education	0.0002	0.0003	0.0002	0.0002
	(0.0019)	(0.0009)	(0.0020)	(0.0009)
Mother-only family	0.0261**	0.0088*	0.0265**	0.0088*
	(0.0114)	(0.0057)	(0.0114)	(0.0058)
Personal characteristics				
Foreign born	0.0484**	−0.0159*	0.0477**	−0.0156*
	(0.0190)	(0.0083)	(0.0189)	(0.0083)
Age	−0.0036	0.0930***	−0.0038	0.0934***
	(0.0244)	(0.0180)	(0.0244)	(0.0183)

Table 8.5 (continued)

	Without heterogeneity		With heterogeneity	
	Part-time work	Full-time work	Part-time work	Full-time work
Agesq	0.0002	−0.0016***	0.0002	−0.0016***
	(0.0005)	(0.0004)	(0.0005)	(0.0004)
Age78_13	−0.0428**	−0.0063	−0.0431**	−0.0063
	(0.0137)	(0.0062)	(0.0138)	(0.0063)
Age78_14	−0.0164	−0.0392***	−0.0164	−0.0392***
	(0.0124)	(0.0054)	(0.0124)	(0.0054)
Age78_15	−0.0300**	−0.0210***	−0.0305**	−0.0210***
	(0.0124)	(0.0053)	(0.0125)	(0.0054)
Labor-market conditions				
Emp. growth	−0.2739*	−0.4824***	−0.2707*	−0.4844***
	(0.1764)	(0.0988)	(0.1770)	(0.0996)
Per-worker income	0.0227***	0.0322***	0.0226***	0.0322***
	(0.0017)	(0.0006)	(0.0017)	(0.0006)

NOTE: Standard errors are in parentheses. Included in the estimates (but not reported) are flags indicating missing values for mother's education, family income, and AFQT score. The variables "high school or GED" and "bachelor's degree or more" are unique to the wage equation. *$P < 0.10$, **$P < 0.05$, ***$P < 0.01$.

tional return on education above and beyond what women reaped from years of school completed, but having achieved a college degree yielded an additional return of 21 percent for part-time employment and 13 percent for full-time work. These "sheepskin" effects were unaltered by consideration of unobserved, person-specific factors.

The work experience effects on employment and wage outcomes are highly differentiated according to whether experience was acquired on a full-time or part-time basis. For example, higher levels of acquired part-time work experience raise the odds of working in a subsequent year, but especially the odds of part-time employment (Table 8.3). Because part-time employment also is associated with school enrollment (the school activity state includes part-time workers who are enrolled full-time), part-time work experience also increases the odds that women will continue in school. Full-time work experience has more pronounced effects on the likelihood of future full-time employment, but it also increases the odds of part-time work relative to remaining enrolled. In sharp contrast to the positive effect of part-time experience on exclusive homemaking, full-time work experience significantly lowered the odds of remaining out of the labor force altogether.

Experience effects on wages present an altogether different picture (Table 8.5). Essentially work experience acquired from part-time employment yields trivial returns for either full- or part-time employment. However, full-time work experience yields a whopping 4.7 to 5.1 percent return on wages received by part-time and full-time workers, respectively. Because the factor loadings were not statistically significant in the wage equation, these effects remain unchanged across specifications. Finally, the AFQT score yields positive wage returns that are slightly higher for women employed full time as compared to those employed only part time.[7]

Labor-Market Conditions

The final question posed at the outset concerns the sensitivity of young women's labor-force decisions to local labor-market conditions. Point estimates indicate zero effects of annual employment growth on women's labor-force or homemaking activity relative to full-time school attendance, but residence in counties with higher incomes pulls women into the labor market relative to attending school and deters them from full-time homemaking (Table 8.3). These average worker income effects are especially pronounced for full-time work and robust across specifications with and without controls for heterogeneity. Similarly, higher average worker incomes are associated with positive wage returns to employed women, on the order of 2.3 percent for part-time workers and 3.2 percent for full-time workers (Table 8.5).

Labor-market conditions also influence women's employment behavior through their effects on fertility (Table 8.4). That is, more favorable market opportunities, as indexed by average per-worker incomes, lower the odds that women employed full or part time will bear another child, but they increase the odds that women enrolled in school will bear a child. The magnitude and statistical significance of market effects on fertility are highly sensitive to the inclusion of statistical controls for unobserved heterogeneity. That is, in addition to personal, human capital, and labor-market conditions, childbearing decisions are governed by unmeasured circumstances, such as family size preferences, early socialization experiences, and the proximate determinants of fertility.

Thus, there is suggestive, but not powerful evidence that favorable labor-market conditions influence young women's employment experiences. More important for predicting young women's labor-market status are the human capital investment choices that generate their stocks of education and experience. To the extent that favorable economic conditions "pulled" these groups out of school and into the labor market, the total effects of labor-market conditions on employment outcomes may be stronger than the direct effects shown here.

CONCLUSIONS

Group differences in family background and other characteristics that are associated with school and work choices produce lower stocks of human capital accumulated by minority women, especially less formal schooling. Once these differences are taken into account, black and Hispanic women are more likely than comparable white women to prolong their investments in education relative to working or becoming homemakers. However, racial and ethnic differences in family formation, which decisively influence work behavior during the early life course, also determine how much and what forms of human capital are acquired during the early life course. Although black mothers are more likely than white mothers to remain enrolled in school, Hispanic mothers are more likely to become full-time homemakers or enter the labor force. Race effects on wages were trivial, but Hispanic women earned 7 to 12 percent more than their white counterparts who were similarly endowed. This result, which differs from most cross-section findings, requires further investigation.

We also find consistent positive effects of education on the likelihood that women will work full time, negative effects on fertility, and approximately a 3 percent wage return for each year of education completed, with the caveat that returns are slightly lower for part-time as compared to full-time workers. Furthermore, as suggested by numerous studies about the rising returns on skill during the 1980s, young women enjoy a substantial wage return on college degrees, but none for completion of high school or its GED equivalent. Finally, we find trivial wage returns on experience acquired through part-time work on subsequent full- or part-time wages but a whopping 5 percent wage return on experience acquired through full-time work to both full- and part-time workers. These results cast doubt on the received wisdom of urging youth to acquire work experience while they are enrolled in school. As shown for young men (Hotz et al. 2002), perhaps the optimal life cycle earnings streams derive from maximizing formal schooling before acquiring work experience either on a full- or part-time basis.

Average county-level per-worker incomes *do* influence the likelihood that young women will be employed either full or part time relative to full-time school enrollment in any given year; moreover, wages received by young workers also depend on the opportunities afforded by the markets in which they reside. However, employment outcomes are insensitive to changes in the annual employment growth rate, which is negatively associated with wage returns on full and part-time employment. This counterintuitive result warrants further investigation and may derive from two sources. One is that employment growth for young workers in recent years has occurred in low-wage industries, particularly services, as relatively well-paying manufacturing and other unionized jobs declined (Danziger and Gottschalk 1993). The other has to do with the level of aggregation at which local market conditions are specified. We have opted to represent local market conditions using counties rather than more conventional units for labor markets, such as Standard Metropolitan Statistical Areas or Primary Metropolitan Statistical Areas, but doing so ignores the fact that women can commute across county lines for work.

Notes

1. Women who were in the military were classified as employed full time if they were not enrolled in school; this group comprises a tiny share of all respondents.
2. Family income and parental education contain large amounts of missing data. Our statistical models include flags for missing values and do not compromise sample sizes or introduce biases in the parameter estimates.
3. Ahituv and Tienda (2004) provide a detailed discussion of this framework and how it applies to modeling the life cycle choices of young women.

4. Hotz et al. (2002) and Ahituv and Tienda (2004) provide details about this specification and the maximum likelihood methods used in estimation.

5. As discussed in Hotz et al. (2002) and Ahituv and Tienda (2004), the products of factor loadings characterize the covariances between the activity-specific utility functions and those in the fertility and wage equations. Thus, the statistical significance of the factor loadings indicates the existence of significant correlations among these disturbances and whether there is statistical evidence consistent with the importance of treating the schooling, work, and homemaking activity and fertility choices and wages as being jointly endogenously determined.

6. The insignificant factor loading for part-time work partly reflects the fact that we did not separate part-time workers who were enrolled in school from those who were not. Hence the contrast with the school-only state may be less sharply defined because many women enrolled in school also work part time.

7. Many cross-section studies show that economic returns to education are lower for part-time workers than for those engaged full time. That the economic returns to skills (AFQT) and years of part-time work experience are lower for part-time than for full-time employment is not totally consistent with a human capital explanation, however, and invokes the possibility that market segmentation may be partly responsible. Our data did not permit a direct exploration of this alternative interpretation.

References

Ahituv, Avner, and Marta Tienda. 2004. "Employment, Motherhood and School Continuation Decisions of Young White, Black and Hispanic Women." *Journal of Labor Economics* 22(1): 115–158.

Ahituv, Avner, Marta Tienda, and V. Joseph Hotz. 2000. "The Transition from School to Work: Black, Hispanic and White Men in the 1980s." In *Restoring Broadly Shared Prosperity*, Ray Marshall, ed. Armonk, NY: M.E. Sharpe, pp. 250–258.

Alon, Sigal, Debra Donahoe, and Marta Tienda. 2001. "The Effects of Early Work Experience on the Establishment of Stable Labor Force Careers among Young Women." *Social Forces* 79(3): 1005–1034.

Bound, John, and Laura Dresser. 1999. "Losing Ground: The Erosion of the Relative Earnings of African American Women during the 1980s." In *Latinas and African American Women at Work: Race, Gender, and Economic Inequality,* Irene Browne, ed. New York: Russell Sage Foundation, pp. 61–104.

Briggs, Vernon M. Jr. 1973. *Chicanos and Rural Poverty.* Baltimore: Johns Hopkins University Press.

Browne, Irene, ed. 1999. *Latinas and African American Women at Work: Race, Gender, and Economic Inequality.* New York: Russell Sage Foundation.

Caspi, Avshalom, Bradley R. Wright, Terrie E. Moffit, and Phil A. Silva. 1998. "Early Failure in the Labor Market: Childhood and Adolescent Predictors of Unemployment in the Transition to Adulthood." *American Sociological Review* 63(3): 424–451.

Danziger, Sheldon, and Peter Gottschalk, eds. 1993. *Uneven Tides: Rising Inequality in America.* New York: Russell Sage Foundation.

Donahoe, Debra, and Marta Tienda. 2000. "The Transition from School to Work: Is There a Crisis and What Can Be Done?" In *Securing the Future: Investing in Children from Birth to College,* Sheldon Danziger and Jane Waldfogel, eds. New York: Russell Sage Foundation, pp. 231–263.

Duncan, Brian, V. Joseph Hotz, and Stephen J. Trejo. 2006. "Hispanics in the U.S. Labor Market." In *Hispanics and the American Future,* Marta Tienda and Faith Mitchell, eds. Washington, DC: National Academies Press, pp. 228–290.

Hotz, V. Joseph, and Marta Tienda. 2002. "Education and Employment in a Diverse Society: Generating Inequality through the School-to-Work Transition." In *American Diversity: A Demographic Challenge for the Twenty-First Century,* N. Denton and S. Tolnay, eds. Albany: SUNY Press, pp. 185–220.

Hotz, V. Joseph, Linxin Xiu, Marta Tienda, and Avner Ahituv. 2002. "Are There Returns to the Wages of Young Men from Working While in School?" *Review of Economics and Statistics* 84(4): 221–236.

Kane, Thomas J. 1994. "College Entry by Blacks since 1970: The Role of College Costs, Family Background, and the Returns to Education." *Journal of Political Economy* 102(5): 878–911.

Keane, Michael P., and Kenneth I. Wolpin. 1997. "The Career Decisions of Young Men." *Journal of Political Economy* 105(3): 473–522.

McLanahan, Sara, and Gary Sandefur. 1994. *Growing Up with a Single Parent.* Cambridge, MA: Harvard University Press.

Neal, Derek, and William Johnson. 1996. "The Role of Pre-Market Factors in Black-White Wage Differences." *Journal of Political Economy* 104 (5): 869–895.

Spain, Daphne, and Suzanne M. Bianchi. 1996. *Balancing Act: Motherhood, Marriage, and Employment among American Women.* New York: Russell Sage Foundation.

Stier, Haya, and Marta Tienda. 2001. *The Color of Opportunity: Pathways to Family, Work, and Welfare.* Chicago: University of Chicago Press.

Tienda, Marta, and Avner Ahituv. 1996. "Ethnic Differences in School Departure: Does Youth Employment Promote or Undermine Educational Attainment?" In *Of Heart and Mind: Social Policy Essays in Honor of Sar A. Levitan,* Garth Mangum, and Stephen Mangum, eds. Kalamazoo, MI: W.E. Upjohn Institute for Employment Research, pp. 93–110.

9

The Misdirected Debate over the Economics of Disabilities Accommodation

Seth D. Harris
U.S. Department of Labor

Vernon Briggs is an unabashed advocate for government regulation of labor markets. Of course, his advocacy has focused primarily on immigration policy (Briggs 1996, 2003; Briggs and Moore 1994). Even if labor markets operate efficiently, he has said, efficiency is not the paramount value in American society. Fairness, equal employment opportunity, and the self-sufficiency of working families are important values that deserve equal respect in debates over labor-market policies (Briggs 1984).

Yet Briggs's arguments do not depend exclusively on a normative appeal. Consistent with his training in institutional economics, and his gentle-but-firm contrariness, Briggs stresses that labor markets do not always operate efficiently. In such cases, he advocates conscientiously designed and properly implemented government intervention to improve efficiency (Briggs 2003). According to Briggs, labor regulation "forces managers to manage," rather than to reflexively slash labor costs in search of competitive advantage (Briggs 1987). A central insight of Briggs's scholarship is that regulation can redirect competition toward more productive and socially desirable outcomes.

This chapter applies Briggs's insight to the economics of workplace accommodations mandated by the Americans with Disabilities Act (ADA). The ADA's Title I prohibits employment discrimination against any "qualified individual with a disability."[1] Along with discrimination's more traditional forms,[2] the ADA defines "discrimination" to include the failure to provide a "reasonable accommodation" to a worker with a known impairment as long as the employer will not suffer an "undue hardship." An accommodation can be any change to a physical environment, work schedule, or job responsibilities that allows a worker with a disability to perform the essential job functions or enjoy the same privileges and benefits as co-workers.

The ADA and its accommodation mandate have been criticized as government meddling in otherwise smoothly operating and efficient labor markets. The attack begins with the premise that accommodations raise employers' costs of hiring workers with disabilities. Critics argue the ADA's accommodations mandate contributes to joblessness by pricing workers with disabilities out of the labor market. The result is a tempting man-bites-dog narrative about labor-market regulation harming its intended beneficiaries. In fact, this is the reasoning behind at least two commentators' calls for the ADA's repeal (DeLeire 2000; Epstein 1992).

Briggs would skewer this type of argument if it were attempted in his scholarly arena. In this chapter, I follow his lead and respond in a similar manner. I will examine certain neoclassical economic assumptions and others that are too seriously flawed to justify the central role they have played in the debate over disabilities accommodations. In essence, this debate began with the wrong premise and, as a result, ruminated over wrong conclusions. These flawed premises have distracted attention from likelier causes of the low and declining employment rate among workers with disabilities—that is, the hypotheses that should have been the debate's starting point. After reviewing how this debate went wrong, I will suggest hypotheses that should have been, and should be, at the center of the debate over the economics of disabilities accommodations.[3]

THE ADA'S EFFECT ON THE EMPLOYMENT OF WORKERS WITH DISABILITIES

Virtually all statistical measures show that workers with disabilities are employed at a much lower rate than workers without disabilities,[4] and there is little debate over the decline in their employment rate since the ADA was enacted (Burkhauser, Houtenville, and Rovba forthcoming; Stapleton and Burkhauser 2003). Instead, the scholarly debate has focused on whether the ADA contributed to the employment rate's decline. From its earliest days, scholars and judges have predicted that the ADA's accommodation mandate would make workers with disabilities more expensive to employ than workers without disabilities and, therefore, less appealing to employers (Barnard 1992; *Borkowski v. Valley Central School District* 1995; Calloway 1995; Donohue 1994; Epstein 1992; Issacharoff and Nelson 2001; Kelman 1999, 2001; McGowan 2000; Rosen 1991; Schwab and Willborn 2003; *Vande Zande v. Wisconsin Department of Administration* 1995). This prediction has been central to the debate.

In particular, this prediction served as the basis for the hypotheses tested by two early and important studies finding a causal relationship between the ADA's passage and a decline in the employment rate. Daron Acemoglu and Joshua Angrist (2001) and Thomas DeLeire (2000) studied data from the Current Population Survey and the Survey of Income and Program Participation, respectively. Acemoglu and Angrist found a decline in the employment rate among both men and women with disabilities between the ages of 21 and 39 beginning in the two years immediately after the ADA took effect in 1992. DeLeire found a substantial decline in the employment rate of men with disabilities beginning in 1990—immediately after the ADA was passed, but two years before it took effect. The proximity of the ADA's passage and the employment-rate decline, and analyses which purported to exclude other potential causes for the decline, led Acemoglu and Angrist and DeLeire to infer a causal relationship between the law and the decline.

A simple syllogism supports these studies' hypotheses. Workers with disabilities need accommodations while workers without disabilities do not. Accommodations cost money; therefore, employing workers with disabilities costs more than employing workers without disabilities. Rational employers seek to maximize profits, which, assuming capital is fixed, result from a worker's net productivity (i.e., productivity minus labor costs). Since workers with disabilities bear higher labor costs because of their accommodations, and the accommodations can be assumed to make these workers only as productive as their co-workers without disabilities, workers with disabilities return lower net productivity to their employers. As a result, employers will not hire them. Only a short logical step is needed to conclude that the ADA's accommodation mandate has caused the employment rate among workers with disabilities to decline. I have called this the "rational-choice" view of the decline in the employment rate for workers with disabilities (Harris 2007a). It justifies employers' choices to eschew workers with disabilities as economically rational.

As with most simply stated economic assertions, the devil is in the details. I challenge two assumptions that are necessary to the rational-choice view. For the purpose of focusing on these assumptions, I will accept that accommodations impose costs that cause the net productivity of workers with disabilities to be lower than that of workers without disabilities. Even when this premise is accepted, the key assumptions supporting the rational-choice view are seriously flawed. Because of these flaws, the rational-choice view can explain, at most, only a small fraction of circumstances in which employers might be asked to provide accommodations to a worker with a disability. Thus, it offers a shaky foundation for any scholar's hypothesis regarding the employment rate for all workers with disabilities.

Competitive Markets and Perfect Information

The first and most important assumption underlying the rational-choice view is that workers' accommodation requests and employers' accommodation decisions occur in perfectly competitive labor markets (Acemoglu and Angrist 2001; Donohue 1994; Jolls 2000). In such markets, there are no transaction costs or other factors interfering with employers' profit-maximization calculations, and net productivity will drive the decision to hire workers without disabilities, rather than workers with disabilities. Yet, perfectly competitive labor markets are not ubiquitous, if they exist at all.

Many incumbent employees bargain with their employers in an "internal labor market" characterized by barriers to competition. Only "external labor markets," in which job applicants and prospective employers search for each other, are presumed to be freely competitive (Harris 2007a). Since internal labor markets are not perfectly competitive, the rational-choice view cannot describe the effects of many incumbent employees' accommodations. To the contrary, as demonstrated by several empirical studies and my own internal labor-market analysis, incumbent employees with disabilities do not necessarily return lower net productivity for their employers than employees without disabilities—in some cases, they yield more (Blanck 1997, forthcoming; Harris 2007a; Hendricks et al. 2005; Schartz et al. 2006). Therefore, the prediction that accommodations will ordinarily price workers with disabilities out of internal labor markets is inaccurate. Thus, the rational-choice view is not relevant to workers with disabilities in internal labor markets.

A presumed characteristic of competitive markets, including external labor markets, is perfect information. Employers are assumed to know everything they need to know to make efficient hiring decisions, including which workers have disabilities and what accommodations they require. Yet information about disabilities and accommodations may not flow freely. Workers who roll their wheelchairs or bring a service animal into a job interview necessarily disclose their impairments. But most employers are not similarly alerted that a prospective employee has epilepsy, diabetes, HIV, vision or hearing limitations, mental disabilities, intellectual and learning disabilities, or other impairments. The ADA does not require job applicants to disclose their impairments and prohibits employers from requesting such information except in limited circumstances.[5]

Further, even when they know a worker has an impairment, employers may not always know whether an impairment requires accommodation. In some cases, it may be obvious. Workers in wheelchairs will very likely need ramps or elevators to access upper-level floors. In other cases, it is less obvious. For example, a worker with cerebral palsy may or may not need an accommodation depending upon factors that the employer may not be able to assess during a job interview, even if the employer knows what those factors are. Only those workers who request an accommodation during the hiring process are effectively forced to disclose that they have an impairment requiring an accommodation.

Thus, workers may have impairments that are unknown to their prospective employers or, even if known, may not require accommodation. Changes in these workers' employment rate cannot be blamed on the costs of their accommodations because, by definition, employers cannot factor those costs into their hiring decisions. The rational-choice view is not relevant to workers with hidden disabilities or workers who do not need accommodation or whose need for accommodation is not apparent.

Many workers acquire impairments after they have been hired. Some suffer industrial accidents or illnesses, and others suffer injury or illness not related to work. Still others experience impairments that are the natural effects of aging or disease. There is substantial evidence that workers in these categories represent a large percentage of all workers with disabilities. For example, incumbent employees, not applicants for jobs, bring a large majority of the ADA charges filed with the U.S. Equal Employment Opportunity Commission (Schwab et al. forthcoming). Also, in 2005, 1.2 million incumbent employees in the private sector suffered workplace illnesses or injuries requiring recuperation away from work beyond the day of the incident (Sengupta, Reno, and Burton 2007). Data drawn from the 1992 Health and Retirement Study, a survey of Americans between the ages of 51 and 61, found that 36 percent of people in that age range with work-limiting impairments acquired those impairments because of an accident, injury, or illness at work. Thirty-seven percent of Social Security Disability Insurance (SSDI) recipients in the same age group were disabled because of an accident, injury, or illness at work (Reville and Schoeni 2003–2004).

As in the case of job applicants with undisclosed impairments or impairments that do not clearly require accommodation, employers could not have made hiring decisions about workers with after-hiring impairments on the basis of accommodations costs. It would have been impossible for employers to know at the hiring stage which workers would need accommodations because of the onset of after-hiring impairments. The rational-choice view is again irrelevant.

In sum, disabilities accommodations issues are not characterized by perfect information in a long list of circumstances. The rational-choice view offers no insight into an employment-rate decline among workers whose disabilities are hidden at the time of hiring, whose prospective employers do not know that their visible impairments require accommodation, or who develop their disabilities any time after hiring (Harris 2007a). For the rational-choice hypothesis to prove true, the employment-rate decline would have to be explained without considering these large groups of workers with disabilities.

It may well be possible to construct an efficiency argument about the ADA's accommodation mandate and workers with disabilities. The argument would likely resemble the debate over statistical race and sex discrimination (Aigner and Cain 1977). Briefly stated, employers may rationally prefer to hire workers without disabilities if assessing the net productivity of workers with disabilities is systematically more costly than assessing the net productivity of workers without disabilities. In the context of disabilities accommodations, the argument would likely depend on an assertion that the costs of determining whether and to what extent workers with disabilities need accommodations are greater than the costs of assessing the net productivity of workers without disabilities.

A full discussion of the statistical-discrimination argument is beyond the scope of this chapter, but two preliminary insights are worth considering. First, as the debate over statistical race and sex discrimination has shown, these arguments do not invariably lead to the rational-choice view's preferred conclusion; it is possible to envision situations in which antidiscrimination policy yields greater economic efficiency than a market shaped by statistical discrimination (Lundberg and Startz 1983; Schwab 1986). Second, like the rational-choice view itself, a statistical-discrimination argument would be relevant only to those workers whose need for accommodation is known to their prospective employers at the hiring stage. In order for employers rationally to prefer low-transaction-cost workers over high-transaction-cost workers, employers must be able to categorize workers correctly. Workers with hidden disabilities would be misclassified into the low-transaction-cost group, as would workers who acquire disabilities after hiring. Thus, at best, a completely successful statistical-discrimination argument would relate to a limited number of cases. Like the rational-choice perspective, the statistical-discrimination argument has nothing to say about workers with hidden disabilities, workers with visible impairments but hidden accommodation needs, and workers who develop impairments after being hired.

In any event, the syllogism that has dominated the debate over the economics of disabilities accommodation was not built on statistical-discrimination arguments. It relied instead on an assumption of perfect information. Eliminating this assumption necessarily makes the rational-choice view irrelevant to the employment prospects of large numbers of workers with disabilities. The next section discusses additional workers with disabilities whose employment status cannot be described by the rational-choice view.

Assuming Workers with Disabilities Would Be Employed without Accommodations

A second assumption underlying the rational-choice view is that workers with disabilities would have found jobs if the ADA did not mandate reasonable accommodations. If there were a causal relationship between the costs of accommodations and employers' decisions not to hire workers with disabilities, then it would also have to be true that the employment rate among workers with disabilities would have remained flat or increased in the absence of the accommodation mandate.[6] In other words, some workers with disabilities must have been able to get jobs in the absence of the accommodation mandate but then unable to get them once the accommodation mandate took effect. This assumption is the essential stepping-stone from the premise that accommodations bear positive costs and the hypothesis that the ADA's accommodation mandate caused disemployment effects. It is also deeply problematic, as a straightforward thought exercise focused on the ADA's text will disclose.

The ADA's definition of the class of workers it protects—"qualified individual with a disability"—illustrates why this causal link is unlikely in a large set of cases. A "qualified individual" is a worker who, with or without accommodations, can perform the essential functions of the job she holds or desires. However, in its definition of "discrimination," the ADA makes clear that employers are not merely obligated to accommodate workers so that they can perform the essential functions of their jobs. Employers must also accommodate workers so that they can enjoy the privileges and benefits of their workplace. Thus, the ADA protects three classes of workers with a disability:

Group 1—workers who can perform the essential functions of their jobs without accommodation *and* do not need accommodation to enjoy the privileges and benefits of their workplace;

Group 2—workers who can perform the essential functions of their jobs only with accommodation; and

Group 3—workers who can perform the essential functions of their jobs without accommodation *but* need accommodation to enjoy the privileges and benefits of their workplace.

The question is: Which of these workers might have gotten jobs in a world *without* an ADA accommodation mandate but could not get jobs in a world *with* one?

The ADA's accommodation mandate should not have affected hiring decisions about workers in Group 1. Since neoclassical economics assumes that the productivity of workers hired in external labor markets is fungible, Group 1's members should have been able to offer prospective employers the same net productivity as workers without disabilities. Without any need for accommodation, their labor costs would be the same. The cost of hiring these workers should not have increased—and, therefore, their net productivity would not decrease—as a result of the accommodation mandate. Thus, both before and after the ADA's mandate took effect, Group 1's members should have been employed at the same rate as workers without disabilities, and the rational-choice view cannot explain any change in these workers' employment rate.

The ADA's accommodation mandate also likely had no effect on the employment rate of Group 2's members, but for the opposite reason. These workers would not have secured their jobs in the absence of the ADA's accommodation mandate because they could not perform their jobs' essential functions without accommodation. Simply, they were unqualified absent accommodations and the law would not have required employers to hire them.[7] By contrast, the accommodation mandate made employment possible for this group at the same time it raised the costs of hiring them. Thus, at worst, the accommodation mandate cannot have had a disemployment effect for these workers, and at best, it may have boosted their employment prospects.

Proponents of the rational-choice view might argue that the ADA changed these workers' job-match expectations. Workers with disabilities might have applied for jobs that they would not have otherwise sought because the prospect of accommodations made these jobs either possible or more desirable. One illustration of this effect might be a worker with a chronic back injury who would not have applied for a job that entails handling heavy packages absent an accommodation mandate. The existence of an accommodation mandate creates a possibility that the employer would provide a mechanical lift, which, in turn, might encourage that worker with a back injury to apply. If so, then the argument would be that the accommodation (here, the mechanical lift) would make the worker with a back injury more expensive to hire than a worker without a back injury. Thus, the worker with the back injury would not win the job in a competition with workers without disabilities.

Even if evidence of this kind of change in job-search behavior were found, it would offer only tepid support for the rational-choice view. There is no reason to believe that Group 2's failure to secure these newly available jobs would cause them to abandon the labor market in a world with an accommodation mandate. Yet, a decline in their employment rate depends upon just that response. More likely, these workers would remain in the labor market and seek out jobs they could perform without accommodations, just as they would in the absence of the ADA's accommodation mandate.

If such workers remained in the labor market, then the most that can be said is that workers with disabilities who were inspired to seek new types of jobs by the ADA's accommodation mandate might have suffered longer spells of unemployment due to a larger number of unsuccessful job searches. Thus, the likeliest effect would have been a modest decline in the employment rate for some period of time after the ADA's effective date followed by a flattening out or a rebound to the pre-ADA employment rate over time. The decline would result from the longer unemployment spells, and the rebound would result from workers with disabilities learning from their experiences and applying for jobs that they could perform without accommodations. Yet, studies of the employment rate do not show a shallow dip in the employment rate after the ADA followed by a rebound in the following years. They show a steady decline after the ADA became law (Acemoglu and Angrist 2001; Burkhauser, Houtenville, and Rovba forthcoming; DeLeire 2000).

Group 3 may contain the only individuals whose employment prospects can be explained by the rational-choice view. Similar to Group 1's members, workers in this group would have been able to perform the essential functions of their jobs without accommodation in the absence of the ADA and, therefore, would have been able to offer prospective employers the same net productivity as workers without disabilities both before and after the ADA became law. Yet, we must assume that Group 3's members saw their labor costs increase and their net productivity decrease because their employers were required to provide non-productivity-related workplace privileges and benefits. Thus, the ADA's accommodation mandate might have caused profit-maximizing employers to prefer workers without disabilities to workers in Group 3, but not to workers in Group 1 or Group 2. In other words, the rational-choice view might explain a decline in Group 3's employment rate but not the employment rates of the other two groups.

Disclosing the flaws in these two assumptions shows that the number of workers with disabilities whose employment prospects might be explained by the rational-choice view is quite small. At most, it might explain changes in the employment rate of 1) workers who were in the external labor market, had impairments at the time of hiring, and those impairments and the workers' needs for accommodation were known to their prospective employers, and 2) workers who could perform the essential functions of their jobs without accommodation but who need an accommodation to enjoy the privileges and benefits of their workplace. In both cases, the prospective employers considering hiring these workers must then also have been able to assess accurately these workers' need for these kinds of accommodations. Simply describing these limitations illustrates the very narrow arena in which the rational-choice view might operate. It is too thin a reed to support the hypothesis that the ADA's accommodations mandate caused a decline in the employment rate of all workers with disabilities.

ALTERNATIVE EXPLANATIONS FOR THE DECLINING EMPLOYMENT RATE OF WORKERS WITH DISABILITIES

If the rational-choice view is not the likeliest explanation for the employment-rate decline among workers with disabilities, what might have been a better hypothesis with which to begin the debate over workplace disabilities accommodations? Answering this question requires the pursuit of two different paths. The first path starts with the premise that the results of the Acemoglu and Angrist and DeLeire studies are accurate—that is, these studies captured a statistically significant decline in the employment rate for working-age people with disabilities associated with the ADA's passage or effective date. Recent studies have also found a decline in the employment rate that is roughly proximate to the ADA's effective date (such as Donohue et al. forthcoming), so this premise should be taken seriously. Pursuing this path requires looking beyond the ADA's accommodation mandate for causes that might explain the association between the ADA's passage and the employment-rate decline that followed.

The second path begins with the premise that any decline in the employment rate among workers with disabilities was not associated with the ADA. Rather, this path assumes that Acemoglu and Angrist, DeLeire, and others examined only one segment of a long-term decline in the employment rate that is unrelated to the ADA. Several critiques of the Acemoglu and Angrist and DeLeire studies have raised doubts about the accuracy of their results, so this premise may also be legitimate (Bound and Waidmann 2000; Burkhauser, Houtenville, and Rovba forthcoming; Kruse and Schur 2003). If so, then pursuing this path requires finding explanations for a long-term employment-rate decline that is unrelated to the ADA's accommodation mandate. In the following sections, each path will be pursued to its logical conclusion.

Path 1: Assuming the Employment-Rate Decline Was Associated with the ADA

In 2004, Christine Jolls and J.J. Prescott produced a landmark study of the ADA's effects on the employment rate of working-age Americans with disabilities (Jolls and Prescott 2004). The study disaggregated the effects of the ADA's prohibition of traditional forms of discrimination from its accommodation mandate. It compared the post-ADA employment rate in states that had pre-ADA employment discrimination regimes that both prohibited the traditional forms of discrimination and mandated accommodations (ADA-like states) with 1) states lacking any pre-ADA disability anti-discrimination laws (no protection states) and 2) states prohibiting the traditional forms of discrimination without mandating accommodations (no accommodation mandate states). Thus, in "no protection" states, all of the ADA's protections for workers with disabilities were an innovation, and in "no accommodation mandate" states, only the ADA's accommodation mandate was an innovation.

Looking at the years immediately following the ADA's passage, Jolls and Prescott found that the employment rate for workers with disabilities in the "no accommodation mandate" states was 10 percent lower than in the group of "ADA-like" states. They found no comparable gap between the "ADA-like" and "no protection" groupings. These results led Jolls and Prescott to conclude that the ADA's accommodation mandate, but not the prohibitions on traditional discrimination, had caused a short-term decline in the employment rate for workers with disabilities (Jolls and Prescott 2004).

The Jolls and Prescott study does not, however, support the rational-choice view. The rational-choice view would have suggested a steady disemployment effect, not the short-term decline found by these scholars. Jolls and Prescott suggest that accommodations costs "may well have been exaggerated or particularly salient in employers' minds just after the ADA's enactment." Contrary to the rational-choice view's assumption of *rationality*, employers may have reacted *irrationally* to the perceived costs of accommodations (Jolls and Prescott 2004).

My own analysis of survey responses by participants in the U.S. Equal Employment Opportunity Commission's (EEOC) mediation program (i.e., workers alleging discrimination and their employers) lends some support to Jolls and Prescott's explanation for the employment-rate decline (Harris 2007b). The responses suggest that mediators faced additional barriers when assisting employers and employees who were negotiating over disabilities accommodations as compared with negotiations over any other employment discrimination issue, including other types of disabilities discrimination charges. One of those added barriers was employers' apparent bias against workers' disabilities accommodations charges. When asked to remedy other allegations of employment discrimination, including other types of disabilities discrimination, employers agreed to solutions proposed in negotiations that were "realistic." In negotiations over accommodations, however, employers were less able or willing to consider new information and new proposals that would lead to settlement. As a result, employers were less likely to agree to an accommodation even if they considered it "realistic." This evidence suggests that employers voluntarily participating in the

EEOC's mediation program systematically doubted the legitimacy of workers' requests for disabilities accommodations, regardless of their merits.

In sum, even assuming some relationship between the ADA's enactment and an employment-rate decline for workers with disabilities, the rational-choice view does not necessarily offer the strongest hypothesis explaining this association. Instead, there is evidence supporting a hypothesis that employers' irrational response to accommodating workers with disabilities contributed to, or even caused, any post-ADA employment-rate decline. Of course, anti-discrimination statutes like the ADA are intended to protect against just this kind of irrationality. There may be enforcement problems with the ADA, but there does not appear to be a conceptual problem.

The irrationality hypothesis has another important advantage over the rational-choice view: it is relevant beyond a narrow group of workers. Employers' negative reaction to workplace accommodations could easily have affected workers in any labor market with any kind of impairment regardless of whether an accommodation was actually required. It would not have been bound by the ADA's scope and the state of employers' knowledge. Thus, an irrationality hypothesis may well have been a better starting place than the rational-choice view for the debate over the economics of disabilities accommodations.

Path 2: Assuming the Employment-Rate Decline Was Not Associated with the ADA

There has been substantial criticism of the research methods employed in the studies of both DeLeire and Acemoglu and Angrist. Early critics argued that the studies did not look beyond the ADA's accommodations mandate so as to properly exclude other possible (even likely) causes of the employment-rate decline among workers with disabilities (Bound and Waidmann 2000; Kruse and Schur 2003). These criticisms would not apply to Jolls and Prescott's cross-state comparison, however (Jolls and Prescott 2004). Any factor with national reach that Acemoglu and Angrist or DeLeire might not have considered fully would have affected employment rates in all states, not merely in "no accommodation mandate" states where Jolls and Prescott found an employment-rate decline. Any critique of the work of Acemoglu and Angrist or DeLeire must also take Jolls and Prescott's study into account.

A recent study revisited the data set used by Acemoglu and Angrist (Burkhauser, Houtenville, and Rovba forthcoming). Burkhauser and his colleagues raised questions about the work of Acemoglu and Angrist that may also extend to Jolls and Prescott's results. First, they reconsidered the population of workers studied. Acemoglu and Angrist studied working-age people who answered "yes" to the following question on the March Current Population Survey in any of the years from 1988 to 1997: "Does [respondent] have a health problem or a disability which prevents him/her from working or which limits the kind or amount of work he/she can do?" (Acemoglu and Angrist 2001). Burkhauser, Houtenville, and Rovba (forthcoming) considered only those workers who answered "yes" in at least two consecutive years; that is, the workers that were the likeliest to be protected by the ADA. This change eliminated Acemoglu and Angrist's evidence of a sharp post-ADA employment-rate decline. While Burkhauser, Houtenville, and Rovba did not also revisit the Jolls and Prescott (2004) study, the pair's data addressed the same group of workers considered by Acemoglu and Angrist. Thus, like Acemoglu and Angrist, Jolls and Prescott's results may also be too sensitive to the definition of "disability" to capture a genuine relationship between the ADA's accommodation mandate and the employment-rate decline.

Second, Burkhauser and his coauthors expanded the time horizon studied to encompass pre-ADA business cycles. They found equivalent employment-rate declines during earlier economic slumps. Economic recession, not the ADA's passage, might have explained Acemoglu and Angrist's post-ADA employment-rate decline. Burkhauser and his coauthors conclude that the employment rate among working-age people with disabilities began its decline long before the ADA became law and lasted long after. Thus, other hypotheses about the causes of the employment rate's decline—hypotheses unrelated to the ADA—should be considered.

They posit that the declining employment rate among working-age people with disabilities is associated with increased reliance on SSDI and Supplemental Security Income (SSI). SSDI provides cash support to people with substantial work histories who have serious or deadly impairments and cannot engage in "substantial gainful activity" in the national economy.[8] People with disabilities or blindness who do not have substantial work histories receive SSI benefits.[9] Studying the households of men with disabilities, Burkhauser, Houtenville, and Rovba found that earnings have represented a declining portion of household incomes over the past 24 years, while SSDI and SSI benefits have represented a growing portion.

One explanation for this increasing reliance on SSDI and SSI is that these programs' eligibility standards were relaxed in the mid 1980s (Burkhauser, Houtenville, and Rovba forthcoming). More readily accessible SSDI and SSI benefits influence more workers' reservation wages. Workers with disabilities can be expected to choose SSDI or SSI benefits over work when the value of those benefits, discounted by the transaction costs associated with obtaining the benefits, exceeds the workers' likely wages. Yet, SSDI and SSI benefits are low: $981.40 per month on average for SSDI beneficiaries in November 2007 and only $519.90 per month on average for working-age SSI beneficiaries in January 2009 (U.S. Social Security Administration 2007, 2009). These cash benefits alone cannot explain the large number of workers with disabilities who have left the labor market.

Three other factors may have also played a contributing role: an educational-attainment gap between workers with and without disabilities, the unavailability and inadequacy of employer-provided health insurance, and workplace and labor-market discrimination.

Educational attainment

Workers' educational attainment affects both their wages and their employment levels. In 2005, workers with high-school diplomas had an 80 percent higher unemployment rate than workers with bachelor's degrees. The unemployment rate for workers without high-school diplomas was nearly triple that of workers with bachelor's degrees. Further, in 2005, workers with bachelor's degrees earned 61 percent more than workers with high-school diplomas. Workers with bachelor's degrees earned more than double the amount earned by workers without high-school diplomas (U.S. Department of Labor 2008).

Adults with disabilities have less education than adults without disabilities. In 2005, adults with disabilities were more than twice as likely as adults without disabilities to have less than a high-school degree. High-school dropout rates among Americans aged 16–24 and students with disabilities have both declined; however, in 2006–2007, 10 percent of students without disabilities dropped out of high school compared with 15 percent of students with disabilities (Individuals with Disabilities Act 2007; National Center for Education Statistics 2009).[10] Further, adults with disabilities were only one-third as likely as adults without disabilities to have at least a bachelor's degree (Rehabilitation Research and Training Center on Disability Demographics and Statistics 2007).

Students with disabilities are less likely than their counterparts without disabilities to enroll in some form of postsecondary education. They are significantly less likely to enroll in a four-year program rather than a two-year degree program and less likely to graduate with a bachelor's or associate's degree (Horn, Bertold, and Bobbitt 1999). Although few workers with disabilities have bachelor's degrees, those with degrees have generally comparable employment rates and salaries to those of baccalaureates without disabilities, and they enrolled in graduate school at similar rates, at least within the first year after earning a bachelor's degree (Horn, Bertold, and Bobbitt 1999). Nonetheless, because of this educational attainment gap, workers with disabilities were more likely to be unemployed and more likely to compete for jobs with wages at or around the level of SSDI benefits. Simply put, less education means higher unemployment, lower wages, and a greater incentive to seek SSDI benefits.

This educational attainment gap is not new, but its importance may have increased as the American economy has demanded ever-higher levels of education from workers.[11] Educational attainment among workers with disabilities has not kept pace with these demands. As a result, it is possible that workers with disabilities have become less employable, as a group, over the past two decades. If so, the educational attainment gap and the growing importance of education in the American economy might help to explain the continuing decline in the employment rate for workers with disabilities.

Discrimination

As Jolls and others have observed, workers who are likely to suffer discrimination in the labor market face lower returns to their human capital investments and, as a result, are likely to pursue less education (Donohue and Heckman 1991; Jolls 2004). Jolls suggested that workers with disabilities might have exited the labor market to increase their investments in human capital after the ADA promised an end to discrimination (Jolls 2004). Yet, it is not clear that this is what happened. In fact, there is evidence that some workers with disabilities faced rising discrimination. Instead of choosing labor-market participation over education, such workers may have pursued a third option—leaving the labor market to join the SSDI rolls.

The Supreme Court drastically narrowed the scope of the ADA's coverage beginning in the late 1990s. As a result, large numbers of workers with disabilities were left without protection against workplace or labor-market discrimination (*Albertson's, Inc. v. Kirkingburg* 1999; *Murphy v. United Parcel Service* 1999; *Sutton v. United Airlines* 1999; *Toyota Motor Mfg. v. Williams* 2002; *Trustees of the University of Alabama v. Garrett* 2001). Without the ADA's protections, workers with disabilities might have rationally opted for the certainty of SSDI and SSI rather than a discriminatory competition they could not win. Those who chose to compete likely did not invest adequately in education because it would yield returns more likely to be unnaturally suppressed by discrimination. In turn, their low level of education likely resulted in worse labor-market outcomes. This rising risk of unremedied discrimination and its effects on both labor-market participation and human capital acquisition may also help explain the continuing employment rate decline among working-age people with disabilities.

Health care

For adults with disabilities, the absence of health insurance can mean irrevocable physical and mental health deterioration. Many people with disabilities need regular care and supervision of their condition by doctors and specialists. Without health insurance, they must pay for these services out of pocket and, as a result, might forego or delay the medical care they need (Williams et al. 2004). Yet, the crumbling employer-provided health insurance system does not provide workers with disabilities adequate relief from this risk. Forty-five million Americans had no health insurance in 2007 (Denvas-Walt, Proctor, and Lee 2008). The number of employees with employer-provided insurance in 2007 has only increased by less than a thousand since 1999 (U.S. Census Bureau 2008), and the percentage of employers providing insurance has remained at about 60 percent since 2004 (Kaiser Family Foundation, Health Research and Educational Trust, and Center for Studying Health System Change 2008, p. 6). Meanwhile, the cost of health insurance to workers has risen substantially: for example, the employee's share of a family premium has doubled since 2000, averaging $3,354 in 2008 (Kaiser Commission on Medicaid and the Uninsured 2008, p. 15).

Workers often lack health insurance because they have lost a job or changed jobs (Committee on the Consequences of Uninsurance 2004). The COBRA system, which allows some laid-off workers to buy into their former employers' health-insurance plans, has proven to be too limited and too expensive.[12] Furthermore, employees with disabilities who find their jobs transformed from full time with benefits to part time without benefits get no protection from COBRA. Even those with insurance may not have adequate benefits. Workers with disabilities are more likely to need specialized health care and to have chronic medical conditions requiring more services, such as frequent doctor's visits or hospitalizations, and larger amounts of prescription drugs. Yet private health insurance plans are structured around providing insurance to relatively healthy people and, as a result, do not take into account the needs of people with disabilities (Crowley and Elias 2003).

By contrast, SSDI and SSI beneficiaries are entitled to Medicare or Medicaid, respectively.[13] These programs also typically provide more comprehensive coverage than private insurance. Adults with disabilities therefore have a substantial reason to seek and continue receiving SSDI or SSI benefits—comprehensive health insurance that cannot be lost or taken away as long as the beneficiary's status is maintained. Thus, the spreading entropy in the employer-provided health-insurance system, perhaps combined with the increasing importance of the education-attainment gap and declining protections against discrimination, may offer the best explanation for the continuing decline in the employment rate (among working-age people with disabilities) and the associated rise in SSDI and SSI recipiency rates.

REDIRECTING THE DEBATE

In this chapter, I have argued that the debate over the economics of workplace disabilities accommodation began with mistaken premises, which misdirected the debate away from consideration of the likeliest causes of the low and declining employment rate among people with disabilities. In an effort to move the debate back onto the right track, I attempted to unmask the faulty assumptions skewing the current debate and proposed alternative explanations for the problems workers with disabilities encounter in the labor market. I offer these arguments in tribute to my teacher and friend Vernon Briggs, who challenged me to question orthodoxies in pursuit of progressive goals. My sincere hope is that this chapter does justice to the example he set.

Notes

1. 42 United States Code §12111(8) (2000) defines a qualified individual with a disability as "an individual with a disability who, with or without reasonable accommodation, can perform the essential functions of the employment position that such individual holds or desires."
2. In the lexicon of employment discrimination lawyers, the traditional forms of discrimination divide into two categories, "disparate treatment" and "disparate impact." Disparate treatment arises when "the employer simply treats some people less favorably than others because of their race, color, religion, sex, or national origin." Disparate impact involves "employment practices that are facially neutral in their treatment of different groups, but that in fact fall more harshly on one group than another and cannot be justified by business" (*International Brotherhood of Teamsters v. United States* 1977).
3. I wish to thank Marisa Baldaccini, Leanne Hamovich, Maria Ingravallo, Damien Maree, Marcelo Martinez, and Michelle Tonelli for diligent and helpful research assistance with this chapter. In addition, Melissa Stevenson's assistance was always essential. Nonetheless, all errors are mine. New York Law School's generous support of my research made this project and many others possible.
4. In 2007, the American Community Survey found employment rates for working-age people with and without disabilities of 36.9 percent and 79.7 percent, respectively. The Survey of Income and Program Participation found that 45 percent of working-age people with "severe disabilities" were employed in 2002, compared with 97.7 percent of working-age people without disabilities. The Bureau of Labor Statistics (BLS) published employment and unemployment rates for workers with a "disability" from the Current Population Survey for the first time in March

2009. In February 2009, the employment-to-population ratio for workers with a disability was 19.8 percent while the ratio for workers without a disability was 64.8 percent (U.S. Department of Labor 2009). Although the levels vary, the differentials are roughly consistent across statistical measures.

5. 42 United States Code § 12112(d)(2)(A)-(B) (2000) states that, with the exception of certain circumstances, an employer or hiring "entity" covered by the act "shall not conduct a medical examination or make inquiries of a job applicant as to whether such applicant is an individual with a disability or as to the nature or severity of such disability . . . [However, a] covered entity may make pre-employment inquiries into the ability of an applicant to perform job-related functions."

6. This statement applies equally to a flat employment rate or a rising employment rate because the population of working-age people with disabilities has grown; therefore, maintaining a steady employment rate means that workers with disabilities are acquiring a larger absolute number of jobs. According to the U.S. Census Bureau, in 1995, 10.1 percent of people aged 16–64 had a work disability. In 2006, the percentage rose to 10.4 percent (U.S. Census Bureau 1995–2006).

7. 42 U.S.C. § 12112 (b) (6) (2000) states that employers may use qualification standards to "screen out . . . individuals" as long as they are "shown to be job-related for the position in question and are consistent with business necessity."

8. 42 U.S.C. § 423 (d) (1) (A) (2000) states that "The term 'disability' means—inability to engage in any substantial gainful activity by reason of any medically determinable physical or mental impairment."

9. 42 U.S.C. § 1382c (a) (3) (B) states that under Title XVI, Supplemental Security Income for the Aged, Blind, and Disabled, one who is disabled and eligible for SSI benefits is one who is "unable to do his previous work but cannot, considering his age, education, and work experience, engage in any other kind of substantial gainful work."

10. These data describe students who received IDEA (Individuals with Disabilities Education Act) services. Virtually all students with disabilities receive IDEA services, so these data are a reasonable proxy for all students with disabilities. In 2006–2007, 675,170 IDEA students exited high school, 100,831 of which were dropouts (Individuals with Disabilities Act 2007; National Center for Education Statistics 2009).

11. The BLS projected in 1996–1997 that 9 of the 20 fastest growing occupations between 1994 and 2005 would require an associate's degree or more education, while BLS projected in 2008–2009 that 12 of the 20 fastest growing occupations between 2006 and 2016 would require an associate's degree or more education (U.S. Department of Labor 1996–1997, 2008–2009).

12. Consolidated Omnibus Budget Reconciliation Act of 1985 ("COBRA"), 29 U.S.C. §§ 1161-1168, 42 U.S.C. §§ 300BB-1 to 300bb-1 (2000).

13. SSDI beneficiaries are eligible for Medicare beginning 24 months after they begin receiving their benefits; see 42 U.S.C. § 1395c (2000). SSI beneficiaries are a "mandatory eligibility group" for Medicaid—that is, states are "required to provide them with health insurance under the Medicaid program" 42 CFR 435.120 (2006).

References

Acemoglu, Daron, and Joshua D. Angrist. 2001. "Consequences of Employment Protection? The Case of the Americans with Disabilities Act." *Journal of Political Economy* 109(5): 915–920.

Aigner, Dennis J., and Glen G. Cain. 1977. "Statistical Theories of Discrimination in Labor Markets." *Industrial and Labor Relations Review* 30(2): 175–187.

Albertson's Inc. v. Kirkingburg, 527 U.S. 555 (1999).

Barnard, Thomas H. 1992. "Disabling America: Costing Out the Americans with Disabilities Act." *Cornell Journal of Law and Public Policy* 2(1): 41–58.

Blanck, Peter. 1997. "The Economics of the Employment Provisions of the Americans with Disabilities Act: Part I—Workplace Accommodations." *DePaul Law Review* 46(Summer): 887–897.

———. Forthcoming. "Workplace Accommodations: Empirical Study of the ADA." In *The Americans with Disabilities Act: Empirical Perspectives*, Samuel Estreicher and Michael A. Stein, eds. Alphen, the Netherlands: Kluwer Law International.

Borkowski v. Valley Central School District, 63 F.3d 131 (2nd Cir. 1995).

Bound, John, and Timothy Waidmann. 2000. "Accounting for Recent Declines in Employment Rates among the Working-Aged Disabled." NBER Working Paper no. 7975. Cambridge, MA: National Bureau of Economic Research.

Briggs, Vernon M. Jr. 1984. *Immigration Policy and the American Labor Force*. Baltimore, MD: Johns Hopkins University Press.

———. 1987. "The Role of Government in the Workplace." *Industrial and Labor Relations Report* 24(2): 7–8.

———. 1996. "Immigration Policy and the U.S. Economy: An Institutionalist Perspective." *Journal of Economic Issues* 30(2): 371–389.

———. 2003. *Mass Immigration and the National Interest*. Armonk, NY: M.E. Sharpe.

Briggs, Vernon M. Jr., and Stephen Moore. 1994. *Still an Open Door? U.S. Immigration Policy and the American Economy*. Washington, DC: American University Press. .

Burkhauser, Richard V., Andrew J. Houtenville, and Ludmila Rovba. Forthcoming. "Accounting for the Declining Fortunes of Working-Age People with Disabilities." In *The Americans with Disabilities Act: Empirical Perspectives*, Samuel Estreicher and Michael A. Stein, eds. Alphen, the Netherlands: Kluwer Law International.

Calloway, Deborah A. 1995. "Dealing with Diversity: Changing Theories of

Discrimination." *St. John's Journal of Legal Commentary* 10(Summer): 481–494.

Committee on the Consequences of Uninsurance. 2004. *Insuring America's Health: Principles and Recommendations*. Washington, DC: Institute of Medicine, National Academies Press. http://books.nap.edu/openbook .php?isbn=0309091055 (accessed July 9, 2007).

Crowley, Jeffrey S., and Risa Elias. 2003. *Medicaid's Role for People with Disabilities*. Washington, DC: Kaiser Commission on Medicaid and the Uninsured.   http://kff.org/medicaid/upload/Medicaid-s-Role-for-People -with-Disabilities.pdf (accessed July 6, 2007).

DeLeire, Thomas. 2000. "The Wage and Employment Effects of the Americans with Disabilities Act." *Journal of Human Resources* 35(4): 693–715.

Denvas-Walt, Carmen, Bernadette D. Proctor, and Cheryl Hill Lee. 2008. *Income Poverty and Health Insurance Coverage in the United States: 2007*. Washington, DC: U.S. Census Bureau. http://www.census.gov/prod/ 2008pubs/p60-235.pdf (accessed March 25, 2009).

Donohue, John J. III. 1994. "Employment Discrimination Law in Perspective: Three Concepts of Equality." *Michigan Law Review* 92(August): 2583– 2612.

Donohue, John J. III, and James J. Heckman. 1991. "The Law and Economics of Racial Discrimination in Employment: Re-evaluating Federal Civil Rights Policy." *Georgetown Law Journal* 79(August): 1713–1735.

Donohue, John J. III, Michael Ashley Stein, Sascha Becker, and Christopher L. Griffin Jr. Forthcoming. "Assessing Post-ADA Employment: Some Econometric Evidence and Policy Considerations." In *The Americans with Disabilities Act: Empirical Perspectives*, Samuel Estreicher and Michael A. Stein, eds. Alphen, the Netherlands: Kluwer Law International.

Epstein, Richard A. 1992. *Forbidden Grounds: The Case against Employment Discrimination Laws*. Cambridge, MA: Harvard University Press.

Harris, Seth D. 2007a. "Law, Economics, and Accommodations in the Internal Labor Market." *University of Pennsylvania Journal of Business and Employment Law* 10(1): 1–62.

———. 2007b. "Disabilities Accommodations, Transaction Costs, and Mediation: Evidence from the EEOC's Mediation Program." *Harvard Negotiation Law Review* 12; also available as York Law School Legal Studies Research Paper no. 06/07-5. New York: New York Law School. http://papers.ssrn .com/sol3/papers.cfm?abstract_id=920110# (accessed March 5, 2009).

Hendricks, D.J., Linda C. Batiste, Anne Hirsh, Helen Schartz, and Peter Blanck. 2005. "Cost and Effectiveness of Accommodations in the Workplace: Preliminary Results of a Nationwide Study." *Disabilities Studies*

Quarterly 25(4). http://www.dsq-sds.org/article/view/623/800 (accessed March 5, 2009).

Horn, Laura, Jennifer Bertold, and Larry Bobbitt. 1999. *Students with Disabilities in Postsecondary Education: A Profile of Preparation, Participation and Outcomes.* Statistical Analysis Report. Washington, DC: National Center for Education Statistics, U.S. Department of Education. http://nces .ed.gov/pubs99/1999187.pdf (accessed March 25, 2009).

Individuals with Disabilities Act. 2007. *Data Table 4-1.* Rockville, MD: Data Accountability Center. https://www.ideadata.org/TABLES31ST/AR_4-1 .htm (accessed March 25, 2009).

International Brotherhood of Teamsters v. United States. 431 U.S. 324, 335 (1977).

Issacharoff, Samuel, and Justin Nelson. 2001. "Discrimination with a Difference: Can Employment Discrimination Law Accommodate the Americans with Disabilities Act?" *North Carolina Law Review* 79(2): 307–358.

Jolls, Christine. 2000. "Accommodation Mandates." *Stanford Law Review* 53(2): 233–242.

———. 2004. "Identifying the Effects of the Americans with Disabilities Act Using State-Law Variation: Preliminary Evidence on Educational Participation Effects." *American Economic Review* 94(2): 447–453.

Jolls, Christine, and J.J. Prescott. 2004. "Disaggregating Employment Protection: The Case of Disability Discrimination." NBER Working Paper no. 10740. Cambridge, MA: National Bureau of Economic Research.

Kaiser Commission on Medicaid and the Uninsured. 2008. *The Uninsured: A Primer. Key Facts about Americans without Health Insurance.* Washington, DC: Kaiser Commission on Medicaid and the Uninsured. http://www.kff .org/uninsured/upload/7451-04.pdf (accessed March 25, 2009).

Kaiser Family Foundation, Health Research and Educational Trust, and Center for Studying Health System Change. 2008. *Employer Health Benefits 2008 Annual Survey.* Washington, DC: Kaiser Family Foundation. http://ehbs .kff.org/pdf/7790.pdf (accessed March 25, 2009).

Kelman, Mark. 1999. *Strategy or Principle? The Choice between Regulation and Taxation.* Ann Arbor: University of Michigan Press.

———. 2001. "Market Discrimination and Groups." *Stanford Law Review* 53(4): 833–896.

Kruse, Douglas, and Lisa Schur. 2003. "Employment of People with Disabilities Following the ADA." *Industrial Relations* 42(1): 31–66.

Lundberg, Shelly J., and Richard Startz. 1983. "Private Discrimination and Social Intervention in Competitive Labor Markets." *American Economic Review* 73(3): 340–347.

McGowan, Miranda Oshige. 2000. "Reconsidering the Americans with Disabilities Act." *Georgia Law Review* 35(1): 27–160.

Murphy v. United Parcel Service. 527 U.S. 516 (1999).

National Center for Education Statistics. 2009. *Digest of Education Statistics: 2008, Table 105.* Washington, DC: U.S. Department of Education. http://nces.ed.gov/programs/digest/d08/tables/dt08_105.asp (accessed June 3, 2009).

Rehabilitation Research and Training Center on Disability Demographics and Statistics. 2007. *2007 Disability Status Report.* Washington, DC: U.S. Department of Education. http://www.ilr.cornell.edu/edi/disabilitystatistics/resources%5CTEXT%20VERSION%202007%20Disability%20Status%20Report.doc (accessed March 25, 2009).

Reville, Robert, and Robert F. Schoeni. 2003–2004. "The Fraction of Disability Caused at Work." *Social Security Bulletin* 65(4): 31–37.

Rosen, Sherwin. 1991. "Disability Accommodation and the Labor Market." In *Disability and Work: Incentives, Rights, and Opportunities,* Carolyn Weaver, ed. Washington, DC: AEI Press, pp. 18–30.

Schartz, Helen A., Kevin M. Schartz, D.J. Hendricks, and Peter Blanck. 2006. "Workplace Accommodations: Empirical Study of Current Employees." *Mississippi Law Journal* 75(Spring): 917–943.

Schwab, Stewart. 1986. "Is Statistical Discrimination Efficient?" *American Economic Review* 76(1): 228–234.

Schwab, Stewart, Susanne M. Bruyere, Andrew J. Houtenville, and S. Antonio Ruiz-Quintanilla. Forthcoming. "Trends in ADA Related Charges: Evidence from EEOC Charge Data." In *The Americans with Disabilities Act: Empirical Perspectives,* Samuel Estreicher and Michael A. Stein, eds. Alphen, the Netherlands: Kluwer Law International.

Schwab, Stewart J., and Steven L. Wilborn. 2003. "Reasonable Accommodation of Workplace Disabilities." *William and Mary Law Review* 44(3): 1197–1284.

Sengupta, Ishita, Virgina Reno, and John F. Burton Jr. 2007. *Workers' Compensation: Benefits, Coverage, and Costs 2005.* Washington, DC: National Academy of Social Insurance.

Stapleton, David C., and Richard V. Burkhauser, eds. 2003. *The Decline in the Employment of People with Disabilities: A Policy Puzzle.* Kalamazoo, MI: W.E. Upjohn Institute for Employment Research.

Steinmetz, Erika. 2006. *Americans with Disabilities: 2002.* Current Populations Reports. Washington, DC: U.S. Census Bureau. http://www.census.gov/prod/2006pubs/p70-107.pdf (accessed July 5, 2007).

Sutton v. United Airlines. 527 U.S. 471 (1999).

Toyota Motor Manufacturing v. Williams. 534 U.S. 184 (2002).

Trustees of the University of Alabama v. Garrett. 531 U.S. 356 (2001).

U.S. Census Bureau. 1995–2006. "Disability Data from the Current Population Survey." Washington, DC: U.S. Census Bureau. http://www.ilr.cornell.edu/edi/disabilitystatistics/resources%5CTEXT%20VERSION%202007%20Disability%20Status%20Report.doc (accessed July 5, 2007).

————. 2008. *Table HI-1: Health Insurance Coverage Status and Types of Coverage by Sex, Race, and Hispanic Origin: 1999 to 2007.* Washington, DC: Housing and Household Economic Statistics Division, U.S. Census Bureau. http://www.census.gov/hhes/www/hlthins/historic/index.html (accessed March 25, 2009).

U.S. Department of Labor. 1996–1997. *Occupational Outlook Handbook, Tomorrow's Jobs.* Washington, DC: U.S. Department of Labor. http://www.umsl.edu/services/govdocs/ooh9697/16.htm (accessed July 6, 2007).

————. 2008. *Employment Projections: Education Pays.* Washington, DC: U.S. Department of Labor. http://www.bls.gov/emp/emptab7.htm (accessed March 25, 2009).

————. 2008–2009. *Occupational Outlook Handbook, 2008–09 Edition: Tomorrow's Jobs.* Washington, DC: U.S. Department of Labor. http://www.bls.gov/oco/oco2003.htm (accessed September 22, 2009).

————. 2009. *New Monthly Data Series on the Employment Status of People with a Disability.* Washington, DC: U.S. Department of Labor. http://www.bls.gov/cps/cpsdisability.htm (accessed March 29, 2009).

U.S. Social Security Administration. 2007. *November 2007: OASDI Monthly Statistics.* Washington, DC: U.S. Social Security Administration. http://www.ssa.gov/policy/docs/statcomps/oasdi_monthly/2007-11/table02.pdf (accessed March 25, 2009).

————. 2009. *January 2009: SSI Monthly Statistics.* Washington, DC: U.S. Social Security Administration. http://www.ssa.gov/policy/docs/statcomps/ssi_monthly/2009-01/table07.pdf (accessed March 25, 2009).

Vande Zande v. Wisconsin Department of Administration. 44 F.3d 538 (7th Cir. 1995).

Williams, Bob, Adrianne Dulio, Henry Claypool, Michael J. Perry, and Barbara S. Cooper. 2004. *Waiting for Medicare: Experiences of Uninsured People with Disabilities in the Two-Year Waiting Period for Medicare.* New York: Commonwealth Fund. http://www.cmwf.org/usr_doc/786_Williams_waiting_for_medicare.pdf (accessed June 26, 2009).

10
Learning Systems for a Globalized Economy

Do Americans Face Tough Choices or Tough Times?

Ray Marshall
University of Texas at Austin

This chapter reflects on two of Vernon Briggs's long-time interests: human resource development and policy-oriented research. Briggs's early research with me on minority participation in apprenticeship programs was designed to increase our understanding of discrimination in these programs and to develop policies and programs to improve minority participation in the skilled trades. Our research helped model, develop, and expand the successful outreach concept that played an important role in overcoming the barriers to minority and female participation in the skilled and professional occupations. Similarly, in this chapter I examine a proposal, being implemented in at least five states (Massachusetts, New Hampshire, Delaware, Arizona, and New Mexico), to radically reform school and workforce-development systems. The design for these proposals is based on extensive international comparative research by the New Commission on the Skills of the American Workforce (NCSAW), sponsored by the National Center on Education and the Economy (NCEE). If these demonstrations are successful, we expect this reform model to spread to many other states now considering our proposal. The NCSAW research also examined the influence of immigrants on workforce quality in the United States and other countries, which is another of Vernon Briggs's research interests.

In its December 2006 report, *Tough Choices or Tough Times*, the NCSAW analyzed some of the daunting economic, labor-market, education, and workforce-development challenges the United States faces after decades of changes in technology, the globalization of product and labor markets, and dramatic demographic twists. These interrelated developments have caused rising skill requirements for family-supporting jobs, declining real wages for most American workers, and growing inequality of income, wealth, and opportunity. A restoration of the broadly shared prosperity Americans experienced before the 1980s is thwarted by obsolete policies and institutions rooted in the less knowledge-intensive and less globally oriented mass-production system that dominated America's twentieth century economy and shaped our education and training institutions.

In this chapter, I focus on the need to modernize our education and workforce-development policies and institutions. However, these reforms, while necessary, are not adequate to restore broadly shared prosperity, which also requires economic policies that increase the demand for skilled workers, social safety nets to promote human resource development and limit labor-market competition, and labor policies to further limit wage competition and give workers a greater voice at work and in the larger society (Marshall 2000). It will be difficult, for example, to achieve equity—our most serious education problem—unless we address the problems associated with poverty. However, it would have been difficult for a diverse, bipartisan group like the NCSAW to reach sufficient agreement on the components of economic, social, and labor-market policies to make meaningful recommendations in the six-month period during which the commission met before issuing its report (even with the 18 months of staff work conducted before the commission was convened). I nevertheless will address these issues in this chapter.

I will also discuss the background of the NCSAW; outline its conclusions, guiding principles, and recommendations; address some of the criticisms of the commission report; and present my conclusions on these matters.[1]

BACKGROUND

In the late 1980s, the NCEE was concerned about the implications of the globalization of product markets for American workers and school systems (Marshall and Tucker 1992). We were particularly worried about growing inequality, American companies' ability to compete in global markets, and declining real wages for workers with a high-school education or less—trends that started in the 1970s. Declining real wages put serious strains on middle- and low-income families, whose earnings could only be maintained by having family members—mainly women—work more hours, a process that not only strained family life, but clearly is self-limiting. The growing college/high-school lifetime income differential, which increased for individuals with a bachelor's degree from 50 percent in the late 1970s to 61 percent by 2006 (Baum and Ma 2007), suggested that improving education and training was at least a partial solution to declining real wages for non-college-educated workers. Individuals with professional degrees have lifetime earnings up to 2.5 times those of high school graduates. NCEE's leaders generally accepted the broad expert opinion that at least two years of college was necessary to enable workers to support themselves and their families.

These considerations prompted the NCEE to create the Commission on the Skills of the American Workforce (CSAW), which I co-chaired. CSAW was a bipartisan group including members from business, labor, government, and education. Its 1990 report, *America's Choice: High Skills or Low Wages*, boosted the movement to improve the standards for schools and workforce-development institutions (CSAW 1990).

The Commission on the Skills of the American Workforce

The CSAW concluded, on the basis of extensive national and international research, that traditional American school systems were not up to the challenge of educating all children to high standards. The problem was not, as many critics alleged—including *A Nation at Risk*, the 1983 report of the Reagan administration's National Commission on Educational Equity—that the system had deteriorated relative to some past golden era (National Commission on Educational Equity 1983). Rather, the problem was that a system that reflected the needs of the mass-production economy was grossly inadequate for a more competitive, knowledge-intensive world. The challenge therefore was to determine the kind of schools and systems needed to enable Americans to compete on terms that would restore broadly shared prosperity under modern conditions.

To explore this question, the CSAW examined available research and conducted extensive interviews with educators, elected officials, scholars, and business and labor leaders in the United States, Singapore, Japan, Ireland, Denmark, Germany, and Sweden. These comparative analyses led the CSAW to conclude that traditional American school systems were too bureaucratic, gave too little autonomy to local schools, lacked coherent instruction systems linked to high standards and diagnostic assessments of student performance, and did not have incentive systems that rewarded schools and teachers for performance.

Traditional school systems were also based on the debilitating theory that learning is mainly due to innate ability, which absolves schools of responsibility for educating all students to high standards and led to school cultures, procedures, and policies that denied high quality instruction to most—especially low-income and minority—students, thus seeming to confirm their learning theory.

Traditional schools were, in addition, based on authoritarian management and governance systems that assumed teachers did not need highly professional training and working conditions to provide basic academic knowledge and skills to most students. Cost became a major success criterion, placing downward pressure on teachers' salaries and subjecting teachers to arbitrary and discriminatory practices.

To protect teachers from these abuses, many states and school districts adopted uniform salary schedules, tenure, and administrative due-process procedures. It was not surprising, therefore, that when teachers acquired the legal right to organize and bargain collectively in the 1960s and 1970s, they became the most unionized college-educated workers in the country. It also was no surprise that the resistance to unionization by school boards and administrators caused teachers to adopt a fairly adversarial industrial union response that limited school managers' discretionary powers and codified many employment practices—for example, seniority and uniform salary schedules—that became institutionalized and therefore difficult to change.

The CSAW's recommendations for reforming American schools included the following (CSAW 1990): internationally benchmarked standards for students; a coherent instruction system linked to these standards that included diagnostic assessments of students' work and more effective curricular materials to help students meet the standards;

professional standards for teachers that included career ladders to enable teachers to improve their incomes while remaining in teaching; and greater autonomy for schools to adopt methods and materials to help students meet the standards.

The recommendations were supported by teachers' unions, many school systems, and by state, local, and federal policymakers. Unfortunately, most states adopted low standards that were less expensive and easier to meet, but they did not adequately prepare students for college or demanding postsecondary learning opportunities.

America's Choice School Design

The CSAW's most enduring legacy is the America's Choice School Design (ACSD), based on the commission's high-performance school concept. The specific features of the ACSD, which has significantly improved the achievement of disadvantaged students in more than 6,000 schools, include:

- High internationally benchmarked student performance standards.

- Continuous, data-driven, and diagnostic assessments that reveal student progress toward these standards, which are conspicuously displayed in America's Choice Schools.

- Curriculum materials that stress mastery of the fundamentals of core subjects, instead of the superficial approach used in most U.S. schools, which relies on drills, memorization, and duplication.

- "Ramp-up" programs that focus materials, time, and resources on preventing dropouts and helping struggling students meet the standards.

- A theory of learning and teaching based on modern cognitive science, which demonstrates that learning is due mainly to hard work and supportive learning systems, not innate ability.

- Professional development for teachers and principals that helps them to create high-performance learning systems in their schools and classrooms. Subject matter coaches, as well as

> model classrooms and schools, are employed to demonstrate best practices for teachers and administrators.

- School management and governance systems that foster a collaborative learning environment, efficient (data-driven, research-based) learning and diagnostic processes, and parental and community involvement in school governance and student learning.

- A support system for participating schools provided by the NCEE's America's Choice division (now America's Choice, Inc. [ACI], a for-profit NCEE subsidiary) that includes cluster leaders for several schools; continuous training for principals, teachers, and coaches; curriculum materials; technical assistance; and research publications on teaching, learning, and school performance in general, as well as in particular subjects.

America's Choice provides technical assistance and other help to schools for five years, after which the schools' professionals take over with help from ACI as needed.

The ACSD has been thoroughly evaluated by the Consortium for Policy Research in Education (CPRE), whose first America's Choice evaluation was titled *Moving Mountains* (Supovitz, Poglinco, and Snyder 2001). CPRE concluded that, compared with traditional schools, the ACSD significantly improved student achievement. NCEE and ACI have continued to improve the model on the basis of internal and external research and evaluation. They have, for example, developed a very effective mathematics curriculum using international benchmarking and relying on pretesting in American schools.

Developments Since 1990

Several developments in the 15 years following the CSAW's 1990 report prompted the NCEE to create the new commission.

Labor markets were globalized by the entry of China, India, and former Soviet-bloc nations into the international trading system, doubling the size of the global labor market. Labor-market competition intensified because of dramatically declining communications costs accelerated by the collapse of high-tech prices and China's emergence as the world's leading exporter of information technology. This caused American college-educated workers to compete directly with similarly educated workers in India, China, and other countries, whose wages were much lower than those in the United States. The NCSAW found, for example, that similarly qualified engineers' salaries in 2005 were $7,500 a year in India and $45,000 in the United States. The implication, of course, was that, with prevailing institutions and policies, international convergence was likely to cause U.S. workers' wages to fall and Indian wages to rise. These developments likewise meant that the CSAW's assumption of high skills or low wages was no longer valid: American workers were competing with workers who had high skills *and* low wages.

A second significant development causing us to reconsider our 1990 *America's Choice* recommendations was the decline of real incomes for college graduates. As Table 10.1 shows, between 2000 and 2007 median incomes for males declined at every educational level except for a slight increase for PhDs ($358 or 0.42 percent), who, in 2007, accounted for only 1.8 percent of male income recipients. Women experienced slight income gains in the bachelor's-degree-or-more category (containing 30 percent of women income recipients) with median income gains of $801 (2.0 percent). Thus, the only significant income gains for college graduates between 2000 and 2007 were for the 1.5 percent (in 2007) of women with professional degrees, who gained $6,328 (11.5 percent). Despite these gains among female professional degree holders, in 2007 such women earned substantially less than men—$61,875 versus $100,000.

These data confirm that in a globalized labor market, even highly educated workers are at risk, causing us to question our 1990 conclusion that education beyond high school would enable American workers to maintain and improve their incomes. Of course, people with more education tend to have higher earnings, but higher education alone will not prevent declining real income.

A third important development was the "demographic twist" caused by escalating immigration and the pending retirement of the baby-boom generation. The American economy benefited greatly from the employment of the 78 million well-educated baby boomers, who are expected

Table 10.1 Median Income, People 25 and Older, by Educational Attainment, 2000–2007 (in 2007 dollars)

Educational attainment	Male				Female			
	Median income 2000	Median income 2007	Change 2000–07	% Change 2000–07	Median income 2000	Median income 2007	Change 2000–07	% Change 2000–07
Less than high school								
Less than 9th grade	17,014	16,625	–389	–2.29	10,290	10,539	242	2.42
9th to 12th (no diploma)	22,774	20,643	–2,131	–9.36	12,116	11,982	–134	–1.11
High school graduate	33,087	31,337	–1,750	–5.29	18,245	18,162	–83	–0.45
Some college, no degree	40,117	37,447	–2,670	–6.66	24,281	23,532	–749	–3.08
Associate degree	45,785	43,006	–2,779	–6.07	27,842	27,668	–174	–0.62
Bachelor's degree or more	64,401	62,421	–1,980	–3.07	39,911	40,712	801	2.00
Bachelor's degree	59,094	56,826	–2,268	–3.84	36,624	36,167	–457	–1.25
Master's degree	71,919	71,097	–822	–1.14	48,907	48,077	–830	–1.69
PhD	85,813	86,171	358	0.42	61,960	61,554	–406	–0.66
Professional degree[a]	100,779	100,000	–779	–0.77	55,487	61,875	6,388	11.50

[a]Professional degrees include MD, DDS, DVM, LLB, JD. Current Population Survey, 2008 Annual Social and Economic [ASEC] Supplement, pp. 8–17. http://www.census.gov/apsd/techdoc/cps/cpsmar08.pdf.
SOURCE: U.S. Census Bureau (2008a).

to retire in droves between 2000 and 2020. The baby boomers are being replaced largely by immigrants, most of whom have much lower levels of education (Ottaviano and Peri 2006). In fact, immigrant education profiles are bimodal: legal immigrants, mainly from Asia and Europe, have more education than natives, wheareas illegal immigrants, mainly from the western hemisphere, have less. The net immediate effect of immigration has been to lower the average educational attainment of our workforce (Ottaviano and Peri 2006).

The net impact of immigration on American wages is hotly debated, but there is little doubt that the large-scale influx of competing foreign workers has lowered real wages for high-school dropouts (Marshall 2007). Because of their bimodal education distribution, immigrants compete at the high and low ends of the educational distribution. According to economic theory, immigrants improve the incomes of natives who are complementary to them but reduce the wages of competitors. In terms of their educational impact, large numbers of immigrants with limited English proficiency create a pressing need for more effective adult education.

Since 1990 international data on education and workforce development has also expanded, including research on the workforce, adult literacy, school performance, and workforce development.

Workforce

Some of the most useful comparative workforce data comes from the Organisation for Economic Co-operation and Development's (OECD) Program in International Student Assessment (PISA) (OECD 2006).

By the end of the 1990s, the United States no longer had the best-educated workforce in the industrialized world, as it had in the 1970s. By 2000, it ranked eleventh out of 20 industrial countries in the percentage of adults who had completed high school, and several lower ranked countries were gaining ground.

The United States was the only OECD country where younger adults (aged 25–34) were not as well educated as the older cohort (aged 45–54). Young Americans not only had lower proportions of high-school graduates but also the lowest proportion of people with associate or baccalaureate degrees (39 percent; Canadians, 54 percent; Japanese, 51 percent; and Koreans, 49 percent).

The United States also had greater inequalities than other OECD countries. Although the United States had the lowest proportion of young adults (aged 25–34) who completed high school or college, it had the highest proportion of older adults (aged 55–64) with this educational attainment (36.2 percent, compared with 34.5 percent for Canada and 19.2 percent for Japan). These statistics reflect the continuing impact of the post–World War II GI Bill, the baby boomers, and rapid improvements in education levels in other countries during the 1980s and 1990s. Ironically, many other countries have lowered the financial barriers to higher education while we, despite the positive effects of the GI Bill, have made higher education less affordable for low- and middle-income students.

Adult literacy

Statistics on years of schooling are less accurate measures of knowledge and skills than those provided by the National Adult Literacy Survey (NALS) and the International Adult Literacy Survey (IALS). The 2003 NALS revealed that 93 million American adults scored at the lowest two of five reading levels. Another 4 million could not take the reading test because of language deficiencies. On assessments of quantitative skills, 123 million adults scored in the lowest two levels. Adults with these literacy levels are unable to read complex material or function very well in society or at work; they therefore have limited earning prospects. Indeed, 70 percent of inmates in U.S. correctional institutions scored at the lowest two literacy levels.

According to a 2004 Educational Testing Service (ETS) study of national and international literacy surveys, "Our overall performance is mediocre at best and . . . as a nation we are among the world's leaders in the degree of inequality between our best and poorest performers" (Sum, Kirsch, and Yamamoto 2004, p. 1). With respect to immigrants, the ETS study had four notable findings:

1) "A majority of our nation's 16–65 year old foreign born demonstrates proficiencies in the lowest literacy level (Level 1) on each of the NALS and IALS literacy scales, while fewer than 10 percent performed at levels 4 or 5, the highest literacy levels" (Sum, Kirsch, and Yamamoto 2004, p. 1).

2) "The average literacy proficiency of the nation's immigrant population is considerably below that of their native born peers in the United States and their foreign born counterparts in most other high-income countries that participated in the IALS assessment" (Sum, Kirsch, and Yamamoto 2004, p. 1). Indeed, on their mean composite proficiency scores, U.S. immigrants ranked eighteenth among the 20 high-income countries (Sum, Kirsch, and Yamamoto 2004, p. 21). The percentile ranking along the world skills' distribution for immigrants with less than a high-school degree—probably the vast majority of undocumented workers—was at the fifth percentile (Sum, Kirsch, and Yamamoto 2004, p. 24).

3) Immigrants' involvement in labor markets, as well as their participation in lifelong learning and civic and political affairs, is strongly associated with their literacy scores (Sum, Kirsch, and Yamamoto 2004, pp. 2–3).

4) The literacy proficiencies of U.S. foreign-born residents have a much higher degree of dispersion than either natives or their peers in other high-income countries, reflecting immigrants' bimodal education distribution.

Although the ETS picture of relative levels of immigrant literacy is pretty grim, it probably understates the severity of the problem because these analyses are partly based on the 1994 IALS, which does not include the subsequent surge in illegal immigration. Immigrants accounted for over half of U.S. civilian workforce growth during the 1990s and 86 percent of the employment growth between 2000 and 2005.

School performance

National and international assessments confirm America's growing disadvantages in school performance, literacy, and school completion levels. The main lesson from the Trends in International Math and Science Survey (TIMSS) is that American students' performance is relatively high at the lower grades, but it is mediocre or worse in the higher grades (National Center for Education Statistics 2003). This is confirmed by the OECD's PISA studies of the performance of 15-

year-olds. The PISA assessments are significant because they come near the end of students' secondary school careers and are performance exams; that is, they test ability to use knowledge and skills, not just the students' ability to memorize. The latest PISA assessments placed U.S. students' mean reading scores at fourteenth of the 22 countries assessed; their mean math scores placed them twentieth of 23 countries (OECD 2006).

The 1999 TIMSS study placed only 5 percent of U.S. students in the top 10 percent of the world's best performing eighth graders; 45 percent of Singaporean students and 32 percent of Japanese students were in this category.

The United States also had relatively low high-school graduation rates. Of 100 students entering the ninth grade, 32 do not graduate and only 18 receive associate or baccalaureate degrees in three to six years. It is estimated that roughly half of the nation's Hispanic and black students do not graduate (NCSAW 2007, p. 34).[2]

The evidence also suggests that American schools are not very efficient. As noted earlier, the performance of our students does not compare very favorably with that of other high-income countries, even though we have the second-highest per-student elementary and secondary school expenditures of any country. Similarly, in 2002, U.S. per-student spending (adjusted for inflation) was 2.64 times as high as in 1971 (from $3,400 to $8,971) (Greene and Forster 2004; NCSAW 2007, p. 4). But, for the same period, fourth-grade National Assessment of Educational Progress reading scores were only slightly higher (from 208 to 219; U.S. Department of Education 2008, Indictors 12 and 17).

Workforce development

It was equally clear that America's workforce-development system was not very effective, especially for low-income workers with limited schooling. And, employer training perpetuates already large inequalities by providing the most training to higher income managerial, professional, and technical workers and relatively little training to frontline workers. One reason employers underinvest in training is that worker mobility makes it uncertain that companies can recoup their training investments (the "free rider" problem).

The federal workforce-development system also does very little to develop human capital. The system, considered to be an extension of the welfare system, is not very clearly connected to either private-sector employers or secondary schools and has grossly inadequate resources to address our mounting workforce needs. In fact, in constant dollars, federal workforce-development resources were cut from $30 billion in 1978 to about $3.1 billion in 2006 (Fischer and Twomey 2007).

Similarly, federal–state adult education programs reach less than 5 percent of those who need these services: as noted previously, about 93 million adults score at the two lowest reading levels (National Commission on Adult Literacy 2008, p. 3) and 123 million in the two lowest math levels, yet only about 3 million participated in federal–state adult education programs. And a large number of these participants are immigrants taking English classes (National Commission on Adult Literacy 2008, p. 10). Given the obvious need for lifelong learning, a system based on educating mainly children and adolescents clearly is inadequate.

Higher education is a bright spot among American learning institutions, especially some of our community colleges, technical institutes, and research universities. But these and other postsecondary institutions could be much more efficient if they were linked to secondary schools and employer training by standards that improved horizontal and vertical mobility and enhanced the measurement, data, and accountability systems needed for continuous improvement.

THE NEW COMMISSION ON THE SKILLS OF THE AMERICAN WORKFORCE

The developments described in the last section caused the NCEE to reconsider the CSAW's underlying assumptions, and the NCSAW was created to address these issues. As with the CSAW, the NCSAW was bipartisan and represented a broad spectrum of former public officials, educators, and business, community, foundation, and union leaders. The commission's deliberations were supported by extensive research for over two years in the United States and 14 other countries, including India and China.

The commission's review of global economic conditions supports two basic conclusions. The first is that earnings in competitive global markets will tend to converge because of rising wages in low-income countries, falling wages in high-income countries, or rising wages in all countries but faster increases in low-income countries. Obviously, the third option would be the best choice for all countries, but since the 1970s, falling wages in high-income countries appears to be the option produced by market forces and prevailing economic and social policies. These trends imply continuing inequality in wealth, income, and opportunity; declining real wages for most American workers; and serious economic, political, and social problems.

The second major conclusion from the NCSAW's deliberations is that to reverse these trends and maintain or improve their incomes, American workers need a creative edge because routine work will either be automated or outsourced to lower wage countries. The commission's main objective was therefore to determine how the United States could foster creativity and innovation. The sources of creativity and innovation are not well understood, but there is general agreement that sound basic education is essential. The necessary skills include complex communications, interpersonal relations, judgment, and problem solving (i.e., the ability to think systematically and strategically, learn, adapt to change, use information and communication technology, and impose order on chaotic information). These kinds of skills and knowledge clearly are not likely to be produced by most traditional American schools, which neither teach nor model higher order thinking skills.

The commission's recommendations were based on several assumptions. The first was that, for reasons discussed earlier, our learning systems must be radically reformed because the nation's education challenges cannot be met effectively by existing schools and workforce-development institutions.

The second assumption was that education and workforce-development policies *alone* cannot restore broadly shared prosperity. The commission did not elaborate on these other policies, but in my view, they include social safety nets (including universal health care), minimum and prevailing wage regulations to prevent low-wage competition, basic labor standards as part of the rules for international economic transactions, and economic policies to promote value-added competition instead of wage competition, including heavy support for research and development.

Much larger and more effective worker adjustment programs for those displaced from noncompetitive industries would be a good human capital investment and could help overcome resistance to an open and expanding international trading system, as they do in other countries. Because of the pervasiveness of globalization's impact, it makes no sense to restrict adjustment services to those who can demonstrate damage from international trade. We could pay for these programs by replacing regressive federal payroll taxes with graduated rates; removing the income cap, currently set at $94,200, and repealing recent tax cuts on incomes above $250,000.

It should be noted that improving productivity in a highly competitive global economy will not necessarily improve workers' incomes because employers now have much more bargaining power with workers and governments than they had in less-global mass-production economies. The ability to outsource and automate means that companies can whipsaw workers and maintain or reduce wages and increase profits even when productivity is rising, as was the case between 1995 and 2005, when productivity rose by 33.4 percent, while average wages and benefits (insurance and pensions) rose by only about half that amount (Mishel, Bernstein, and Allegretto 2007, p. 111). And, as noted earlier, between 2000 and 2007, among income recipients 25 and older, over 98 percent of men and over two-thirds of women were in education categories with declining real income (Table 10.1).

Labor policies are required to balance worker and employer power, including strengthening workers' ability to organize and participate in workplace decisions. In a global economy, labor standards must be part of the international economic rules in order to prevent companies from whipsawing workers and countries. In addition, fiscal policy should be used to moderate growing income inequalities in more competitive markets.

Even if it is not politically feasible to promote broadly shared prosperity, improving education and workforce-development systems is good public policy because of the high returns on education. Under these conditions, better educated people and nations will improve productivity and incomes.

Principles and Recommendations

The commission's recommendations were based on the following principles.

- Improve teacher quality through better pay and working conditions, teacher training, and professional development.
- Reprogram funds for higher performance.
- Let students advance when they are ready.
- Create positive performance-based incentives for teachers, schools, and students.
- Give schools the flexibility to innovate and educate all students to high standards.
- Create a fair school finance system based on student needs.
- Reform the nineteenth century school governance system to enable schools to more efficiently educate all students to high standards through a lean, performance-oriented managerial system and standards-driven instruction processes with reciprocal accountability (i.e., hold schools accountable for results and elected officials accountable for providing the resources needed to achieve those results).
- Provide fewer, much higher quality tests that are diagnostic and linked to internationally benchmarked standards and high-quality curricula material.
- Create the same opportunities for working adults as for full-time students.
- Create seamless, lifetime learning systems connected by standards, with easy access and supports.

The NCSAW's recommendations were designed to accelerate the establishment of high-performance schools and school systems, as well as to create much stronger and more highly coordinated workforce-development systems to provide training, education, and labor-market services for adults. The commission recommendations were intended to be suggestions, not a blueprint for all states and school districts.

Schools and School Systems

Create a coherent system of standards, assessments, and curricula

Curricula should be based on the mastery of key ideas, concepts, core facts, and the capacity for creativity and innovation. The K–12 standards should be designed to get all students ready for college or demanding postsecondary training. The commission envisioned the creation of a set of Board Examinations similar to those used in other high-performing countries. These examinations could be created by states or national and international organizations, and they would be in a set of core subjects based on syllabi provided by the Board.

The commission assumed that, for most students, the first Board Exam (BE1) would come at the end of the tenth grade, but since students would be allowed to advance at their own pace, they might take BE1 earlier or later. Students would be allowed to take BE1 as many times as needed to pass. The standards for BE1 would be benchmarked to the exams given by the countries that do the best job of educating their students. In any case, the standard should be no lower than the requirements for entering the state's community colleges without remediation.

Students who pass BE1 would be guaranteed the right to enter a community college to work toward a two-year technical degree or the requirements needed to transfer to a four-year state college. Students who have good enough scores on BE1 could stay in high school to prepare for BE2, which could be like the exams given by the International Baccalaureate, Advanced Placement, or other state or private equivalents. Students who do well enough on BE2 could enroll in colleges or universities of their choice (subject to admission) and receive college credit for the courses leading to BE2. Some of these students might start college as juniors.

These Board Exams should be designed to motivate students to meet high standards. Continuing student assessments at the elementary and secondary levels would be linked coherently to the standards required for BE1, as would syllabi and instruction materials. School professionals and instruction systems would provide students enough assistance to allow them to proceed at their own pace but never to fall too far behind. Experience with ACSD, and other high-performance school designs, suggests that these procedures could greatly improve graduation rates.

Create high-performance schools and districts

Several actions must be taken to create high-performance schools and districts. One of the most important is to break schools' dependence on local property taxes by having education funded mainly by states, supplemented by the federal government.

Funding equity should be improved by allocating funds to schools on the basis of student-weighted budgeting, based on the educational needs of different categories of students. Schools with the most disadvantaged students would receive larger allocations of resources. Combining student-weighted budgeting with district-wide public-school choice, as is done in Seattle, for example, would give schools incentives to recruit disadvantaged students.

Teacher quality is very important for high-performance schools. States and school districts therefore should work with teachers' organizations to design systems that would compensate teachers more for performance (as is done in Denver, Toledo, and some other districts) and less for seniority. The main objective should be to recruit teachers from the top third of college students. Traditionally, schools have had many very good teachers because discrimination limited the nonteaching opportunities for women and minorities. As discrimination declines and the pay and working conditions for teachers fail to improve, fewer academically talented students are attracted to teaching. The National Council on Teacher Quality, for example, concluded that a disproportionately high number of teacher candidates came from the lower end of the academic ability distribution measured by SAT and ACT scores (U.S. Department of Education 2002). And a 2002 National Bureau of Economic Research study concluded that the likelihood of a highly talented (ranked in the top 10 percent of high school students) female entering teaching fell from 20 percent in 1964 to 11 percent in 2000 (Corcoran, Evans, and Schwab 2002).

Fortunately, recent evidence suggests that more teachers are now being recruited from the top half of college classes (Gitomer 2007). This is being done in part through initiatives like the University of Texas's UTeach initiative, an innovative teacher preparation program for math and science majors.

Beginning teachers' salaries should be raised to the current median—about $45,000 a year; there should be high standards for beginning, intermediate, and master teachers; and career ladders should enable educators to improve their earnings and remain in teaching. All teachers should be hired by local schools but paid by the states.

School boards should no longer operate schools. Instead, they should contract with autonomous local schools that agree to meet performance standards for students and school professionals. These contracts should encourage performance incentives for teachers and schools to improve student performance and provide incentives to attract teachers to hard-to-fill positions in math, science, special education, or low-performing schools.

In addition to negotiating and monitoring performance contracts, school districts would support schools in various ways, including certifying helping organizations to provide technical assistance, professional development, or other services and providing data and research to promote continuous improvement.

These recommendations could end the conflict over charter schools and private-school vouchers. Any school that met the prescribed standards could become a contract school, but no school that refused (or failed) to meet these standards could receive state funds.

The commission's recommendations could change the role of teachers' unions in several ways. Teachers' unions would negotiate compensation contracts with states and working conditions with districts and schools. Those unions could also be certified as helping organizations to assist schools with school performance, as is currently being done in New York City, Boston, Newark, Minneapolis, Toledo, and other urban school districts. Indeed, teachers' unions have comparative advantages in helping urban school districts design instructional systems tailored to urban conditions, as is currently the case with the American Federation of Teachers (AFT), the National Education Association (NEA), and some local unions affiliated with the Teachers Union Reform Network

(TURN), especially the United Federation of Teachers (UFT) in New York City. The teachers' unions would continue to represent teachers in negotiating rules for economic and working conditions, but they could assume larger roles in promoting teachers' professional interests in advancing their knowledge and skills and improving their schools. For example, several TURN unions have followed the Toledo Federation of Teachers' lead in taking greater responsibility for teacher quality through peer assistance and review programs (Marshall 2008).

Promote more efficient resource utilization

The commission assumes its recommendations could yield a net national savings of $58 billion per year as a result of students spending fewer years in high school, requiring less remediation, and avoiding course duplication (since different class levels and schools would be linked with performance standards). These savings would be divided equally between increased investments in universal preschool for three- and four-year-olds, higher teachers' salaries, and stronger support for disadvantaged students.

Provide universal high-quality preschool for three- and four-year-olds

There is abundant evidence that good preschool programs that allow children to start school ready to learn are a very efficient use of education resources. Research suggests that a dollar spent in early education can save $7 to $17 in social and education costs over children's lives. Unfortunately, only about a fourth of the nation's eligible children are enrolled in publicly funded preschool programs. Since the quality of these schools is very important, major efforts should be made to improve the standards, training, and compensation for preschool caregivers.

Provide greater support for disadvantaged students

The most important challenge for American school systems is to narrow the large performance gaps between advantaged and disadvantaged students. This problem becomes more important as immigrants with limited English proficiency and levels of schooling become a larger proportion of school populations. This is a particularly serious problem for many poor rural and urban school districts. Federal and state governments therefore should give high priority to educational equity and allocate funds to schools on the basis of student-weighted budgeting.

In addition, equity requires school professionals to do the following: abandon the theory that learning is mainly due to innate ability; change teacher compensation and assignment policies to attract the best teachers to schools with the greatest need; give more time and support to disadvantaged students; and provide diagnostic assessment, data, and school-specific research to strengthen educators' ability to diagnose and prescribe interventions to help disadvantaged students. Schools and districts also need to provide creative ways to involve minority and disadvantaged parents in their children's education.

Workforce Development and Adult Education

Rising and rapidly changing skill requirements and the displacement of workers by technology and global competition, combined with the declining education attainment of many new workers, make it critical that we create much more coherent and effective systems to meet workers' training, information counseling, family support, and labor-market adjustment needs. The absence of an effective workforce-development system will cause workers to incur most of the costs and realize few of the benefits of change, as well as prevent the whole economy from adjusting smoothly to economic and technological changes and promoting high-value-added economic development policies. The absence of an effective workforce-development system also will intensify resistance to an open and expanding global economy. To function more effectively, workforce investment boards must have more resources, status, authority, and ability to coordinate easily with schools and community colleges, as well as with adult education, social service, and preschool providers.

To strengthen workforce development, the commission made several proposals. First, provide education paid for by the federal government to enable all adults to meet the same academic standards required for high-school graduates. A possible division of responsibility would be for the states to provide free adult education up to the ninth grade level and for the federal government to provide additional education to enable adults to meet the BE1 standard.

Adults should also be given more resources to invest in their own education through tax-advantaged individual development accounts (IDAs). The NCSAW recommended that the federal government create IDAs for every child by depositing $500 in such accounts at birth and $100 every year thereafter until age 16. Employers, individual family members, and others could make pretax contributions to IDAs, which would accumulate tax-free and be used only for career-related education purposes.

In addition, regional competitiveness authorities (RCAs) that combine regional workforce- and economic-development activities should be created. The RCAs would align workforce investment, economic development, and adult education and community college districts into common regions based on logical economic and labor markets to form new regional and state jobs, skills, and growth authorities. These authorities would coordinate with community colleges and other education and training institutions to provide learning systems for adults without diplomas, immigrants, and others who need basic literacy skills. The RCAs should be empowered to issue tax-exempt bonds, raise money from private sources, and have considerable flexibility in the use of state and federal funds for developmental purposes.

The RCAs would have much more power than existing workforce, adult education, and economic development boards to formulate and execute regional development plans. They also would be responsible for a reformed adult education system, including establishment of standards for program providers and instructors and creation of a process for identifying and accrediting providers who met the standards, and for monitoring compliance and quality. To link adult, career, and continued learning functions, community colleges could be designated as the primary adult education provider, assisted by other institutions, including career centers, libraries, and other adult education providers.

Like high-performance school systems, the RCAs should be performance based. They should also generate data and analyses to assess the impact of various training providers and programs on different categories of learners.

The RCAs could become important institutions for addressing America's serious adult education and training problems. These entities are called "authorities" to distinguish them from the fragmented boards that ostensibly have had oversight of federal workforce, economic development, and adult education programs, but actually have little autonomy and inadequate financial and legal independence to work with elected officials to develop effective regional development plans.

CONCLUSIONS: DO WE FACE TOUGH CHOICES OR TOUGH TIMES?

An examination of the principal criticisms of *Tough Choices* clarifies the relationships between education and the economy, as well as the challenge involved in improving our learning systems. At the outset, it is worth noting that the media and political responses to the NCSAW's report generally have been positive.[3] There seems to be widespread agreement that America's schools have not improved enough since the 1980s to overcome their most serious problems, especially the wide achievement gaps between advantaged and disadvantaged students. Although these gaps have narrowed in some districts, as measured by the National Assessment of Educational Progress, there has not been much change overall. Progress in some districts, and with the ACSD and other comprehensive models, nevertheless provides insights into the kinds of interventions that can narrow the achievement gaps and improve overall school performance. In particular, these experiences demonstrate the importance of developing efficient, high-performance learning processes based on coherent instruction systems driven by high standards and closely linked diagnostic assessments, high-quality curricula materials, and data systems administered by highly motivated professional educators supported by effective helping organizations such as ACI.

There also seems to be broad support for some of our specific recommendations, especially universal preschool, higher teachers' pay, student-weighted budgeting, and strengthening workforce-development and adult education systems.

Some defenders of existing school systems doubt that their performance justifies the radical systemic changes the commission proposes. They point out that the schools' main shortcomings are due to poverty, racism, or other societal problems unrelated to the schools themselves.

Since the schools cannot solve these problems, critics argue, it is unfair to blame them for the achievement gaps.

As noted earlier, the commission did not argue that education policy alone would return us to broadly shared prosperity—or perhaps even reverse the broad declines in real wages. It would be a serious mistake, however, to argue that our school systems have no responsibility for inequality or that improving education for disadvantaged students would not enhance their life chances.

Part of the equity problem is due to the schools' dependence on local property taxes. There is reason to believe that student-weighted budgeting and state and federal financing could help narrow the grossly unacceptable financial gaps. Moreover, the gaps are due in part to the still widespread assumption that learning is due to innate ability, thus absolving schools from the responsibility to educate poor and minority students to high standards. Again, experiences with the ACSD, the Comer school model (Comer 1980), and others using similar designs based on sound theories of learning and teaching, demonstrate that all students can be educated to high standards.

Inequality also is perpetuated by the widely used single-salary schedule and the common practice of assigning teachers to schools based on seniority, which usually means that the best teachers are assigned where they are needed least. There is abundant evidence, however, that a systemic approach to transforming low-performing schools, including providing financial and other incentives to attract teams of master teachers and principals to troubled schools, can significantly improve their performance.

In short, while school systems are not entirely responsible for the achievement gaps, they bear some of the responsibility; additionally, systemic changes can narrow the gaps, despite the continuation of poverty and other serious social problems. Indeed, the most effective interventions coordinate education, social services, and other support activities. It would be inexcusably fatalistic to argue that we have to solve our poverty problems before making the necessary systemic changes to significantly improve the education of disadvantaged students.

Other traditional school defenders contend that the American economy's superior performance with workers educated in these institutions proves there is nothing seriously wrong with our schools. However, the NCSAW did not argue that all of our schools performed poorly. On the contrary, many of our suburban high schools and higher education institutions, especially community and technical colleges and research universities, perform well despite the waste of resources caused by the absence of high standards for high-school graduation, which necessitates considerable remedial work. Moreover, the American economy continues to benefit from immigrants and the baby boomers who will retire in greater numbers after 2010, a benefit that will continue long after these workers retire because of the technology they have developed. It is, however, prudent to note the negative effects on our future workforce from the demographic twist in the 20 years before and after 2000. Finally, although it has had undesirable effects on our workers, American productivity has benefited from outsourcing lower value-added work to foreigners. Given these realities, it would be a real stretch to argue that our economic performance has been due mainly to the soundness of our traditional K–12 schools or that systemic reforms in those schools would not significantly improve the life chances for their students.

Some criticisms are based on misinterpretations of the commission's recommendations. Some, for example, reject the contract school idea by equating it to charter schools, which have an uneven record, but on average have not so far performed as well as public schools serving similar students (Schemo 2004). There are, however, considerable differences between contract schools, which have to meet high standards for students, teachers, and schools, and charter schools, which do not. Moreover, contract schools would be required to affiliate with a state-approved helping organization and would be closely monitored by the contracting district (although they would have considerable autonomy to hire teachers and principals and establish a coherent instruction system required to meet state-imposed standards, which, hopefully, would be more demanding than the low standards currently used by most states). The funding system proposed by the commission could obviate the high-income school districts' fiscal reasons for opposing high standards—especially if states adopted the concept of reciprocal accountability.

A final criticism of *Tough Choices* is that we are naïve to assume that federal and state authorities will adopt such radical recommendations. Of course, these critics could be right. Whether or not we can gain political support depends on the credibility of our evidence that the problems we face are very serious, that our existing institutions are not up to the challenges they face, that marginal changes are not likely to do much good, and that a failure to act would have serious negative consequences for our nation's future.

The media, political, and scholarly responses to *Tough Choices* have been encouraging, and there are grounds for optimism about support from the federal government and enough states to initiate the process of institutional change. By 2009, at least 20 states had shown strong interest in *Tough Choices'* recommendations and five have become part of the first cohort to implement the recommendations (Massachusetts, New Hampshire, Delaware, Arizona, and New Mexico). If the first cohort of states produces dramatic improvements in student performance, then it is likely that others will join; we expect support to spread, as it did with the ACSD. Transforming our obsolete education and training institutions will not be easy, but real change in deeply entrenched institutions never is.

Notes

1. I chair the NCEE's board of trustees, served on the NCSAW, and agree with the main thrust of the commission's analyses and recommendations. But, as is commonly true of commission reports, I do not necessarily agree with either all of the details of that report or some of the wording of the recommendations. Similarly, my colleagues at NCEE and on the commission would not necessarily endorse all of the ideas presented in this chapter.

2. Heckman and LaFontaine (2008, p. 3) estimate that "the U.S. high school graduation rate peaked in the late 1960s and then dropped 4–5 percentage points" and "about 65 percent of blacks and Hispanics leave school without a high school diploma." These analysts find "no evidence of convergence in minority-majority graduation rates over the past 35 years."

3. The link to media reports can be found at http://www.skillscommission.org/news.htm.

References

Baum, Sandy, and Jennifer Ma. 2007. *Education Pays: The Benefits of Higher Education for Individuals and Society.* Washington, DC: College Board.

Comer, James. 1980. *School Power.* New York: Free Press.

Commission on the Skills of the American Workforce (CSAW). 1990. *America's Choice: High Skills or Low Wages.* Washington, DC: National Center on Education and the Economy.

Corcoran, Sean, William N. Evans, and Robert M. Schwab. 2002. "Changing Labor Market Opportunities for Women and the Quality of Teachers, 1957–1992." NBER Working Paper no. 4180. Cambridge, MA: National Bureau of Economic Research.

Fischer, David Jason, and John Twomey. 2007. *A Thousand Cuts.* Report prepared for Center for an Urban Future and New York Association of Training and Employment Professionals. New York: Center for an Urban Future. http://www.nycfuture.org/images_pdfs/pdfs/FINAL%20MATRIX.pdf (accessed February 24, 2009).

Gitomer, Drew H. 2007. *Teacher Quality in a Changing Policy Landscape: Improvements in the Teacher Pool.* Educational Testing Service Policy Report. Princeton, NJ: Educational Testing Service.

Greene, Jay P., and Greg Forster. 2004. *Dollars in the Classroom.* http://www.worldandi.com/subscribers/feature_detailasp?num=23934 (accessed February 23, 2009).

Heckman, James, and Paul LaFontaine. 2008. "The Declining American High School Graduation Rate: Evidence, Sources, and Consequences." *NBER Reporter* 2008(1). http://www.nber.org/reporter/2008number1/heckman.html (accessed 15 June 2009).

Marshall, Ray, ed. 2000. *Back to Shared Prosperity.* Armonk, NY: M.E. Sharpe.

———. 2007. "Getting Immigration Reform Right." *Challenge* 50(4): 26–48.

———. 2008. *The Case for Collaborative School Reform.* Washington, DC: Economic Policy Institute.

Marshall, Ray, and Marc Tucker. 1992. *Thinking for a Living: Education and the Wealth of Nations.* New York: Basic Books.

Mishel, Lawrence, Jared Bernstein, and Sylvia Allegretto. 2007. *The State of Working America 2006/2007.* Ithaca, NY: ILR Press.

National Center for Education Statistics. 2003. *Trends in International Math and Science Survey.* Washington, DC: National Center for Education Statistics.

National Commission on Adult Literacy. 2008. *Reach Higher America: Over-*

coming Crisis in the U.S. Workforce. New York: Council for Advancement of Adult Literacy.

National Commission on Educational Equity. 1983. *A Nation at Risk: The Imperative for Educational Reform.* Washington, DC: U.S. Government Printing Office.

New Commission on the Skills of the American Workforce (NCSAW). 2007. *Tough Choices or Tough Times: The Report of the New Commission on the Skills of the American Workforce.* Washington, DC: National Center on Education and the Economy.

Organisation for Economic Co-operation and Development (OECD). 2006. *Education at a Glance.* Paris: Organisation for Economic Co-operation and Development.

Ottaviano, Gianmarco I.P., and Giovanni Peri. 2006. "Rethinking the Effects of Immigration on Wages." NBER Working Paper no. 12497. Cambridge, MA: National Bureau of Economic Research.

Schemo, Diana J. 2004. "Charter Schools Trail in Results, U.S. Data Reveals." *New York Times,* August 17, A:1. http://www.nytimes.com/2004/08/17/education/17charter.html (accessed June 15, 2009).

Sum, Andrew, Irwin Kirsch, and Kentaro Yamamoto. 2004. *A Human Capital Concern: The Literacy Proficiency of US Immigrants.* Washington, DC: Educational Testing Service.

Supovitz, Jonathan A., Susan M. Poglinco, and Brooke A. Snyder. 2001. *Moving Mountains: Successes and Challenges of the America's Choice Comprehensive School Reform Design.* Philadelphia: Consortium for Policy Research in Education.

U.S. Census Bureau. 2008a. *Historical Income Tables—People.* Washington, DC: U.S. Census Bureau. http://www.census.gov/hhes/www/income/histinc/p18.html (accessed August 10, 2009).

———. 2008b. *Historical Income Tables—Households.* Washington, DC: U.S. Census Bureau. http://www.census.gov/hhes/www/income/histinc/h13.html (accessed February 24, 2009).

U.S. Department of Education. 2002. *Condition of Education 2002.* Washington, DC: Government Printing Office.

———. 2008. *Condition of Education 2008.* Washington, DC: Government Printing Office.

11

Sectoral Approaches to Workforce Development

Toward an Effective U.S. Labor-Market Policy

Robert W. Glover
Christopher T. King
University of Texas at Austin

Labor-market policies refer to government interventions to support and improve labor-market operations for workers and employers. All major industrialized nations have some form of labor-market policy, but such policies differ widely in design, size and scope, and implementation.

Economists generally distinguish between active and passive labor-market policies (Kletzer and Koch 2004), and nations typically offer a mix of active and passive policy elements. Active labor-market policies include five types of activity: job matching and job search assistance (such as public employment services), enhancing the supply of labor (e.g., training), reducing labor supply (by means such as encouraging early retirement or prorating unemployment benefits to accommodate reduced work weeks), creating stronger labor demand (e.g., through public works or public service employment), and changing the structure of demand (e.g., by the use of employment subsidies) (Auer, Efendioglu, and Leschke 2008). An example of a passive policy is a program that extends or expands unemployment insurance. Active labor-market policies have also been called "selective labor-market policies" to distinguish them from macroeconomic policies and to emphasize their targeted nature (Marshall 1984). Sweden and other European nations, as well as a few Asian countries, provide examples of countries that have long pursued labor-market policies emphasizing active elements, whereas the United Kingdom and the United States are often seen as examples of countries that have adopted more passive forms (Kletzer and Koch 2004).

Active labor-market policies can aim at a variety of goals, including promoting the expansion of employment, facilitating adjustments to changes in technology or the economy, and reducing inequality and the incidence of poverty. In his career, Vernon Briggs conducted research on all of these topics, with a particular concern for the effective implementation of programs. Yet, a key theme of his work has been reducing poverty and improving the well-being of poor people, especially African Americans and Latinos (e.g., Briggs 1973; Briggs and Marshall 1967). Among the lessons learned from that work about effective workforce-development programs since the 1960s is that the best programs operate on both the supply and demand sides of the labor market.

In this chapter, we examine major changes in the context within which modern labor-market policies operate, the nature of the current U.S. workforce- and economic-development "systems," and the major challenges and opportunities these systems face. We then look at an important strategy that appears to be effective in bringing together key elements of workforce- and economic-development policies: sectoral workforce development. A belief motivating many sectoral programs is that people who work full time should not be poor. We present emerging evidence on the effectiveness of such sectoral approaches and outline guiding principles for policymakers and program administrators to follow in pursuing them. Sectoral workforce-development approaches offer a much needed, major step toward implementing more active labor-market policies in the United States.

THE ECONOMIC, LABOR-MARKET, AND DEMOGRAPHIC CONTEXT

In the early 1960s, the United States began moving toward development and implementation of comprehensive workforce-development policies.[1] Since that time, the economic, labor market, and demographic context within which these policies and their accompanying programs operate has changed dramatically. Many of these contextual changes have important implications for workforce policies and programs.

The mid to late 1950s were a time of unprecedented economic growth and broadly shared prosperity. Employment was expanding in most sectors of the economy (including manufacturing), real wages were rising, and many more workers found that they were part of a "social contract" that offered them health benefits, opportunities for training and career advancement, as well as economic security in return for their commitment to working hard and long for their employer (see King, McPherson, and Long 2000; Marshall and Tucker 1992; Osterman 2007). Moreover, immigration was at relatively low levels as the domestic workforce expanded to meet the growing demands of a booming post–World War II economy (Borjas 2007). The United States had emerged from World War II with an intact economy and faced limited economic competition from other nations.

This is not to say that serious labor-market problems were completely absent. Some groups of workers—especially minorities and low-skilled workers—were largely bypassed or did not participate fully in the postwar economic successes (Harrington 1963). Moreover, there was a trend toward "creeping prosperity unemployment," attributed to the effects of technological change and disproportionate demand for highly skilled and educated workers (Killingsworth 1968; Long 1972). U.S. policymakers began to enact legislation to address these and related problems by means of a "system" of diverse policies and programs. Current economic, labor-market, and demographic conditions, however, bear little resemblance to the context and conditions facing policymakers in those earlier periods. Several points serve to illustrate the breadth and depth of the changes.

First, the U.S. economy has become overwhelmingly a producer of services. The share of employment in the traditional goods-producing industries—which includes mining, manufacturing, and construction—fell from 35.6 percent in 1958 to a low of just over 16 percent in 2007 (BLS n.d.). Within the goods-producing sector, the share of employment in manufacturing fell even more precipitously, from a high of 28.5 percent in 1958 to a postwar low of 10.1 percent in 2007. The service sector, including the government, now accounts for nearly 84 percent of all nonfarm jobs. Moreover, as this shift to services was continuing its relentless pace, the economy also was becoming far more tied to information. A large majority of workers are now employed in knowledge-based or information-related jobs. As Marshall and Tucker (1992) phrased it, more and more workers are now "thinking for a living."

Second, as Tom Friedman argued in his 2005 book *The World Is Flat*, a number of major developments have "flattened the world" and dramatically opened up global interconnectedness in many respects. These include the fall of the Berlin Wall and the collapse of barriers impeding trade with the former Communist countries starting in 1989; the rise of the Internet and tools for using it more effectively in the 1990s; and the rapid growth of off-shoring and both out- and in-sourcing of production, among others.[2] Friedman found that these world-flattening forces led to a "triple convergence" through which a new global playing field was being created at the beginning of the twenty-first century. New forms of business and organizational practices and employee skills emerged to take advantage of the new interconnected world, and 1.5 billion new "plug and play" workers from China, India, and the former Soviet Union joined the global workforce. Increased globalization and interdependence in world markets means that a far greater share of the American economy now is exposed to global markets, and more U.S. workers are competing with much cheaper labor elsewhere in the world than ever before. A few short decades ago, workers with limited skills and education felt most of the pain, but now even those possessing relatively high levels of skill and education are adversely affected by globalization (Friedman 2005).

Rob Atkinson (2005) describes the evolution of the American economy as proceeding from a Mercantilist, craft-based economy during the 1840s through the 1880s; to a factory-based, industrial economy during the 1890s through the 1940s; to a corporate, mass-production economy from the 1950s through the late 1970s; and finally, after several decades of "turbulent transition," to the "new economy," which is decidedly entrepreneurial and knowledge-based since 1994. Atkinson's comparison of the two most recent periods, summarized in Table 11.1, captures the transition that Friedman's book describes.

Third, the nature of work and the workplace has also changed dramatically, as many analysts have noted (e.g., Cappelli 1999; Cappelli et al. 1997; Marshall and Tucker 1992; Osterman 2007). Where work

Table 11.1 A Comparison of Mass Production and Entrepreneurial, Knowledge Economies

Issue	Mass production economy	Entrepreneurial, knowledge economy
Economy-wide traits		
Markets	Stable	Dynamic
Competition scope	National	Global
Organization form	Hierarchical	Networked
Production system	Mass	Flexible
Key production factor	Capital, labor	Innovation, knowledge
Key technology driver	Mechanization	Digitization
Competitive advantage	Economies of scale	Innovation/quality
Importance of research	Moderate	High
Relations between firms	Go it alone	Collaborative
Workforce		
Policy goal	Full employment	High incomes
Skills	Job-specific	Broad, sustained
Nature of employment	Stable	Dynamic
Government		
Business-government relations	Impose requirements	Assist firm growth
Regulation	Command & control	Market tools/flexibility

SOURCE: Atkinson (2005, p. 96).

had long been highly structured, repetitive, and hierarchical, it has now become flexible and fluid, and built more around tasks than jobs. The types of skills required to succeed in the new economy are quite different (Levy and Murnane 2004), as are those needed for long-term job retention and career advancement.

Fourth, the United States has experienced increasing disparities of income and wealth in the past few decades, as have other nations (see, for example, Galbraith 1998; Marshall 2000). Real earnings have flattened or declined for all but the most highly educated males, while they have grown only marginally for females, even as female labor-force participation has increased markedly (Mishel, Bernstein, and Shierholz 2009). The gap between the haves and have-nots has grown. In fact, as *Tough Choices or Tough Times*, the 2006 report of the New Commission on Skills of the American Workforce (2007) has noted, real earnings appear to be flattening even for workers with four-year college degrees.

Fifth, as a recent Aspen Institute report pointed out, in sharp contrast to recent periods in its history, the United States faces three critical gaps over the next few decades: workers, skills, and wages (Aspen Institute 2003). The native-born workforce will be flat or declining for the near future, meaning that we will have to rely more on foreign-born workers, shift even more work off shore, or introduce more labor-saving technology into the workplace. In addition, new workers are expected to enter the workforce with lower education and skill levels than they did in the preceding period. At the same time, real wages are expected to decline in the future for many groups in the labor market. The latter two issues were addressed in several works by Briggs, who argued that the influx of large numbers of low-skilled, undocumented Mexican workers adversely affected job opportunities and substantially depressed real wages for African-American males in Los Angeles and other urban areas for many years (Briggs 1984, 2003).

Finally, workers are experiencing a breakdown of the "social contract" that prevailed in many workplaces during the early postwar era (Cappelli 1999; King, McPherson, and Long 2000; Osterman 2007). A growing majority of workers can no longer count on being rewarded to the same extent as in earlier decades when they devote their working lives to their employer, especially with respect to job security, opportunities for training and career advancement, and secure retirement income.

Labor economists once could clearly articulate the "career ladders" that workers could use to advance within a given employer or industry if they obtained the requisite education, skills, and experience. In today's labor markets, this is no longer the case. Several as yet imperfect metaphors are emerging to describe and understand the way labor-market advancement works. Two such metaphors—the "career lattice" and the "climbing wall"—suggest that progression may sometimes require sideways or even downward movement for workers as they navigate today's labor markets.[3] As the metaphors suggest, workers will require different types of safety nets in this new environment. There may also be related, nonlinear work-arounds for potential skill shortages, such as community-college skill training and certification for graduates of four-year colleges who have general knowledge but need practical skills or experience applying that knowledge before they can secure better paying positions (Glover et al. 2005).

Research made possible by the recently available (longitudinal, linked) employer-employee data files from the Longitudinal Employer-Household Dynamics Program (LEHD), a joint initiative of the U.S. Census Bureau and the U.S. Department of Labor's Bureau of Labor Statistics, has led to new insights on career development in today's labor markets. Brown, Haltiwanger, and Lane (2006) studied job ladders and actual career paths of workers over a decade in five industries: semiconductors, software, financial services, trucking, and retail food. Their research documented that the quality of career paths varies by industry as well as by firm. In general, workers improved their career paths by moving *into* semiconductors, software, trucking, or financial services and by moving *out* of retail food. The researchers also found a general pattern with regard to inter-firm differences and their effects. While acknowledging significant variations across firms, they write: "The basic message here is that businesses with higher-quality workforces and lower churning are more likely to survive" (Brown, Haltiwanger, and Lane 2006, p. 54). For the individual worker, it made a big difference whether the person got a job with a high-wage, career-oriented firm.

Andersson, Holzer, and Lane (2005) also used LEHD data to follow and analyze the experiences of low-income workers in California, Florida, Illinois, Maryland, and North Carolina during the late 1990s.[4] They found considerable mobility into and out of low-earnings categories during the six years tracked by the study. But earnings increased only from $12,000 to $15,000 per year for these workers. Success differed by racial group. White males and Asians had the highest transition rates. In cases involving a transition into construction and manufacturing, African-American males were underrepresented relative to whites and Latinos. Of particular interest were the findings about successful transitions out of low earnings. Transitions out of low earnings were "associated with subsequent employment in high-wage industrial sectors, larger firms, firms with lower turnover, and, especially, high-wage firms" (Andersson, Holzer, and Lane 2005, p. 143). They were also more common among workers who changed jobs rather than stayed in them. Increased earnings for job-changers tended to accrue to those who changed jobs from a low-paying to a higher paying position early on and subsequently remained with that firm.

Taken together, this new, transformed context suggests that the old approaches to workforce development, based on outmoded conceptions of the economy and labor markets, are unlikely to perform well, now or in the foreseeable future. New workforce organizational forms appear to be needed to respond to the changing nature of labor markets. Before we can say that with confidence, however, we need to examine American workforce- and economic-development systems more closely. In many respects, these aren't really "systems" at all, but fragmented sets of strategies and programs addressing ad hoc problems for varying target groups with widely differing needs and expectations.

THE AMERICAN WORKFORCE-DEVELOPMENT "SYSTEM"

Frederick Harbison, in his classic 1973 volume, *Human Resources as the Wealth of Nations*, explained that human resource development—what we now more commonly refer to as workforce development—encompasses three broad functions:

- *Maintenance*, including cash welfare benefits (such as Temporary Assistance for Needy Families), in-kind support (e.g., food stamps, assistance with transportation, and child-care subsidies), Unemployment Insurance payments, and income supplements for the working poor available through the Earned Income Tax Credit;

- *Utilization*, including basic labor exchange services through the Employment Service or one-stop core services supported by the Workforce Investment Act (WIA) of 1998, as well as similar private efforts matching workers and jobs (such as CareerBuilder.com and Monster.com); and

- *Development*, including a broad array of efforts intended to build workers' skills at all levels, by means of adult basic education (ABE), occupational skills training, customized training, on-the-job training, and apprenticeship.

Yet, on the surface, it would appear that very little about our current approach to workforce development in this country can accurately be characterized as a "system." In fact, as noted above, what has evolved over the decades is really a hodgepodge of programs and initiatives funded by various federal, state, local, and private entities and operated by a similarly varied mix of public and private organizations with widely divergent goals and expected outcomes.[5]

Osterman (2007) outlined a framework for publicly funded workforce development. He spelled out several key functions of this system, starting with improving skill levels—its "core" function—and job matching to better connect workers and employers in the labor market. He also envisioned a series of demand-side functions, including working directly with employers and their associations to help them become more economically competitive and provide training and career opportunities to less-educated and low-skilled workers. According to Osterman (2007, p. 125), the publicly funded system for less-skilled adults and dislocated workers comprises six main "buckets" (with Fiscal Year [FY] 2005 federal budget amounts shown in parentheses):[6]

- WIA programs geared primarily toward poor adults ($1.5 billion);

- WIA and Trade Adjustment Assistance programs for dislocated workers ($1.6 billion);

- ABE programs funded by federal and state governments ($570 million in federal grants to states; totaling around $2.1 billion, including state-reported matching funds);

- State-funded programs providing training to incumbent workers ($270 million);[7]

- The Employment Service or one-stop system supported largely by WIA for job matching ($0.9 billion); and

- Community and technical college programs (totaling $12 billion to $20 billion, including state and local contributions along with $1.2 billion in federal Perkins funding).[8]

To this list, apprenticeship programs need to be added. Although apprenticeship programs received only $21 million from the U.S. Department of Labor in FY 2005, this covered only the expense of administering the apprenticeship registration system and a few demonstration grants. Apprenticeship is primarily financed by employers and, in the union sector, through collective bargaining. In some areas, apprenticeship training is provided in collaboration with community and technical colleges.

To fully characterize the broader system, we must add employer-provided training, education, and career development to these public "buckets."[9] U.S. employers are responsible for the lion's share of workforce-development activity. The American Society for Training and Development (ASTD) estimates that employer spending on formal workplace learning—on such activities as on-the-job training, customized training, work-based learning, and tuition assistance—exceeded $139 billion in 2007, about two-thirds of which was spent on internal workplace learning (Paradise 2008). Employers in the ASTD survey spent $1,103 per worker/year, about 2.15 percent of payroll.

Employer spending disproportionately favors better educated and higher skilled workers (Lerman, McKernan, and Riegg 2004). Employers across industries tend to provide far better training access and financing to their most skilled workers. The low level of training offered to the least skilled employees makes it more difficult for them to advance. Advancement out of low-wage work has become a critical issue, posing a serious obstacle for workers who want to move up to jobs with family-supporting incomes.

America's workforce development efforts fall far short of being a coherent "system" and have many serious shortcomings, among them the following:

- Public workforce-development programs have too often failed to effectively engage employers. With few exceptions, the publicly funded workforce system does not connect well with employers. Despite the fact that workforce investment boards must be composed of a majority of business representatives, a study of the implementation of the WIA in eight states concluded that employer involvement in workforce development is weak in many areas (Barnow and King 2005; Rockefeller Institute of Government 2004a,b).

- Most public workforce training programs have not been well connected to educational institutions, especially community colleges (Grubb 1996a,b; Grubb et al. 1999). Although community and technical colleges generally enjoy a better reputation with employers as a source of trained workers than do workforce programs (Laufer and Winship 2004), their completion rates are very low (McIntosh and Rouse 2009). Few students obtain any form of credential. Further, community colleges rarely offer effective job placement services.

- The training in American public workforce development is generally too short term to have the necessary impact (King 2008). In a study of persistence and outcomes of community college in Washington State, Prince and Jenkins (2005) found that at least one year of community college work with a credential is needed to make significant advancements in employment and earnings.

- Even short-term follow-up services are rarely provided in workforce-development programs, yet the highest turnover of new employees occurs during the early stages of their employment (Price 1977, p. 84).

- Federal support for workforce development, broadly considered, has been on the decline for decades, despite a growing need for publicly funded efforts in an increasingly global marketplace.

Despite these shortcomings, in the past decade new approaches to workforce development have emerged that show real promise to help improve the employment and earnings of low-income individuals. These so-called sectoral strategies, utilizing workforce intermediaries as key actors, appear in part to succeed by making explicit connections to economic development, among other important steps. A brief review of economic development follows in the next section.

ECONOMIC DEVELOPMENT
AND WORKFORCE DEVELOPMENT

In the United States, the traditional approaches to economic development and workforce development have differed substantially.[10] In economic development, the key focus is on marketing or "branding" to attract firms and jobs to the area. Attention to specific workforce issues, if any, is typically limited to recruiting high-level out-of-area talent to fill top positions in management, engineering, and marketing. Economic developers tend to leave details to the market after an initial assist through public sector incentives. In contrast, workforce developers are concerned about these details, including which occupations might be critical for a given industry cluster to flourish, how *local residents* might best be prepared for these jobs, how long the process to prepare the workforce might take, and how this process will be financed.

A market approach may take many years to accomplish, during which time area residents will not be prepared for jobs, so companies will incur added costs to recruit out-of-town employees for the available jobs. Also, individual employers typically do not foresee skill shortages until they are imminent. Firms in growing clusters frequently do not identify or project their workforce needs more than a few months into the future and are generally unwilling to commit significant resources to planning.

Successful, timely preparation of area residents often requires considerable planning and sustained investment—and coordination—of public and private resources. To be effective, a workforce-development system must give attention to the need for workers across the spectrum of skill levels. Workforce developers are aware that one must plan ahead to develop and deploy effective training programs. Traditionally, the workforce system has been charged primarily with addressing *current* workforce demands and training for *existing* jobs. However, workforce development systems have begun moving toward innovation and capacity building for the emerging future.

The Rise of Cluster-Driven Economic Development

The initial description of industry clusters traces back to economist Alfred Marshall, who described the advantages found in externalities of specialized industry locations in his *Principles of Economics* (1890). Michael Porter of the Harvard Business School popularized the modern concept of industry clusters (Porter 1990). Although Porter's initial work on competitive advantages was originally applied to nations, he soon recognized that most economic activities take place at the regional level. So, he extended his theory and applied it to regional, state, and metropolitan economies as well (Porter 2000). According to Porter, clusters are a striking feature of the economy of virtually every country, region, state, and even metropolitan area, especially in advanced economies (Porter 1998b). It is now common for states and regions to use clusters to help them target economic development activities. Porter defines a cluster as "A geographically proximate group of interconnected companies, specialized suppliers, service providers, firms in related industries, and associated institutions (such as universities, standard-setting agencies, trade associations) in a particular field, linked by commonalities and complementarities" (Porter 2000, p. 16).

Clusters can take varying forms, depending on their depth and sophistication, but a majority of them include end-product or service companies; suppliers of specialized inputs, components, machinery, and business services; financial institutions; and firms in related industries. They may also include the producers of complementary products and specialized infrastructure providers, including governmental entities (Porter 1998b, p. 199). Porter argues that clusters may be considered an alternative way of organizing a value chain (Porter 1998a, p. 80).

In *The Competitive Advantage of Nations*, Porter (1990) developed the Diamond Model in which the competitive advantage of nations lies in four interlinked factors: 1) demand conditions, 2) industry strategy or rivalry, 3) related and supporting industries, and 4) factor conditions. In the model, government plays a role as catalyst and challenger—encouraging and pushing businesses to raise their aspirations and move to higher levels of competitive performance, stimulating early demand for advanced products, focusing on specialized factor creation, and stimulating local rivalry by limiting direct cooperation and enforcing anti-trust regulations. Porter used his "diamond of advantage" notion to determine which firms, sectors, or industries had competitive advantages, and his emphasis on the importance of related and supporting firms or industries encouraged interest in clusters.

Clusters offer an organizing framework for understanding regional economies and for developing economic strategies. Cluster analysis can help diagnose a region's economic opportunities and challenges and identify what a region might do to influence its economic future. It can help highlight a region's competitive strengths and weaknesses and clarify an area's economic drivers.

Regional economies are composed of three main types: natural-resource clusters, local clusters, and traded clusters, which can be characterized as follows:

- *Natural-resource clusters* are found in regions where a particular natural resource is abundant.

- *Local clusters* are found in every region and produce goods and services that are needed by the local population (these include retail and personal-services firms, and hospitals and other medical-services institutions).

- *Traded clusters* in a region produce goods and services that are in competition with other regions and nations. They trade across the nation and even the globe (semiconductors and medical devices, for example) and tend to be concentrated in only a few regions.

Traded clusters tend to drive regional prosperity. Although local clusters account for roughly two-thirds of employment in an average region, traded clusters are usually the keys to the prosperity and growth of the region. This is because traded clusters can achieve higher productivity and attain growth that is unconstrained by the size of the local market. The success of traded clusters creates much of the demand for the services and products of local clusters. Traded clusters bring new value to a region, rather than simply shifting value within a region (Porter 2003).

Stuart Rosenfeld, who has conducted research with regions, states, and community colleges, defines an industry cluster as "a geographically bounded concentration of similar, related or complementary businesses, with active channels for business transactions, communications and dialogue, that share specialized infrastructure, labor markets and services, and that are faced with common opportunities and threats" (Rosenfeld 1997, p.10). In a more recent publication, he explains the concept in more operational terms: "A cluster consists of groups of companies and/or services and all of the public and private entities on which they in some way depend, including suppliers, consultants, bankers, lawyers, education and training providers, business and professional associations and government agencies" (Rosenfeld 2002, p. 8).

Rosenfeld further explains the minimum requirements of a cluster as follows: "A scale of demand sufficient to produce externalities (i.e., sufficient number of firms with common or overlapping needs to create or attract more services and resources, including labor, than would be available to more isolated firms)." He identifies the externalities produced by mature and growing clusters. They include mid-skilled technical labor-force members who are educated locally and area professionals (such as bankers, consultants, and accountants) with a depth of understanding regarding the needs of local firms. "There is a depth of relationship among members within the region. The dynamics of clusters are embodied in the value-added and knowledge-adding chains among its members" (Rosenfeld 2002, pp. 9–10).

Rosenfeld's explanation highlights the importance of the mid-skilled labor force and the workforce-development system's role in creating it, as does a recent work by Holzer and Lerman (2007). Of course, workforce quality is one of several factors that influence economic development by means of a regional industry cluster. Others include innovation, entrepreneurship, and business incubation, venture capital funding, infrastructure development, product characteristics, the location of suppliers, availability of professional services, competitors, and the customer base.

In the past decade, a number of states have begun pursuing cluster-based economic-development strategies to bolster the competitiveness of their economies and have attempted to link them much more closely to their workforce-development strategies. The National Governors Association's (NGA) Center for Best Practices has played a key role in fostering the development and use of such strategies over the past decade, using multi-state "policy academies" as a key tool (see NGA

Center for Best Practices 2002; Simon and Hoffman 2005). For example, six states—Idaho, Missouri, Montana, New Jersey, Ohio, and Virginia—participated in NGA's Next-Generation of Workforce Development Project, with support from the Ford Foundation and the U.S. Department of Labor, and have continued to develop policies and activities that better link their economic- and workforce-development systems.

SECTORAL APPROACHES TO WORKFORCE DEVELOPMENT

Labor-market intermediaries have been in existence for a long time (see Levitan, Mangum, and Marshall 1981, chapter 24; National Commission for Manpower Policy 1978). They range from the public employment service to union hiring halls and staffing agencies. A new form of labor-market intermediary has been developed since the 1990s, which has come to be called a "workforce intermediary" (Giloth 2004). These intermediaries have several distinguishing features, including an explicit "dual-customer" focus on both participants and employers, serving as integrators of varied funding streams, fostering new ideas and solutions and the pursuit of high-skills, high-wage strategies rather than simply promoting labor-force attachment, among others (Giloth 2004, p. 7). Workforce intermediaries often pursue sectoral approaches to workforce development, operating in partnership with industry clusters. These sectoral partnerships connect supply and demand for a cluster of firms. They generally focus their efforts on improving the economic status of low-income residents in American cities (Clark and Dawson 1995).

A sectoral strategy to workforce development functions as follows. It *targets* a specific industry or cluster of occupations, developing a deep understanding of the interrelationships between business competitiveness and the workforce needs of the targeted industry. It *intervenes* through a credible organization or set of organizations, crafting workforce solutions tailored to that industry and its region. It *supports workers* in improving their range of employment-related skills, improving their ability to compete for higher quality work opportunities. It *meets the needs of employers*, improving their ability to compete in the marketplace. And it *creates lasting change* in the labor-market system to the benefit of both workers and employers (Conway et al. 2007).

Sectoral approaches offer promise to help resolve problems that have long plagued workforce development in America. In particular, such programs:

- Offer a means to effectively engage employers in public workforce development by focusing on selected industries and firms, developing a keen knowledge of their situation, and implementing strategies to meet their needs.

- Help integrate funding streams, putting pieces together to provide effective services to reach successful outcomes. This is achieved through advocacy and expert knowledge of the fragmented array of available public workforce, social services, tuition assistance, and work-support programs.

- Work with community colleges as partners, improve their performance, and help provide more substantial training tailored to employer needs.

- Provide support and follow-up services that help clients keep the jobs they obtain.

In short, sectoral programs serve as integrators. They convene the parties and establish public/private partnerships. They fill the gaps in service needs to help ensure successful completion of training and entry into career paths.

Sectoral workforce-development programs target a particular industry—and specific occupations within it—to improve the quality of job opportunities available to low-income and disadvantaged individuals. They take a dual customer approach, serving both employers and job seekers. They establish sustained relationships with firms over extended periods of time and develop deep knowledge of the industry. They match workers to jobs through careful screening, and address whatever skills are needed for the jobs, including "soft" skills, life skills, language skills, literacy and basic skills, and occupational skills. At the same time, they develop expertise in overcoming barriers of disadvantaged workers and implement support and follow-up services to help assure training completion, certification, and job retention.

Sectoral workforce-development programs operate on both the supply and demand sides of the labor market. They take a systems approach, and the lasting changes they seek may involve the modification of industry practices, educational institutions, training programs, or public policy. Sectoral programs seek to promote access to jobs by removing barriers to getting good jobs or advancing to better jobs. Alternatively, where jobs offer low wages, few benefits, and poor working conditions, sector strategists may focus on improving the quality of jobs. According to *A Governors Guide to Cluster-Based Economic Development*:

> The best sectoral organizations are more than brokers or bridges between disadvantaged communities and industry; they help articulate career paths and advancement opportunities, develop standardized industry training, establish standards for job quality and working conditions, assist with market coordination, broker business networks, and help develop strategic plans. Successful intermediaries employ staff with solid cluster experience and expertise, people who understand employers' needs but also have the trust of the communities they serve. (NGA Center for Best Practices 2002, p. 32)

Sectoral workforce development can provide an effective complement to economic-development activities, especially as cluster-driven economic development has become an increasingly popular approach. Indeed, combining the two offers the logical and practical means to promote a regional economy and help ensure that local residents benefit from the job growth that occurs. Sectoral programs have the potential to address three goals simultaneously: increase skills, improve productivity, and enhance regional competitiveness. Sectoral workforce-development programs aim to create value for employers and to strengthen their targeted industry sector(s) while creating pathways to employment and advancement for low-income individuals (Giloth 2004).

Sectoral workforce-development programs began during the 1990s with funding from philanthropic organizations. Since then, variations of the sectoral approach have become more widely adopted. A recent survey of sectoral workforce programs made by the Workforce Strategies Initiative at the Aspen Institute found 227 organizations targeting approximately 20 industries (Conway et al. 2007, p. 82). In 2001, the U.S.

Department of Labor funded 39 Workforce Investment Boards to participate in a Sectoral Employment Demonstration project (Pindus et al. 2004). Subsequent Labor Department initiatives—including the High Growth Job Training Initiative and the Community-Based Job Training Initiative, which sought to link workforce-development organizations with high-growth industries in need of skilled workers—included elements of sectoral approach. In 2006, the NGA, in collaboration with the Corporation for a Skilled America and the National Network of Sector Partners, began a project with 11 states to accelerate state adoption of sectoral approaches to workforce development.

Sectoral programs are undertaken by collaborations, usually including community colleges as training partners. The collaborations can be initiated, organized, and led by any of a variety of organizations, including community-based organizations, local workforce-investment boards, educational institutions, faith-based organizations, or industry associations.

The Effectiveness of Sectoral Workforce Development

Evidence is emerging on the effectiveness of sectoral workforce-development approaches. The National Economic Development and Law Center and the National Network of Sector Partners have documented sectoral workforce practices.[11] Evaluations of sectoral programs have been conducted by several organizations, including the Aspen Institute, Public/Private Ventures (P/PV), Abt Associates, the Ray Marshall Center, and others. Some of these studies include longitudinal data on participant outcomes, and a few have actually estimated program impacts on employment, earnings, or other measures.

The Aspen Institute and P/PV have conducted the most extensive field research on sectoral workforce programs. As part of its Sectoral Employment Development Learning Project, Aspen's Workforce Strategies Initiative group conducted case studies of six sectoral programs and collected data on participants at the start of training, and at 90 days, at one year, and at two years after training. The six programs and their industry targets are presented in Table 11.2.

The Aspen Institute's in-depth case studies—which relied on pre- and post-training comparisons rather than an experimental or

Table 11.2 Six Sectoral Workforce Programs Studied by the Aspen Institute

Program (location)	Target industry
Asian Neighborhood Design (San Francisco, CA)	Construction industry
Garment Industry Development Corporation (New York, NY)	Garment industry
Focus: HOPE (Detroit, MI)	Metalworking manufacturing
Jane Addams Resource Corporation (Chicago, IL)	Metalworking manufacturing
Paraprofessional Healthcare Institute (Bronx, NY)	Home care (home health aides)
Project QUEST (San Antonio, TX)	Health services; business systems and information technology; and maintenance, repair, and overhaul (including heavy equipment/diesel mechanics, aircraft mechanics, auto collision repair technicians, and electricians)

SOURCE: Conway et al. (2007).

quasi-experimental design—found that 87 percent of participants completed their training and, on average, participants increased their earnings by 41 percent within one year after training. Across all the programs, average earnings rose from $9,036 shortly before or during training to $19,809 two years after training. This increase reflected a rise in both wages and hours worked. Also, significant proportions of those placed in jobs were receiving fringe benefits. In the second year of employment, large shares of participants reported receiving health-care benefits (65 percent), paid vacation (77 percent), paid sick leave (64 percent), and pensions other than Social Security (59 percent). Fully 82 percent of respondents reported that they were satisfied with the quality of their jobs, and the same percentage believed that their future job prospects improved due to their participation in the sectoral program (Zandniapour and Conway 2002, pp. 9–11).

P/PV studied a wider array of nine sectoral initiatives, including six skills-training organizations, two social enterprises (to place day laborers and home health-care providers), and a membership organization (for family child-care providers). These programs are listed in Table 11.3.

The P/PV study included baseline and one- and two-year follow-up studies administered by Abt Associates. Although two of the initiatives, ARCH and PhAME, tried to establish in-house training and failed, the others were able to recruit and place low-income, less-educated, and minority individuals into employment previously unavailable to them. Participants experienced more stable employment, higher hourly wages, and better quality jobs. P/PV concluded that the most successful organizations sought to combine employment and training services for job seekers with efforts to influence the practices of employers and educators or to change state policies to do so (Roder, Clymer, and Wyckoff 2008).

Table 11.3 Sectoral Programs Studied by Public/Private Ventures

Program (location)	Target industry/occupation
Skills-training organizations	
Action to Rehabilitate Community Housing (ARCH) (Washington, DC)	Paralegal profession
Philadelphia Area Accelerated Manufacturing Education, Inc. (PhAME)	Manufacturing
Southern Good Faith Fund (Pine Bluff, AR)	Certified nursing assistants
Training, Inc. (Newark, NJ)	Information technology
Project QUEST (San Antonio, TX)	Health services; business systems/ information technology; and maintenance, repair, and overhaul
WIRE-Net (Cleveland, OH)	Metalworking
Social enterprises	
Quality Care Partners New Hampshire Community Loan Fund	Health care
Primavera Works (Tucson, AZ)	Day laborer
Membership organization	
Day Care Justice Co-op Direct Action for Rights and Equality (DARE) (Providence, RI)	Child care

SOURCE: Roder, Clymer, and Wyckoff (2008).

Examples of Successful Sectoral Programs

Project QUEST is a training and support services program in San Antonio aimed at working poor people with high-school degrees (Rademacher, Bear, and Conway 2001). Project QUEST was founded as a nonprofit organization in 1992 by two community organizations, Communities Organized for Public Service (COPS) and Metro Alliance, both affiliated with the Industrial Areas Foundation (see chapter in this volume by Ernesto Cortés Jr.). The program identifies jobs in high demand that pay a living wage and works with firms to identify job openings and the skills required. Training is provided through local community colleges and usually lasts from one to four semesters. The program provides modest financial support, extensive counseling, and follow-up services.

Lautsch and Osterman (1998) estimated that post-program earnings for Project QUEST participants increased over their pre-program earnings by $7,457 (p. 221). Zandniapour and Conway (2002) compared pre- and post-program earnings of participants in San Antonio's Project QUEST and five other sectoral workforce programs over a two-year period and found significant improvements in hourly pay and hours of work earnings, and proportions of participants covered by fringe benefits, as previously summarized. To be sure, these results are based only on simple pre–post comparisons of gross outcomes and do not address the value-added issue. The impacts of Project QUEST are currently being evaluated by P/PV. In addition, P/PV has evaluated three other sectoral programs using a random assignment design and found strong positive impacts, as previewed in a brief published in May 2009. The evaluated programs are Jewish Vocational Services in Boston, MA, Per Scholas in New York, NY, and the Wisconsin Regional Partnership in Milwaukee, WI (Maguire et al. 2009).

Project QUEST has been replicated by four sister organizations in Texas and Arizona: Capital IDEA (Austin), VIDA (Rio Grande Valley), Project ARRIBA (El Paso), and JobPath (Tucson). All of these programs were established during the mid to late 1990s by their local interfaith organizations, multi-denominational coalitions of congregations from churches and synagogues established through the Southwest Chapter of the Industrial Areas Foundation. Key benefits of this model are that the local interfaith organizations help in providing political support and raising funds for the programs, assist in identifying suitable candidates for participation, and provide mentoring and motivational support.

Capital IDEA offers occupational skills training and extensive support services to low-income residents, concentrating on long-term engagement to improve education and labor-market outcomes. It takes a sectoral approach, focusing on occupations in high demand, typically with starting wages of $14 per hour or more in health care, information technology, accounting, wireless technologies, utilities, and education. Fully three-quarters of Capital IDEA's training in the 2003–2006 period was in nursing and allied health careers, and its training is usually provided through Austin Community College.

The evaluation results for Capital IDEA's efforts are noteworthy. Whereas the previous studies were only able to make simple comparisons of participant earnings before and after training, Smith, King, and Schroeder (2007, 2008) documented the gross labor-market outcomes for participants from Capital IDEA and estimated labor-market impacts for participants using a quasi-experimental design. They measured the value added of intensive occupational skills investments with wrap-around support services provided through Capital IDEA relative to registration for or receipt of low-intensity labor-force attachment services. Comparison group members drawn from the local Employment Service, and WIA "core services" rolls were closely matched on an array of variables, including age, race/ethnicity, gender, and prior employment and earnings patterns, through a technique known as weighted multivariate matching.[12] Incremental training impacts were estimated over a five-year period following program entry. The study is continuing, so longer term impacts will be documented as additional data become available.

Five years (20 quarters) after their initial entry into training, Capital IDEA participants, a group that entered in the 2003–2005 period and included both graduates and program dropouts, enjoyed a substantial earnings advantage over comparison group members (Figure 11.1).[13] At the end of five years, the statistically significant advantage was about $1,500 per quarter (or about $6,000 per year) and still widening. By the end of the period, participants were experiencing roughly a 100 percent gain in quarterly earnings compared with their two-year pre-program

Figure 11.1 Quarterly Earnings for Capital IDEA Participants and Members of a Comparison Group

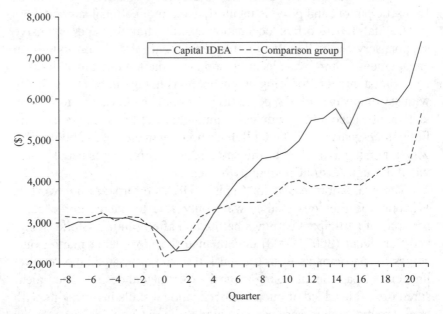

NOTE: "0" represents the participant's entry into the training program.
SOURCE: Smith, King, and Schroeder (2008).

average. In contrast, the earnings of the comparison group members who only had the benefit of less intensive labor-force attachment services flattened out for much of the post-entry period.

Further analysis suggests that, much like the results reported in a "tipping point" study in Washington State (Prince and Jenkins 2005), the earnings impacts appear to be strongly associated with program completion and attaining the occupational (nursing/allied health) certificates. As Figure 11.2 shows, program completers actually garnered most of the impacts. In addition to enjoying substantial continuing earnings effects from Capital IDEA's sectoral workforce-training program, Capital IDEA participants were also significantly more likely to qualify for Unemployment Insurance benefits and much less likely to claim them in the follow-up period than were their comparison group counterparts (Smith, King, and Schroeder 2008).

**Figure 11.2 Quarterly Earnings for Capital IDEA Program Completers
and Members of a Comparison Group**

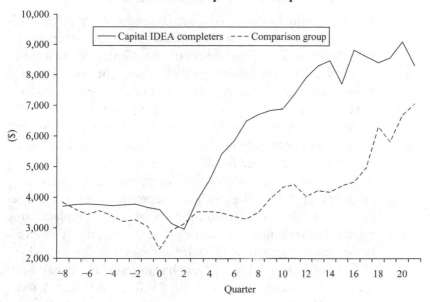

NOTE: "0" represents the participant's entry into the training program.
SOURCE: Unpublished results for 2003–2005 Capital IDEA program completers (Ray
  Marshall Center).

These results provide compelling empirical evidence that a sectoral
training strategy can be successfully implemented through an established workforce intermediary with strong employer engagement and
commitment to a high-skills, high-wage strategy for its participants.

Promising sectoral training programs have been operating and
are now emerging in other parts of the country as well, including the
following.

- *Workforce Solutions—The Gulf Coast Workforce Board* (Houston, TX). For the past several years, Houston's workforce board
  has been operating a large-scale sectoral initiative focused
  on the region's expansive health-care industry sector, which
  includes numerous hospitals and universities, among other employers (see Love et al. 2006). This effort has been driven by
  perceived shortages of nurses in the region, and the initiative

has advocated successfully for improvements in Texas state policies and budgets for nursing education.

- *The Wisconsin Regional Training Partnership* (WRTP) (Milwaukee, WI). WRTP is a nonprofit organization begun during the 1990s with the assistance of the Center on Wisconsin Strategy at the University of Wisconsin. The initiative is a collaboration of employers, unions, and community residents developed in response to the devastating decade of the 1980s, during which Milwaukee lost a third of its industrial base, and poverty and unemployment rose dramatically. WRTP helped manufacturing recover in Milwaukee by assisting local companies to modernize plants and adopt innovative workplace practices; upgrading the skills of incumbent workers; and recruiting, training, and mentoring new workers to replace large numbers of retiring workers. By the year 2003, the WRTP collaboration had grown to 125 worksite partners covering about 125,000 employees. The partners had invested more than $100 million in education and training. WRTP had placed more than 1,400 community residents into jobs at family-supporting wages. In short, WRTP has benefited employers, workers, unions, and the community (Bernhardt, Dresser, and Rogers 2004). In recent years, WRTP has expanded to replicate its collaboration model in other Milwaukee industries, including construction, health care, transportation, and utilities.

- *The Investing in Workforce Intermediaries Initiative/National Fund for Workforce Solutions* (multisite). This initiative, which was initially created and funded by the Annie E. Casey, Ford, and Rockefeller Foundations, began in 2004–2005 in five sites and one state—Austin, Baltimore, Boston, New York, San Francisco, and Pennsylvania. Sites with workforce-intermediary organizations and supporting partners were provided with seed funding and encouraged to focus their efforts on a few growth sectors of their local economies while creating career pathways for less-skilled workers. Health care was chosen as a target sector in most of the sites. The initiative has grown into a larger effort involving about a dozen sites around the country with funding from the National Fund for Workforce Solutions, which includes support from foundations, corporations, and the U.S. Department of Labor's Employment and Training Administration (see Griffen 2008; National Fund for Workforce Solutions 2008). A related initiative, the *Jobs-to-Careers Initiative*, supports a number of intermediary-driven, work-based learning and career advancement projects in health care with funding from the Robert Wood Johnson and Hitachi Foundations and others. Boston-based Jobs for the Future is coordinating all of these efforts.

- *WIRED Initiative* (multisite). The U.S. Department of Labor's Employment and Training Administration began the *Workforce Innovation in Regional Economic Development (WIRED)* demonstrations in 13 regions in late 2006 and has since expanded to a total of 39 regions across the country.[14] Regional WIRED projects, not surprisingly, vary widely in their sectoral emphases, funding mix, and participating actors, but all of the projects are explicitly focused on more closely aligning economic and workforce-development strategies in key sectors, often with the active involvement of workforce-intermediary organizations.

- *Tulsa Initiative* (Tulsa, OK). The Ray Marshall Center is currently working with colleagues in a project led by Harvard's Center for the Developing Child to design and implement a sectoral jobs strategy for the parents of children in local Head Start and Early Head Start programs in a unique dual-generation anti-poverty initiative. The initiative draws on findings of the interdisciplinary science of early childhood and early brain development, as well as emerging evidence that children in families with stable and growing incomes have significantly improved academic and behavioral outcomes (Yoshikawa, Weisner, and Lowe 2006). Candidate target sectors for the Tulsa Initiative include health care, manufacturing (including aerospace), early childhood development, and construction.

GUIDING PRINCIPLES FOR COORDINATED
SECTORAL DEVELOPMENT

Sectoral workforce programs are labor-market intermediaries that serve dual customers—both employers and workers (and job applicants) in an industrial cluster of firms that they come to know well. Successful sectoral strategies can address multiple goals simultaneously, including strengthening regional competitiveness and workforce preparedness and promoting broadly shared prosperity and family self-sufficiency. They can align workforce development with economic development to benefit local residents. The National Center on Education and the Economy (NCEE) has conducted a series of case studies of local initiatives to combine workforce development with economic development (NCEE 2007).

Effective industry engagement is critical to success. Success begins with careful selection of industries and firms facing shortages of skilled workers, collaborating with employers to clearly identify the skills needed, and finding ways to fulfill those needs. Sectoral workforce programs usually focus selectively on good jobs offering high pay along with benefits and opportunities for advancement. Alternatively, they may target low-wage jobs that are key entry points into the labor market for low-skilled individuals but the jobs could be improved through restructuring or connecting them with pathways leading to higher wage jobs. Sectoral workforce development aims at long-term retention and career advancement, whether through ladders or lattices, in the "right" firms and industries. As programs build capacity, they can partner with multiple sectors, enabling them to offer participants a wider array of occupational opportunities.

Sectoral workforce programs operate as intermediaries between the supply and demand sides of the labor market, serving as interpreters, integrators, and facilitators. There is a critical need for good communication between economic developers and workforce developers, between industry and educators, and between participants and social service agencies. Sectoral workforce programs can use a variety of approaches that benefit low-income workers by producing "systems changes" in industry practices, education and training, and/or public policy.

Training is geared to employer needs. Appropriate preparation in math and reading and in acquisition of English language is usually a key beginning, but effective accelerated remediation strategies and preparation in these foundation skills should be closely connected to occupational skill preparation. Such connections are often missing.

Sectoral programs partner with community colleges and help them become more effective at producing the skills that employers need. At least one and often two years of education or training beyond high school plus certification are needed to produce levels of knowledge and skills that are meaningful to industry. This is not a new message. Similar recommendations have been made by the New Commission on Skills for the American Workforce in their 2006 report, *Tough Choices or Tough Times*, and by the Skills2Compete campaign.[15] Long-term, serious training is markedly different from workforce development of the past. As LaLonde concluded in his 1995 review of evaluations of public training programs: "The best summary of evidence about the impact of past programs is that we got what we paid for . . . Not surprisingly, modest investments usually yield modest gains—too small to have much effect on poverty rates" (LaLonde 1995, p. 149).

Wherever possible, classroom instruction is joined with work-based learning, combining earning with learning through paid internships, apprenticeships, or other hands-on practical experience. This not only enhances learning but also gives job seekers early exposure to the types of work involved, provides an important technique for engaging employers, and offers a source of income for households during long-term training.

Case/care management is provided through the program to encourage completion of training. This includes individual counseling, peer group meetings, tuition assistance, and work supports (such as child care, transportation, social services, and income supplements). Follow-through services are available afterward to help ensure retention on the job after graduation.

To be sustained, a sectoral workforce program needs to maintain good records and build a track record of performance through credible evaluation of results achieved, producing outcomes for workers, employers, and the public. Evaluation not only documents program success to justify continued funding, but also feeds a process of continuous improvement.

Revitalizing Active Labor-Market Policy in America

Evidence is accumulating to demonstrate that many workforce-development programs yield strong rates of return to participants, employers, and the public (King 2008; King et al. 2008; Smith, King, and Schroeder 2007). Yet for decades, workforce development has been relegated to a minor role in American economic policy for reasons that are now well documented. As noted in this chapter, substantial work has been under way in recent years to more closely align economic- and workforce-development policy through sectoral strategies and to introduce new organizational forms—workforce intermediaries—that could and should raise its profile. Sectoral workforce strategies—bolstered through the use of workforce intermediaries and pressing for high skills and high wages for all workers, including those who have not had access to good opportunities—represent the way forward.

Notwithstanding the deep recession that has been under way since 2007, there are likely to soon be real opportunities for turning the nation's current workforce-development situation around through such active labor-market policies. First, while many older workers may choose to work longer to restore the value of their severely depleted retirement savings, jobs will open up in the future as the baby boom generation begins to retire in large numbers. Second, as the Aspen Institute's 2003 report suggested, the United States will face three important gaps in the near future: workers, skills, and wages. More effective workforce strategies are needed to ensure that workers will be there with the right skills to address these gaps as they surface. Third, considerable knowledge and experience have been developed—at all levels—about how to connect economic and workforce policies for enhanced, lasting impacts that can benefit employers and workers; the result is insight that can now be put to use more broadly. Finally, there seems to be a growing, though grudging, recognition that the labor-market policy mix the United States has been content with for years, one tilted heavily toward passive rather than active elements, has not worked all that well and that new, more active approaches are in order.

The challenge will be to secure the necessary resources and reach a sufficient scale in order to truly make such policies work at the level we now need. The sectoral workforce-development approaches outlined in this chapter hold enormous promise and would move the United States much more toward the active labor-market policy that is sorely needed.

Notes

1. Mangum (1976) and Clague and Kramer (1976) document the early history and evolution of what were then known as "manpower" policies.
2. In-sourcing involves arranging for previously subcontracted work to be done in-house, often in a stand-alone facility.
3. For example, Stevens (2001) describes the climbing wall metaphor and discusses its implications for workforce-development policy, while the Council for Adult and Experiential Learning (2005) outlines the way career lattices are being used in designing effective interventions for training and employing nurses.
4. This research is reinforced and expanded upon in a follow-up volume using LEHD data by Brown, Haltiwanger, and Lane (2006).
5. Barnow and King (2005) describe the "system" in a report prepared for the Rockefeller Institute of Government. Two companion volumes (Rockefeller Institute of Government 2004a, b) offer details for the eight states and more than a dozen local areas that participated in the field network study, which was funded by the U.S. Department of Labor's Employment and Training Administration and led by the Rockefeller Institute of Government.
6. These amounts are derived mainly from the President's FY 2006 budget request and related documents. Kletzer and Koch estimate that, including all active and passive labor-market activities, U.S. spending in 2000 amounted to only about 0.38 percent of gross domestic product.
7. State Unemployment Insurance–funded training programs, their key features, and the literature on their effectiveness are reviewed in King and Smith (2007).
8. Federal funds have historically accounted for only about 6–10 percent of total Perkins spending. Overall community and technical college spending on workforce-related programs is likely to be many times greater than the total shown here.
9. This discussion draws on King (2008).
10. This discussion draws on Glover et al. (2005).
11. The National Economic Development and Law Center has recently been renamed Insight Center for Community Economic Development. See http://www.insightcced.org/.
12. Details of the matching procedure, a variation of "nearest-neighbor" matching, are provided in Smith, King, and Schroeder (2008).

13. Krueger (2003) observed a similar pattern of earnings for similar investments in training and workforce services.
14. See http://www.doleta.gov/wired/ for more information.
15. See http:// www.skills2compete.org for more information.

References

Andersson, Frederik, Harry J. Holzer, and Julia I. Lane. 2005. *Moving Up or Moving On: Who Advances in the Low-Wage Labor Market.* New York: Russell Sage Foundation.

Aspen Institute. 2003. *Growing Faster Together or More Slowly Apart.* Washington, DC: Aspen Institute.

Atkinson, Robert D. 2005. *The Past and Future of America's Economy: Long Waves of Innovation That Power Cycles of Growth.* Northampton, MA: Edward Elgar.

Auer, Peter, Umit Efendioglu, and Janine Leschke. 2008. *Active Labor Market Policy around the World: Coping with the Consequences of Globalization.* Washington, DC: International Labor Organization and Brookings Institution Press.

Barnow, Burt S., and Christopher T. King, eds. 2000. *Improving the Odds: Increasing the Effectiveness of Publicly Funded Training.* Washington, DC: Urban Institute Press.

———. 2005. *The Workforce Investment Act in Eight States.* Occasional Paper 2005-01. Washington, DC: Employment and Training Administration, U.S. Department of Labor. http://www.doleta.gov/reports/searcheta/occ/eta_occasional_papers.cfm (accessed March 7, 2009).

Bernhardt, Annette, Laura Dresser, and Joel Rogers. 2004. "Taking the High Road in Milwaukee: The Wisconsin Regional Partnership." In *Partnering for Change: Unions and Community Groups Build Coalitions for Economic Justice*, David Reynolds, ed. New York: M.E. Sharpe, pp. 231–247.

Borjas, George. 2007. "Immigration Policy and Human Capital." In *Reshaping the American Workforce in a Changing Economy,* Harry J. Holzer and Demetra S. Nightingale, eds. Washington, DC: Urban Institute Press, pp. 183–200.

Briggs, Vernon M. Jr. 1973. *Chicanos and Rural Poverty.* Baltimore: Johns Hopkins Press.

———. 1984. *Immigration Policy and the American Labor Force.* Baltimore: Johns Hopkins Press.

———. 2003. *Mass Immigration and the National Interest: Directions for a New Century.* Armonk, NY: M.E. Sharpe.

Briggs, Vernon M. Jr., and Ray Marshall. 1967. *The Negro and Apprenticeship.* Baltimore: Johns Hopkins Press.

Brown, Claire, John Haltiwanger, and Julia Lane. 2006. *Economic Turbulence: Is a Volatile Economy Good for America?* Chicago, IL: University of Chicago Press.

Bureau of Labor Statistics (BLS). n.d. *Databases, Tables and Calculations by Subject.* Washington, DC: U.S. Department of Labor. http://www.bls.gov/data (accessed September 22, 2009).

Cappelli, Peter. 1999. *The New Deal at Work: Managing the Market-Driven Workforce.* Boston: Harvard Business School Press.

Cappelli, Peter, Laurie Bassi, Harry Katz, David Knoke, Paul Osterman, and Michael Useem. 1997. *Change at Work.* New York: Oxford University Press.

Clague, Ewan, and Leo Kramer. 1976. *Manpower Policies and Programs: A Review, 1935–1973.* Kalamazoo, MI: W.E. Upjohn Institute for Employment Research.

Clark, Peggy, and Steven L. Dawson. 1995. *Jobs and the Urban Poor: Privately Initiated Sectoral Strategies.* Washington, DC: Aspen Institute.

Conway, Maureen, Amy Blair, Stephen L. Dawson, and Linda Dworak-Muñoz. 2007. *Sectoral Strategies for Low Income Workers: Lessons from the Field.* Washington, DC: Workforce Strategies Initiative, Aspen Institute.

Council for Adult and Experiential Learning. 2005. *How Career Lattices Solve Nursing and Other Workforce Shortages in Healthcare: A Guide for Workforce Investment Boards, One-Stop Career Centers, Healthcare Employers, Industry Alliances, and Higher Education Providers.* Chicago, IL: Council for Adult and Experiential Learning.

Friedman, Thomas. 2005. *The World Is Flat: A Brief History of the Twenty-First Century.* New York: Farrar, Straus, and Giroux.

Galbraith, James K. 1998. *Created Unequal: The Crisis in American Pay.* A Century Foundation Book. New York: Free Press.

Giloth, Robert P., ed. 2004. *Workforce Intermediaries for the Twenty-First Century.* Philadelphia: Temple University Press.

Glover, Robert W., Suzanne Hershey, Christopher T. King, and Deepshikha Roychowdhury. 2005. *Critical Skills Shortage Report.* Austin, TX: Ray Marshall Center for the Study of Human Resources, University of Texas.

Griffen, Sarah. 2008. *Sustaining the Promise: Realizing the Potential of Workforce Intermediaries and Sectoral Projects.* Boston: Jobs for the Future.

Grubb, Norton W. 1996a. *Working in the Middle: Strengthening Education and Training for the Mid-skilled Labor Force.* San Francisco: Jossey-Bass Publishers.

————. 1996b. *Learning to Work: The Case for Reintegrating Job Training and Education.* New York: Russell Sage Foundation.

Grubb, Norton W., N. Badway, D. Bell, B. Chi, C. King, J. Herr, H. Prince, R. Kazis, L. Hicks, and J. C. Taylor. 1999. *Toward Order from Chaos: State Efforts to Reform Their Workforce Development Systems.* MDS-1249. Berkeley, CA: National Center for Research in Vocational Education.

Harbison, Frederick. 1973. *Human Resources as the Wealth of Nations.* New York: Oxford University Press.

Harrington, Michael. 1963. *The Other America: Poverty in the United States.* New York: Penguin Books.

Holzer, Harry J., and Robert I. Lerman. 2007. *America's Forgotten Middle-Skill Jobs: Education and Training Requirements in the Next Decade and Beyond.* Washington, DC: The Workforce Alliance. http://www.skills2 compete.org/atf/cf/{8E9806BF-4669-4217-AF74-26F62108EA68}/ ForgottenJobsReport%20Final.pdf (accessed January 22, 2007).

Killingsworth, Charles. 1968. "The Labor Market 'Twist' Hypothesis." *Monthly Labor Review* 91(9): 12–17.

King, Christopher T. 2008. "Does Workforce Development Work?" Paper prepared for the Workforce Narrative Project. Baltimore: Annie E. Casey Foundation. http://www.aecf.org/~/media/PublicationFiles/doeswkfdevewkr .pdf (accessed March 7, 2009).

King, Christopher T., Robert E. McPherson, and Donald W. Long. 2000. "Public Labor Market Policy for the Twenty-First Century." In *Back to Shared Prosperity: The Growing Inequality of Wealth and Income in the United States,* Ray Marshall, ed. Armonk, NY: M.E. Sharpe, pp. 275–286.

King, Christopher T., and Tara Carter Smith. 2007. "State Unemployment Insurance–Supported Training Funds." In *Strategies for Financing Workforce Intermediaries: Working Papers*, Heath Prince, ed. Boston: Jobs for the Future, pp. 69–122.

King, Christopher T., Ying Tang, Tara Carter Smith, Daniel Schroeder, and Burt S. Barnow. 2008. *Returns from Investments in Workforce Services: Texas Statewide Estimates for Participants, Taxpayers, and Society.* Austin, TX: Ray Marshall Center for the Study of Human Resources, University of Texas.

Kletzer, Lori G., and William L. Koch. 2004. "International Experience with Job Training: Lessons for the United States." In *Job Training Policy in the United States*, Christopher O'Leary, Robert Straits, and Stephen Wander, eds. Kalamazoo, MI: W.E. Upjohn Institute for Employment Research, pp. 245–288.

Krueger, Alan B. 2003. "Inequality, Too Much of a Good Thing." In *Inequality in America: What Role for Human Capital Policies?* Benjamin M. Friedman, ed. Cambridge, MA: MIT Press, pp. 1–75.

LaLonde, Robert J. 1995. "The Promise of Public Sector–Sponsored Training Programs." *Journal of Economic Perspectives* 9(2): 149–168.

Laufer, Jessica, and Sian Winship. 2004. "Perception vs. Reality: Employer Attitudes and the Rebranding of Workforce Intermediates." In *Workforce Intermediaries for the Twenty-First Century*, Robert P. Giloth, ed. Philadelphia: Temple University Press, pp. 216–240.

Lautsch, Brenda, and Paul Osterman. 1998. "Changing the Constraints: A Successful Employment and Training Strategy." In *Jobs and Economic Development: Strategies and Practice*, Robert Giloth, ed. Thousand Oaks, CA: Sage Publications, pp. 214–233.

Lerman, Robert I., Signe-Mary McKernan, and Stephanie Riegg. 2004. "The Scope of Employer-Provided Training in the United States: Who, What, Where and How Much." In *Job Training Policy in the United States*, Christopher O'Leary, Robert Straits, and Stephen Wander, eds. Kalamazoo, MI: W.E. Upjohn Institute for Employment Research, pp. 211–244.

Levitan, Sar A., Garth L. Mangum, and Ray Marshall. 1981. *Human Resources and Labor Markets: Labor and Manpower in the American Economy*, 3d ed. New York: Harper and Row.

Levy, Frank, and Richard Murnane. 2004. *The New Division of Labor.* New York: Russell Sage Foundation.

Long, Clarence D. 1972. "A Theory of Creeping Unemployment and Labor Force Replacement." In *An Anthology of Labor Economics: Readings and Commentary*, Ray Marshall and Richard Perlman, eds. New York: John Wiley & Sons, pp. 323–335. Reprint of Long's 1960 address to the Catholic Economic Association Annual Meeting, St. Louis, Missouri.

Love, Karen, Robert McPherson, Susan Distefano, and Tabitha Rice. 2006. "The Gulf Coast Health Services Steering Committee: A Business-Education Partnership to Solve the Registered Nurse Shortage." *Journal of Nursing Administration* 36(12): 558–566.

Maguire, Sheila, Joshua Freeley, Carol Clymer, and Maureen Conway. 2009. *Job Training That Works: Findings from the Sectoral Employment Impact Study*. Philadelphia: Public/Private Ventures.

Mangum, Garth L. 1976. "Manpower Policies and Worker Status Since the 1930s." In *Federal Policies and Worker Status since the Thirties,* Joseph P. Goldberg, Eileen Ahern, William Haber, and Rudolph A. Oswald, eds. Madison, WI: Industrial Relations Research Association.

Marshall, Alfred. 1890. *Principles of Economics*. London: McMillan and Co.

Marshall, Ray. 1984. "Selective Employment Programs and Economic Policy." *Journal of Economic Issues* 18(1): 117–142.

————, ed. 2000. *Back to Shared Prosperity: The Growing Inequality of Wealth and Income in America.* Armonk, NY: M.E. Sharpe.

Marshall, Ray, and Marc Tucker. 1992. *Thinking for a Living: Education and the Wealth of Nations.* New York: Basic Books.

McIntosh, Moly F., and Cecelia Elena Rouse. 2009. *The Other College: Retention and Completion Rates among Two-Year College Students.* Washington, DC: Center for American Progress. http://www.americanprogress.org (accessed March 7, 2009).

Mishel, Lawrence, Jared Bernstein, and Heidi Shierholz. 2009. *The State of Working America 2008/2009.* An Economic Policy Institute Book. Ithaca, NY: ILR Press.

National Center on Education and the Economy (NCEE). 2007. *Under One Roof.* 3 vols. Washington, DC: National Center on Education and the Economy.

National Commission for Manpower Policy. 1978. *Labor Market Intermediaries.* Special Report no. 22. Washington, DC: U.S. Government Printing Office.

National Fund for Workforce Solutions. 2008. *National Fund for Workforce Solutions: Experience and Evidence.* Boston, MA: Jobs for the Future.

National Governors Association (NGA) Center for Best Practices. 2002. *A Governor's Guide to Cluster-Based Economic Development.* Report prepared by Stuart A. Rosenfeld. Washington, DC: NGA Center for Best Practices.

New Commission on Skills of the American Workforce. 2007. *Tough Choices or Tough Times.* Washington, DC: National Center on Education and the Economy.

Osterman, Paul. 2007. "Employment and Training Policies: New Directions for Less Skilled Adults." In *Reshaping the American Workforce in a Changing Economy,* Harry J. Holzer and Demetra S. Nightingale, eds. Washington, DC: Urban Institute Press, pp. 119–154.

Paradise, Andrew. 2008. *2008 State of the Industry Report: ASTD's Annual Review of Trends in Workplace Learning and Performance.* Alexandria, VA: American Society for Training and Development.

Pindus, Nancy M., Carolyn O'Brien, Maureen Conway, Conaway Haskins, and Ida Rademacher. 2004. *Evaluation of the Sectoral Employment Demonstration Program.* Washington, DC: Urban Institute.

Porter, Michael E. 1990. *The Competitive Advantage of Nations.* London: Macmillan.

————. 1998a. "Clusters and the New Economics of Competition." *Harvard Business Review* 76(6): 77–90.

————. 1998b. *On Competition*. Boston: Harvard Business School Publications.

————. 2000. "Location, Competition, and Economic Development: Local Clusters in a Global Economy." *Economic Development Quarterly* 14(1): 15–34.

————. 2003. "Economic Performance of Regions." *Regional Studies* 37(6/7): 549–578.

Price, James L. 1977. *The Study of Turnover*. Ames, IA: Iowa State University Press.

Prince, David, and Davis Jenkins. 2005. *Building Pathways to Success for Low-Skill Adult Students: Lessons for Community College Policy and Practice from a Longitudinal Student Tracking Study*. CCRC Brief no. 25. New York: Community College Research Center, Teachers College, Columbia University. http://ccrc.tc.columbia.edu/Publication.asp?uid=288 (accessed March 7, 2009).

Rademacher, Ida, Marshall Bear, and Maureen Conway. 2001. *Project QUEST: A Case Study of a Sectoral Employment Development Approach*. Washington, DC: Aspen Institute, Economic Opportunity Program.

Rockefeller Institute of Government. 2004a. *The Workforce Investment Act in Eight States: State Case Studies from a Field Network Evaluation, Volume One*. Occasional Paper 2004-02. Washington, DC: Employment and Training Administration, U.S. Department of Labor http://www.doleta.gov/reports/searcheta/occ/eta_occasional_papers.cfm (accessed March 7, 2009).

————. 2004b. *The Workforce Investment Act in Eight States: State Case Studies from a Field Network Evaluation, Volume Two*. Occasional Paper 2004-03. Washington, DC: Employment and Training Administration, U.S. Department of Labor. http://www.doleta.gov/reports/searcheta/occ/eta_occasional_papers.cfm (accessed March 7, 2009).

Roder, Anne, with Carol Clymer and Laura Wyckoff. 2008. *Targeting Industries, Training Workers and Improving Opportunities*. Final Report from the Sectoral Employment Initiative. Philadelphia: Public/Private Ventures.

Rosenfeld, Stuart A. 1997. "Bringing Business Clusters into the Mainstream of Economic Development." *European Planning Studies* 5(1): 3–25.

————. 2002. *Just Clusters: Economic Development Strategies that Reach More People and Places*. Chapel Hill, NC: Regional Technology Strategies.

Simon, Martin J., and Linda Hoffman. 2005. *The Next Generation of Workforce Development Project: A Six-State Policy Academy to Enhance Connections between Workforce and Economic Development Policy.* Final Project Report. Washington, DC: National Governors Association Center for Best Practices.

Smith, Tara Carter, Christopher T. King, and Daniel G. Schroeder. 2007. *Local Investments in Workforce Development: Initial Evaluation Findings*. Final Report. Austin, TX: Ray Marshall Center for the Study of Human Resources, University of Texas.

———. 2008. *Local Investments in Workforce Development: Evaluation Update*. Austin, TX: Ray Marshall Center for the Study of Human Resources, University of Texas.

Stevens, David W. 2001. "Welfare to Work Policy—Getting a Job is a Good First Step: What Should Follow?" Baltimore, MD: Jacob France Institute, University of Baltimore. Revised version of a paper presented at the America's Workforce Network Research Conference, held in Washington, DC, June 26–27, 2001.

Yoshikawa, Hiro, Thomas S. Weisner, and Edward D. Lowe, eds. 2006. *Making It Work*. New York: Russell Sage Foundation.

Zandniapour, Lily, and Laureen Conway. 2002. *Gaining Ground: The Labor Market Progress of Participants of Sectoral Economic Development Programs*. SEDLP Research Report no. 3. Washington, DC: Aspen Institute.

Appendix A

Vernon M. Briggs Jr. Bibliography

BOOKS AND MONOGRAPHS

The Negro and Apprenticeship. (With Ray Marshall.) Baltimore: Johns Hopkins University Press, 1967, 278 pp.

Equal Apprenticeship Opportunities: The Nature of the Issue and the New York Experience. (With Ray Marshall.) Policy Papers in Human Resources no. 10, A Joint Publication of the Institute of Labor and Industrial Relations, University of Michigan, and the National Manpower Policy Task Force, November 1968, 57 pp.

They Have the Power—We Have the People: The Status of Equal Employment Opportunity in Houston, Texas. Washington, DC: U.S. Equal Employment Opportunity Commission, 1970, 103 pp.

Negro Employment in the South, Vol. I: The Houston Labor Market. Manpower Research Monograph no. 23. Washington, DC: Manpower Administration, U.S. Department of Labor, 1971, 97 pp.

Chicanos and Rural Poverty. Baltimore: Johns Hopkins University Press, 1973, 81 pp.

The Mexico–United States Border: Public Policy and Chicano Economic Welfare. Studies in Human Resource Development no. 2. Austin: Center for the Study of Human Resources and Bureau of Business Research of the University of Texas, 1974, 28 pp.

Mexican Migration and the U.S. Labor Market: A Mounting Issue for the Seventies. Studies in Human Resource Development no. 3. Austin: Center for the Study of Human Resources and Bureau of Business Research of the University of Texas, 1975, 37 pp.

The Chicano Worker. (With Walt Fogel and Fred Schmidt.) Austin, TX: University of Texas Press, 1977, 129 pp. (Paperback version published in August 1979.)

Employment, Income, and Welfare in the Rural South. (With John Adams, Brian Rungeling, and Lewis Smith.) New York: Praeger Publishing, 1977, 357 pp.

The Feasibility of Bilingual Vocational Training through the Border College Consortium Approach. (With Domingo Arechiga, Thomas Deliganis, and Hiram Goad.) Laredo, TX: Border Junior College Consortium, 1978, 171 pp.

Human Needs and Income Supplement Programs in the Rural South. (With Brian Rungeling and Lewis H. Smith.) Oxford, MS: Center for Manpower Studies, University of Mississippi, 1978, 29 pp.

Labor Economics: Wages, Employment, and Trade Unionism. (With Ray Marshall and Allan King.) Homewood, IL: Richard D. Irwin, 1980, 594 pp.

Youth Employment Programs in the Southwest. Austin, TX: Bureau of Business Research of the University of Texas, 1980, 47 pp.

Apprenticeship Research: Emerging Findings and Future Trends. (With Felician Foltman.) Ithaca, NY: New York State School of Industrial and Labor Relations, Cornell University, 1981, 224 pp.

Labor Economics: Wages, Employment, Trade Unionism, and Public Policy. (With Ray Marshall and Allan King.) Homewood, IL: Richard D. Irwin, Inc., 1984, 676 pp. (Translated into Spanish in 1987 and published by the Centro de Publicaciones of the Ministerio de Trabajo y Seguridad Social, Madrid, Spain.)

Public Service Employment in the Rural South. (With Brian Rungeling and Lewis Smith.) Austin, TX: Bureau of Business Research, Graduate School of Business, University of Texas, 1984, 144 pp.

Immigration Policy and the American Labor Force. Baltimore: Johns Hopkins University Press, 1984, 293 pp.

Immigration: Issues and Policies. (With Marta Tienda.) Salt Lake City, UT: Olympus Publishing Company, 1985, 146 pp.

The Internationalization of the U.S. Economy: Its Labor Market Implications. Salt Lake City, UT: Olympus Publishing Company, 1986, 98 pp.

The Population and Labor Force of New York: 1990–2050. (With Leon Bouvier.) Washington, DC: Population Reference Bureau, 1988, 90 pp.

Labor Economics: Theory, Institutions, and Public Policy. (With Ray Marshall.) Homewood, IL: Richard D. Irwin, 1989, 654 pp.

Mass Immigration and the National Interest. Armonk, NY: M.E. Sharpe, 1992, 276 pp. (Paperback version published simultaneously.)

Immigration Policy: A Tool of Labor Economics? Policy Brief no. 7. Annandale-on-Hudson, NY: Jerome Levy Economics Institute, 1993, 40 pp.

Still an Open Door? U.S. Immigration Policy and the American Economy. (With Stephen Moore.) Washington, DC: American University Press, 1994, 167 pp. (Paperback version published simultaneously.)

Mass Immigration and the National Interest, 2nd ed., Armonk, NY: M.E. Sharpe, 1996, 283 pp. (Paperback version published simultaneously.)

Immigration and American Unionism. Ithaca, NY: Cornell University Press, 2001, 254pp. (Paperback version published simultaneously.)

The U.S. Population and Its Civilian Labor Force: Evolving Incongruity. Ithaca, NY.: Cornell University Book Store custom publishing, 2002, 62 pp.

Mass Immigration and the National Interest: Policy Directions for a New Century. Armonk, NY: M.E. Sharpe, 2003, 320 pp. (Paperback version published simultaneously.)

ARTICLES

NOTE: Many of the following articles may be viewed on the Digital Commons of the School of Industrial and Labor Relations, Cornell University. See http://digitalcommons.ilr.cornell.edu/hrpubs (accessed September 23, 2009).

"The Mutual Aid Pact of the Airline Industry." *Industrial and Labor Relations Review* (October 1965), pp. 3–20.

"The Strike Insurance Plan of the Railroad Industry." *Industrial Relations* (February 1967), pp. 205–212.

"Negro Participation in Apprenticeship Programs." (With Ray Marshall.) *Journal of Human Resources* (Winter 1967), pp. 51–69.

"Remedies for Discrimination in Apprenticeship Programs." (With Ray Marshall.) *Industrial Relations* (May 1967), pp. 303–320.

"Labor in the South: Manpower Programs and Regional Development." *Monthly Labor Review* (March 1968), pp. 55–61.

"A Review Article: The Report of the Commission on Civil Disorders." *Journal of Economic Issues* (June 1968), pp. 200–210.

"The Negro in American Industry: A Review of Seven Studies." *Journal of Human Resources* (Summer 1970), pp. 371–381. Reprinted in *The Economics of Black America* by Harold Vatter and Thomas Palm. New York: Harcourt Brace, 1972, pp. 122–130.

"National Manpower Policy." *The Encyclopedia of Education.* New York: Macmillan Company, Vol. 6, 1971, pp. 60–65.

"Chicanos and Rural Poverty: A Continuing Issue for the 1970s." *Poverty and Human Resources* (March 1972), pp. 3–24.

"The Emergency Employment Act of 1971: The Texas Experience." In *The Emergency Employment Act: An Interim Assessment.* Washington, DC: U.S. Congress, Committee on Labor and Public Welfare (May 1972), pp. 153–186.

"The Federal Emergency Employment Act of 1971: An Appraisal of the Texas Experience." *Public Affairs Comment.* Austin, TX: Lyndon B. Johnson School of Public Affairs (May 1973), pp. 1–6.

"Mexican Immigrants and the Labor Market." *Texas Business Review* (April 1975), pp. 85–90.

"Mexican Workers in the United States Labour Market: A Contemporary Dilemma." *International Labour Review* (November 1975), pp. 351–368. (Simultaneously published in the French and Spanish editions of the journal.)

"Illegal Aliens: The Need for a More Restrictive Border Policy." *Social Science Quarterly* (December 1975), pp. 477–484.

"Illegal Immigration and the American Labor Force: The Use of 'Soft' Data for Analysis." *American Behavioral Scientist* (January–February 1976), pp. 351–363.

"Railroad Brotherhoods." *Dictionary of American History.* Charles Scribner's Sons, Vol. 5, 1976, pp. 19–20.

"The Problem of Illegal Immigration." *Texas Business Review* (August 1977), pp. 171–175.

"Issues in Full Employment Policy: Immigration." *Labor Law Journal* (August 1977), pp. 495–500.

"La Confrontacion del Chicano con el Immigrante Mexicano." *Foro Internacional.* Publicada por el Colegio de Mexico (Enero–Marzo 1978), pp. 514–521.

"Welfare Reform and the Plight of the Poor in the Rural South." (With Brian Rungeling and Lewis Smith.) *Monthly Labor Review* (April 1978), pp. 28–30.

"Wage and Occupational Differences between Black and White Men: Labor Market Discrimination in the Rural South." (With Lewis Smith, Brian Rungeling, and James Smith.) *Southern Economic Journal* (July 1978), pp. 250–257.

"The Quest for an Enforceable Immigration Policy." *Thrust: The Journal for Employment and Training Professionals* (Fall 1979), pp. 385–400.

"Youth Employment Programs: Three Southwestern Case Studies." *Texas Business Review* (May 1980), pp. 149–154.

"Economic Development: A Poverty Solution for the Rural South?" (With Brian Rungeling.) *Growth and Change* (October 1980), pp. 31–35.

"Illegal Immigration: A Continuing Issue for the 1980s." *Bell Journal* (Spring 1981), pp. 10–19.

"Employment and Income Issues in the Southwest for the 1980s." *Adherent: A Journal of Comprehensive Employment Training and Human Resource Development* (July 1981), pp. 41–58.

"Report of the Select Commission on Immigration and Refugee Policy: A Critique." *Texas Business Review* (January 1982), pp. 11–15.

"Illegal Immigration from Mexico and Its Labor Force Implications." *ILR Report* (Spring 1983), pp. 7–12.

"Non-Immigrant Labor Policy in the United States." *Journal of Economic Issues* (September 1983), pp. 609–630.

"Methods of Analysis of Illegal Immigration into the United States." *International Migration Review* (Fall 1984), pp. 623–641.

"An Immigration Policy for Today." *Business Forum*, Journal of the School of Business and Economics of California State University at Los Angeles (Fall 1985), pp. 9–13.

"The 'Albatross' of Immigration Reform: Temporary Worker Policy in the United States." *International Migration Review* (Winter 1986), pp. 995–1019.

"Immigration Reform's Unfinished Agenda." *Human Resource Executive* (May 1987), pp. 42–43.

"Human Resource Development and the Formulation of National Economic Policy." *Journal of Economic Issues* (September 1987), pp. 1207–1240.

"Youth Employment and Training Programs: A Review." *Industrial and Labor Relations Review* (October 1987), pp. 137–140.

"The Growth and Composition of the U.S. Labor Force." *Science* (a publication of the American Association for the Advancement of Science) (October 9, 1987), pp. 176–180.

"Efficiency and Equity as Goals for Contemporary U.S. Immigration Policy." *Population and Environment: A Journal of Interdisciplinary Studies* (Fall 1989), pp. 7–24.

"Forum: Immigration Policy and Skill Shortages." *BNA's Employee Relations Weekly* (August 20, 1990), pp. 1073–1074.

"Labor Market Transformation: The Role of U.S. Immigration Policy." *Population and Environment: A Journal of Interdisciplinary Studies* (Fall 1990), pp. 81–92.

"The Role of Public Policies in Rural Labor Markets." *Food and Life Sciences Quarterly* Vol. 20, Nos. 1–2 (1990), pp. 17–21.

"Immigration Policy and Workforce Preparedness." *ILR Report* (Fall 1990), pp. 18–23.

"Employer Sanctions and the Question of Discrimination: The GAO Study in Perspective." *International Migration Review* (Winter 1990), pp. 803–815.

"Comments on 'The Findings and Policy Implications of the GAO Report and the Urban Institute Hiring Audit.'" *The International Migration Review* (Winter 1990), pp. 828–830.

"The Changing Nature of the Workforce." *Looking Ahead* (a publication of the National Planning Association) (March 1991), pp. 8–17.

"Immigration Reform and the Urban Labor Force." *Labor Law Journal* (August 1991), pp. 537–544.

"Immigration Policy: Political or Economic?" *Challenge: The Magazine of Economic Affairs* (September–October 1991), pp. 12–19.

"The Immigration Act of 1990: Retreat from Reform." *Population and Environment: A Journal of Interdisciplinary Studies* (Fall 1991), pp. 89–93.

"The Mexican Free Trade Agreement: An Idea Whose Time Has Not Yet Come." *Social Contract* (Winter 1991–92), pp. 111–115.

"Despair Behind the Riots: The Impediment of Mass Immigration to Los Angeles Blacks." *Scope* (a publication of the Center for Immigration Studies) (Summer 1992), pp.1–3.

"Policy Dilemmas in Urban Education: Addressing the Needs of Poor, At-Risk Children." *Journal of Urban Affairs* Vol. 14, Nos. 3/4 (1992), pp. 263–290.

"Memorial Session: Reflections on Dudley Dillard's Career." (With Jeffrey A. Raffel, William Lowe Boyd, Eugene E. Eubanks, and Roberto Fernandez.) *Journal of Economic Issues* (June 1993), pp. 593–596.

"A Dead-End Street: Female Immigrants and Child Care." *Child Care Action News* (March–April 1993), Vol. 10, No. 2, pp. 3 and 7.

"Immigrant Labor and the Issue of 'Dirty Work' in Advanced Industrial Societies." *Population and Environment: A Journal of Interdisciplinary Studies* (July 1993), pp. 503–514.

"U.S. Asylum Policy and the New World Order." *People and Place: The Australian Forum for Population Studies* (Vol. 1, No. 3, 1993), pp. 1–8.

"The Administration of U.S. Immigration Policy." *Social Contract* (Spring 1994), pp. 192–197.

"Mass Immigration, Free Trade, and the Forgotten American Worker." *Challenge: The Magazine of Economic Affairs* (May–June 1995), pp. 37–44.

"Mass Immigration Worsens Plight of Urban Underclass." *Forum for Applied Research and Public Policy* (Fall 1995), pp. 45–50.

"Immigration Policy and the U.S. Economy: An Institutional Perspective." *Journal of Economic Issues* (June 1996), pp. 371–389. (Reprinted in *Race and Ethnicity in the United States*, Stephen Steinberg, ed. Oxford: Blackwell Publishers Ltd., 2000, pp. 253–266.)

"Ethics Trumping Economics? The Economics of Immigration Control." *Social Contract* (Winter 1997), pp. 117–120.

"Error Discovered in Unemployment Rate." *Immigration Review* (Winter 1998), pp. 10–11.

"Malthus: The Economist." *The Social Contract* (Spring 1998), pp. 206–215. (This appeared in a special issue commemorating the bicentennial of Malthus's *Essay on Population*.)

"American-Style Capitalism and Income Disparity: The Challenge of Social Anarchy." *Journal of Economic Issues* (June 1998), pp. 473–480.

"Henry George's Contribution to Political Economy." *Encyclopedia of Political Economy,* Vol. 1, 1999, pp. 397–398.

"U.S. Immigration Policy and the Plight of Unskilled Workers." *People and Place: The Australian Forum for Population Studies* (Vol. 7, No. 2, 1999), pp. 1–6. (Reprinted in *The Social Contract* [Fall 1999], pp. 13–17.)

"Reining-in a Rogue Policy: The Imperative of Immigration Reform." *University of Miami Inter-American Law Review* (Winter–Spring 1999), pp. 612–627.

"Immigration Policy and Human Resource Development." *HR Spectrum* (July–August 1999), pp. 1–4.

"American Unionism and U.S. Immigration Policy." *Backgrounder*, Center for Immigration Studies (August 2001), pp. 1–11.

"At a Crossroad: Immigration Reform and American Unionism." *Social Contract* (Winter 2002), pp. 122–125.

"Immigration and Poverty Reduction: Policy Making on a Squirrel Wheel." *Journal of Economic Issues* (June 2003), pp. 325–331. (Reprinted in *Social Contract* [Fall 2004], pp. 37–41.)

"The Economic Well-Being of Black Americans: The Overarching Influence of U.S. Immigration Policy." *Review of Black Political Economy* (Summer–Fall 2003), pp.15–42.

"Guestworker Programs: Lessons from the Past and Warnings for the Future." *Backgrounder*, Center for Immigration Studies (March 2004), pp. 1–7. (Reprinted in *The Social Contract* [Summer 2006], pp. 237–240.)

"Immigration: A Rogue Labor Market Policy." *Perspectives on Work* (Summer 2004), pp. 28–30.

"Parting Shots: Immigration." *Yale Economic Review* (Summer 2006), p. 49.

"Living Standards, Scarce Resources, and Immigration." *Social Contract* (Summer 2006), pp. 227–236. (A biographical interview conducted by John Rohe.)

"Immigration Reform: The Key Issue is Enforcement." *Voices—Immigration* No. 4 (2007), pp. 8–12.

"Revisiting the Administration of Immigration Policy." *Social Contract* (Spring 2007), pp. 180–183.

"Immigration Policy and Organized Labor." *Social Contract* (Summer 2007), pp. 260–268.

"The Heart of the Matter: Illegal Immigration." *Stanford Review* Vol. 40, No. 5 (March 18, 2008), p. 5.

"The Report of the Commission on Immigration Reform (i.e., the Jordan Commission): A Beacon for Real Immigration Reform." *Progressives for Immigration Reform*. Policy Brief no. 09-1, January 2009, pp. 1–6.

"The State of U.S. Immigration Policy: The Quandary of Economic Methodology and the Relevance of Economic Research to Know." *Journal of Law, Economics and Policy* (Vol. 5, No. 1, 2009), pp. 177–193.

CHAPTERS OF BOOKS

"The Administration of Training Programs." In *Compendium of Papers for an Economic Analysis of Federal Programs for the Development of Human Resources.* (With Ray Marshall.) U.S. Congress, Joint Economic Committee, Washington, DC (March 1968), Vol. 1, pp. 165–186.

"Texas." In *Emergency Employment Act*, Sar Levitan and Robert Taggart, eds. Salt Lake City, UT: Olympus Publishing, 1974, pp. 221–234.

"The Employment and Income Experience of Black Americans." In *Career Behavior of Special Groups*, J. Steven Picou and Robert E. Campbell, eds. Columbus, OH: Charles E. Merrill Publishing, 1975, pp. 382–403.

"Illegal Immigration and the American Labor Force." In *Current Issues in Social Policy*, W. Boyd Littrell and Gideon Sjoberg, eds. Beverly Hills, CA: Sage Publications, 1976, pp. 113–126.

"Labor Market Aspects of Mexican Migration to the United States." In *Views across the Border*, Stanley R. Ross, ed. Albuquerque, NM: University of New Mexico Press, 1978, pp. 204–225.

"Special Labor Market Segments." In *Manpower Research and Labor Economics*, Gordon Swanson and Jon Michaelson, eds. Beverly Hills, CA: Sage Publications, 1979, pp. 243–276. (A report prepared for the National Research Council of the National Academy of Sciences.)

"The Impact of the Undocumented Worker on the Labor Market." In *The Problem of the Undocumented Worker*, Robert S. Landmann, ed. Albuquerque, NM: Latin American Institute, University of New Mexico, 1979, pp. 31–38.

"La Migracion Como Un Fenomeno Socio-Politico." In *Estudios Fronterizos*. Mexico City: Asociacion National de Universidades e Institutos de Ensenaza Superior, 1981, pp. 239–258.

"Unemployment and Underemployment." In *Nonmetropolitan America in Transition*, Amos H. Hawley and Sara Mills Mazie, eds. Chapel Hill, NC: University of North Carolina Press, 1981, pp. 359–381.

"Foreign Labor Programs as an Alternative to Illegal Immigration: A Dissenting View." In *The Border That Joins*, Peter G. Brown and Henry Shue, eds. Totowa, NJ: Rowman and Littlefield, 1982, pp. 223–245.

"Nonimmigrant Labor Policy. Future Trend or Aberration?" In *The Unavoidable Issue: U.S. Immigration Policy in the 1980s*, Demetrios G. Papademetriou and Mark J. Miller, eds. Philadelphia: Institute for the Study of Human Issues, 1983, pp. 93–122.

"Employment Trends and Contemporary Immigration Policy: The Macro Implications." In *Immigration: Issues and Policies*, Vernon M. Briggs and Marta Tienda, eds. Salt Lake City, UT: Olympus Publishing, 1985, pp. 1–31.

"Employment Trends and Contemporary Immigration Policy." In *Clamor at the Gates*, Nathan Glazer, ed. San Francisco: Institute for Contemporary Studies, 1985, pp. 135–160.

"Immigration Reform and U.S. Employment Policy." In *In Defense of the Alien*, Vol. 8, Lydio Tomasi, ed. New York: Center for Migration Studies, 1986, pp. 42–60.

"The Imperative of Immigration Reform." In *Essays on Legal and Illegal Immigration*, Susan Pozo, ed. Kalamazoo, MI: W.E. Upjohn Institute for Employment Research, 1986, pp. 43–72.

"Rural Labor Markets: The Role of Government." In *Symposium on Rural Labor Markets Research Issues*, Molly Killian et. al., eds. Washington, DC: Economic Research Service of the U.S. Department of Agriculture, 1986, pp. 160–183.

"Human Resource Development and the Formulation of National Economic Policy." In *Evolutionary Economics: Foundations of Institutional Thought*, Vol. 1, Mark Tool, ed. Armonk, NY: M.E. Sharpe, 1988, pp. 257–290.

"The Mexican Free Trade Agreement: An Idea Whose Time Has Not Yet Come." In *In Defense of the Alien*, Vol. 14, Lydio Tomasi, ed. New York: Center for Migration Studies, 1992, pp. 63–70.

"Political Confrontation with Economic Reality: Mass Immigration in the Postindustrial Age." In *Elephants in the Volkswagen: Facing the Tough Questions about Our Overcrowded Country*, Lindsey Grant, ed. New York: W.H. Freeman and Company, 1992, pp. 72–84.

"Mass Immigration, Free Trade, and the Forgotten American Worker." In *In Defense of the Alien*, Vol. 17, Lydio Tomasi, ed. New York: Center for Migration Studies, 1995, pp. 20–32.

"International Migration and Labor Mobility: The Receiving Countries." In *The Economics of Labour Migration*, Julien van den Broeck, ed. Cheltenham, UK: Edward Elgar, 1996, pp. 115–158.

"Achieving National Economic and Social Goals." In *Of Heart and Mind: Social Policy Essays in Honor of Sar A. Levitan*, Garth Mangum and Stephen Mangum, eds. Kalamazoo, MI: W.E. Upjohn Institute for Employment Research, 1996, pp. 239–254.

"Income Disparity and Unionism: The Workplace Influences of Post-1965 Immigration Policy." In *The Inequality Paradox: Growth of Income Disparity*, James A. Auerbach and Richard Belous, eds. Washington, DC: National Policy Association, 1998, pp. 112–132.

"Immigration Policy and the U.S. Economy: An Institutional Perspective." In *Race and Ethnicity in the United States*, Stephen Steinberg, ed. Oxford: Blackwell Publishers, 2000, pp. 253–266.

"A Legal Immigration Policy for the 21st Century." In *Blueprints for an Ideal Legal Immigration Policy*, Richard D. Lamm and Alan Simpson, eds. Washington, DC: Center for Immigration Studies, 2001, pp. 21–27.

"Immigration Policy and American Unionism: A Reality Check." In *The Future of the American Labor Movement*, Jack Getman and Ray Marshall, eds. Austin, TX: University of Texas Press and the Lyndon B. Johnson School of Public Affairs, University of Texas, 2004, pp. 161–180.

"The Economic Well-Being of Black Americans: The Overarching Influence of U.S. Immigration Policy." In *The Impact of Immigration on African Americans*, Stephen Shulman, ed. New Brunswick, NJ: Transactions Publishers, 2004, pp. 1–26.

"Immigration and Income Disparity." In *The Ethics of Immigration Policy: A Collection of Essays*, John Rohe, ed. Petoskey, MI: Social Contract Press, 2006, pp. 6–7.

WORKING PAPERS

"Foreign Labor Programs as an Alternative to Illegal Immigration into the United States: A Dissenting View." Working paper NB-1. College Park, MD: Center for Philosophy and Public Policy, University of Maryland, 1980. (Reprinted in *U.S. Immigration Policy and the National Interest*, Appendix F to the Staff Report of the Select Commission on Immigration and Refugee Policy. Washington, DC: U S. Government Printing Office, 1981, pp. 141–174.)

"Efficiency and Equity as Goals for Contemporary U.S. Immigration Policy." Center for Advanced Human Resource Studies working paper no. 89-02. Ithaca, NY: Cornell University, 1989.

"The Changing Nature of the Workforce: The Influence of U.S. Immigration Policy." Center for Advanced Human Resource Studies working paper no. 91-01. Ithaca, NY: Cornell University, 1991.

"Immigration and the U.S. Labor Market: Public Policy Gone Awry." Center for Advanced Human Resource Studies working paper no. 92-41. Ithaca, NY: Cornell University, 1992.

"International Migration and Labor Mobility: The Receiving Countries." Center for Advanced Human Resource Studies working paper no. 94-19. Ithaca, NY: Cornell University, 1994.

"Reining In a Rogue Policy: The Imperative of Immigration Reform." Center for Advanced Human Resource Studies working paper no. 99-04. Ithaca, NY: Cornell University, 1999.

"U.S. Immigration Policy and the Plight of Its Unskilled Workers." Center for Advanced Human Resource Studies working paper no. 99-05. Ithaca, NY: Cornell University, 1999.

PUBLISHED PROCEEDINGS AND SPECIAL REPORTS

"Negro Participation in Apprenticeship Programs." (With Ray Marshall.) In *Research in Apprenticeship Training*. Madison, WI: University of Wisconsin Press, 1967, pp. 159–177.

"Equal Apprenticeship Opportunities in New York City." (With Ray Marshall.) In *Education and Training of Racial Minorities*. Madison, WI: University of Wisconsin Press, 1968, pp. 3–25.

"Texas." In *The Emergency Employment Act: Second Interim Assessment*. Washington, DC: National Manpower Policy Task Force, 1972, pp. 8–22.

"Texas." In *Case Studies of the Emergency Employment Act in Operation*. U.S. Senate Committee on Labor and Public Welfare. Washington, DC: U.S. Government Printing Office, 1973, pp. 1055–1172.

"The Impact of New Immigrants in Low Wage Labor Markets: Discussion." In *Proceedings of the Twenty-Seventh Annual Winter Meetings of the Industrial Relations Research Association*. Madison, WI: Industrial Relations Research Association, 1974, pp. 359–361.

"The Migration of Mexican Nationals into the United States: A Mounting Issue for the 1970s." In *International Conference on Migrant Workers*. Berlin: The International Institute for Comparative Social Studies, 1975, pp. 142–176. (Also published simultaneously in the German edition of the conference proceedings.)

"Issues in Full Employment Policy: Immigration." In *Proceedings of the 1977 Spring Meetings of the Industrial Relations Research Association*. Madison, WI: Industrial Relations Research Association, 1977, pp. 495–500.

"The Significance of Welfare Reform for the Rural South." (With Brian Rungeling and Lewis Smith.) In *Proceedings of the Thirtieth Annual Winter Meetings of the Industrial Relations Research Association*. Madison, WI: Industrial Relations Research Association, 1977, pp. 226–234.

"Alternatives to Immigration Laws and Policies." In *Immigration and the Mexican National*, Guy Poitras, ed. San Antonio, TX: Trinity University, 1978, pp. 52–61.

"The Youth Employment and Demonstration Projects Act in Albuquerque, New Mexico, the Costal Bend Consortium, and El Paso, Texas." In *The Unfolding Youth Initiatives: The Prime Sponsor Experience in Implementing the Youth Employment and Demonstration Projects Act*. Washington, DC: National Council on Employment Policy, 1978, pp. B1–B21. (Reprinted in *Youth Knowledge Development Report: Program Evaluation*. Report no. 3.14. Washington, DC: U.S. Government Printing Office, 1980, pp. B1–B21.)

"Comments on Rural Employment Statistics." In *Rural Employment and Unemployment Statistics*. Washington, DC: National Commission on Employment and Unemployment Statistics, 1978, pp. 48–51. (Reprinted in National Commission on Employment and Unemployment Statistics, *Data Collection, Processing, and Presentation*, Appendix Vol. 2, Washington, DC: U.S. Government Printing Office, 1980, pp. 561–563.)

"Area Descriptions: Albuquerque–Bernalillo County, New Mexico, Coastal Bend Manpower Consortium, and El Paso and El Paso County, Texas." In *Youth and the Local Employment Agenda: An Analysis of Prime Sponsor Experience Implementing the Youth Employment and Demonstration Projects Act*, Gregory Wurzburg, ed. Washington, DC: National Council on Employment Policy, 1980, pp. C1–C25.

"Public Service Employment in the Rural South: The Prospects for Job Transition." (With Brian Rungeling and Lewis Smith.) In *Proceedings of the Thirty-Second Annual Meetings of the Industrial Relations Research Association*. Madison, WI: Industrial Relations Research Association, 1979, pp. 195–202.

"The Need for a Contingent Countercyclical PSE Program." In *An Employment Policy to Fight Recession and Inflation*. A background paper prepared for the National Council on Employment Policy. Washington, DC: National Council on Employment Policy, 1980, pp. 9–14.

"The Youth Employment and Demonstration Project Act of 1977: Albuquerque, N.M., El Paso, Texas, and Coastal Bend Areas of Texas." Interim Report no. 3, *Youth Knowledge Development: Program Evaluations*. Report no. 3.15. Washington: U.S. Government Printing Office, 1980, pp. B1–B18.

"Albuquerque–Bernalillo County, New Mexico, Coastal Bend Manpower Consortium, and City and County of El Paso, Texas: Final Report." In *Youth Knowledge Development Report: Program Evaluations of Youth and the Local Employment Agenda*. Report no. 3.16. Washington, DC: U.S. Government Printing Office, 1980, pp. C1–C25.

"The Revival of Job Creation Programs in the 1970s: Lessons for the 1980s." In *Proceedings of the Thirty-Fourth Annual Meetings of the Industrial Relations Research Association*. Madison, WI: Industrial Relations Research Association, 1982, pp. 258–265.

"Immigration and Employment: Discussion." In *Proceedings of the Thirty-Sixth Annual Meetings of the Industrial Relations Research Association*. Madison, WI: Industrial Relations Research Association, 1984, pp. 174–176.

"Automation and Robotics: A Labor Economics Point of View." In *Proceedings of the 41st Conference of the Society for the Advancement of Food Service Research*. Lake Placid, FL: Society for Advancement of Food Service Research Association, 1985, pp. 131–136.

"The Purpose of Legal Immigration." In *Proceedings of Conference on Immigration Reform*. Washington, DC: Federation of Americans for Immigration Reform, 1988, pp. 104–111.

"Immigration Reform and the Urban Labor Market: Resolved and Unresolved Data Issues." In *Proceedings of the 1988 Meetings of the Social Statistics Section of the American Statistical Association*. Alexandria, VA: American Statistical Association, 1989, pp. 12–16.

"Political Confrontation with Economic Reality: Mass Immigration in the Post-Industrial Age." In *The NPG Forum*. Teaneck, NJ: Negative Population Growth, 1990, pp. 1–8.

"Changes in the Labor Market." In *Meeting the Challenges of Change: Unions and the White Collar Work Force*. Washington, DC: Department for Professional Employees, AFL-CIO, 1990, pp. 1–4.

"Foreword." In *Plebiscite: Puerto Rico at a Political Crossroad*, Felix Masud-Piloto, Hector Velez-Guadalupe, and Irma Almirall-Padamsee, eds. Ithaca, NY: Hispanic American Studies Program, Cornell University, 1991, p. 2.

"Immigration Reform and the Urban Labor Force." In *Proceedings of the 1991 Spring Meeting of the Industrial Relations Research Association*. Madison, WI: Industrial Relations Research Association, 1991, pp. 537–544.

"Introduction of the 1993 Recipient of the Veblen-Commons Award: Ray Marshall." *Journal of Economic Issues* (June 1993), pp. 297–300.

"Immigration: The Neglected Orphan of Economic Policy." *Backgrounder*, Center for Immigration Studies, no. 6-93 (September 1993), pp. 1–6.

"Unz vs. Them: A Debate on Immigration." *Policy Review* (Winter 1995), pp. 88–89.

"Institutional Barriers to Effective Employment Policy: The Case of the United States." In *Institutions, Economic Integration, and Restructuring*. Athens: European Association for Evolutionary Political Economy, 1997, Vol. 1, pp. 90–98.

"Immigration and Poverty." In *Employment Policies to Reduce Poverty*. Annandale-on-the-Hudson, NY: Jerome Levy Economics Institute, 1999, pp. 7–8.

PUBLISHED TESTIMONY FROM PUBLIC HEARINGS

NOTE: Most of the following public testimonies are available on the Digital Commons of the School of Industrial and Labor Relations at Cornell University. See http://digitalcommons.ilr.cornell.edu/briggstestimonies (accessed September 23, 2009).

"Equal Employment Opportunity in the Construction Industry." Testimony before the Massachusetts State Advisory Committee of the United States Commission on Civil Rights. Contract Compliance and Equal Employment Opportunity in the Construction Industry. Washington, DC: U.S. Government Printing Office, 1969, pp. 3–14.

"Labor Market Implications of Prevailing Immigration Policies and Practices." Testimony before Select Committee on Population, U.S. House of Representatives, April 5, 1978. *Immigration to the United States: Hearings*, pp. 462–471. (See also pp. 94–111 for oral comments.)

"Foreign Policy Implications of Illegal Immigration from Mexico." Testimony before Subcommittee on Inter-American Affairs of the Committee on International Relations, U.S. House of Representatives, May 24, 1978. *Undocumented Workers: Implications for U.S. Policy in the Western Hemisphere: Hearings*, pp. 245–255. (See also pp. 84–92 for oral comments.)

"Employer Sanctions on the Hiring of Illegal Immigrants." Testimony before the Subcommittee on Immigration and Refugee Policy of the Committee on the Judiciary, U.S. Senate (September 20, 1981). *The Knowing Employment of Illegal Immigrants: Hearings*, pp. 194–199.

"The Rural Labor Force: Unemployment and Underemployment Issues." Testimony before the Subcommittee on Agriculture and Transportation of the Joint Economic Committee of the Congress (June 13, 1985). *The Economic Evolution of Rural America: Hearings*, pp. 226–237. (See also pp. 220–225.)

"Employment Implications of U.S. Immigration Policy." Testimony before the Subcommittee on Immigration, Refugees, and International Law of the Committee on the Judiciary, U.S. House of Representatives (July 21, 1987). *Legal Immigration—Occupational Preferences: Hearings*, pp. 17–26. (See also pp. 42–71 for oral comments.)

"The Reform of the Legal Immigration System." Testimony before the Subcommittee on Immigration and Refugee Affairs of the Committee on the Judiciary, U.S. Senate (December 11, 1987). *Legal Immigration Reform: Hearings*, pp. 371–379. (See also pp. 405–410 for oral comments.)

"Labor Market Transformation: The Role of U.S. Immigration Policy." Testimony before the Joint Hearings of the Subcommittee on Immigration, Refugees, and International Law of the Committee on the Judiciary and the Immigration Task Force of the Committee on Education and Labor of the U.S. House of Representatives (March 1, 1990). *Immigration Act of 1989*. Washington, DC: U.S. Government Printing Office, 1990, pp. 235–243. (See also pp. 232–234.)

"Illegal Immigration and the U.S. Labor Market." Testimony before Hearings of the Subcommittee on Immigration and Claims, Committee of the Judiciary, U.S. House of Representatives (April 5, 1995). *Impact of Illegal Immigration on Public Benefit Programs and the American Labor Force*, pp. 95–100. (See also pp. 93–94 for oral comments.)

"Immigration Reform: Comments on H.R. 1915." Testimony before Hearings of the Subcommittee on Immigration and Claims of the Committee on the Judiciary, U.S. House of Representatives (June 29, 1995). *Immigration in the National Interest Act of 1995*, pp. 89–90. (See also pp. 88 and 92 for oral comments.)

"Immigration Reform and the U.S. Labor Force." Testimony before the Subcommittee on Immigration, Committee on the Judiciary, U.S. Senate (September 13, 1995), Hearings.

"Statement." Testimony before Hearings of the Subcommittee on Immigration and Claims of the Committee on the Judiciary, U.S. House of Representatives. *Impact of Immigration on Recent Immigrants and Black and Hispanic Citizens* (March 11, 1999), pp. 71–75. (See also pp. 69–71 for oral comments.)

"Immigration Policy and Low Wage Workers: The Influence of American Unionism." Testimony before Hearings of the Subcommittee on Immigration, Border Security, and International Claims of the Judiciary Committee of the U.S. House of Representatives (October 30, 2003).

"Guestworker Programs for Low-Skilled Workers: Lessons from the Past and Warnings for the Future." Testimony before Hearings of the Subcommittee on Immigration, Border Security, and Citizenship of the Judiciary Committee of the U.S. Senate (February 12, 2004).

"Immigration Reform and the U.S. Labor Force: The Questionable 'Wisdom' of S 2611 (the Comprehensive Immigration Reform Act of 2006)." Testimony before Hearings of the Judiciary Committee of the U.S. House of Representatives, Evansville, IN (August 29, 2006).

"Real Immigration Reform: The Path to Credibility." Testimony before Hearings of the Subcommittee on Immigration and Border Security of the Committee of the Judiciary of the U.S. House of Representatives. *U.S. Economy, U.S. Workers, and Immigration Reform*, Washington, DC (May 3, 2007), pp. 79–87.

"Immigration Policy and Organized Labor: A Never-Ceasing Issue." Testimony before Hearings of the Subcommittee on Immigration and Border Security of the Committee of the Judiciary of the U.S. House of Representatives. *Comprehensive Immigration Reform: Labor Movement Perspectives*. Washington, DC (May 24, 2007), pp. 40–48. (Reprinted in *The Social Contract* [Summer 2007], pp. 260–269.)

UNPUBLISHED STUDY

The Emergency Jobs Program of 1983: Its Implementation by the Tennessee Valley Authority. A consulting report to TVA that was conducted under Contract #TV61589A (July 15, 1984), pp. 82.

BOOK REVIEWS

The Lean Years: A History of the American Worker, 1920–1933, by Irving Bernstein. In *Journal of Economic History* (March 1967).

The Negro in Federal Employment: The Quest for Equal Opportunity, by Samuel Krislov. In *Journal of Human Resources* (Fall 1968).

The Negro and Equal Employment Opportunity: A Review of Management Experiences in Twenty Companies, by Louis Ferman. *Journal of Human Resources* (Spring 1970).

The Mexican-American People: The Nation's Second Largest Minority, by Leo Grebler, Joan W. Moore, and Ralph C. Guzman. In *Industrial and Labor Relations Review* (January 1972).

The Unions and the Cities, by Harry K. Wellington and Ralph K. Winter, and *Managing Local Government under Union Pressure*, by David T. Stanley. In *Texas Law Review* (August 1973).

Opening the Skilled Construction Trades to Blacks: A Study of the Washington and Indianapolis Plans for Minority Employment, by Richard Rowan and Lester Rubin. In *Industrial and Labor Relations Review* (January 1974).

Mexican Americans Tomorrow: Educational and Economic Perspectives, Gus Tyler, ed. In *Monthly Labor Review* (July 1976).

The Opportunities Industrialization Centers: A Decade of Community-Based Manpower Services, by Bernard Anderson. In *Industrial and Labor Relations Review* (January 1978).

Mexican Illegal Alien Workers in the United States, by Walter Fogel. In *Industrial and Labor Relations Review* (July 1979).

Immigrants—and Immigrants: Perspectives on Mexican Labor Migration to the United States, by Arthur Corwin. In *Journal of Economic Literature* (September 1979).

A Popularized Version of 21 Doctoral Dissertations, by Lawrence R. Klein and Susan Ghozeil. In *Growth and Change* (January 1980).

Mexican Workers in the United States: Historical and Political Perspectives, by George Kiser and Martha Kiser. In *Southwestern Historical Quarterly* (April 1980).

Creating Jobs: Public Employment Programs and Wage Subsidies, John L. Palmer, ed. In *Children and Youth Services Review*, Vol. 2, 1980. (Reprinted in *Confronting Youth Unemployment in the 1980s: Rhetoric versus Reality*, Ray Rist, ed. New York: Pergamon Press, 1980. pp. 232–234.)

The United States–Mexico Border: A Politico-Economic Profile, by Raul A. Fernandez. In *International Migration Review* (Fall 1980).

The Long Road North: The Story of a Mexican Worker's Perilous Crossing into the United States, by John Davidson. In *Southwestern Historical Quarterly* (October 1980).

Comparative Metropolitan Employment Complexes, by Dale Heistand and Dean Morse. In *Industrial and Labor Relations Review* (April 1981).

Democracy, Authority, and Alienation, by John F. Witte. In *Journal of Economic Issues* (December 1981).

Administering Foreign Worker Programs: Lessons from Europe, by Mark J. Miller and Philip L. Martin. In *Industrial and Labor Relations Review* (January 1983).

Jobs for Disadvantaged Workers: The Economics of Employment Subsidies, by Robert H. Haveman and John Palmer. In *Journal of Economic Issues* (September 1983).

CETA: Accomplishments, Problems, Solutions, by William Mirengoff, Lester Rindler, Harry Greenspan, and Charles Harris. In *Industrial and Labor Relations Review* (July 1983).

Labor Displacement and Public Policy, by Philip L. Martin. In *Journal of Economic Issues* (December 1984).

Interregional Migration, National Policy and Social Justice, by Gordon L. Clark. In *Journal of Economic Issues* (June 1985).

For We Are Sold, I and My People, by Maria Patricia Fernandez-Kelly. In *Industrial and Labor Relations Review* (October 1985).

Studies in International Labor Migration, by W. R. Bohning, In *Journal of Economic Issues* (September 1985).

The Immigration Reform Law of 1986, by Nancy Montwieler. In *Industrial and Labor Relations Review* (January 1988).

Industries, Firms, and Jobs, by George Farkas and Paula England. In *Social Forces* (March 1990).

The Trade Threat and U.S. Trade Policy, by John M. Culbertson. In *Population and Environment* (Spring 1990).

Illegal Aliens: Their Employment and Employers, by Barry Chiswick. In *Industrial and Labor Relations Review* (April 1990).

For the Common Good: Redirecting the Economy toward Community, the Environment, and a Sustainable Future, by Herman Daly and John Cobb. In *Population and Environment* (Fall 1990).

The Invisible Work Force: Transforming American Business with Outside and Home-Based Workers, by Beverly Lozano. In *Administrative Science Quarterly* (September 1990).

Friends or Strangers: The Impact of Immigrants on the U.S. Economy, by George Borjas. In *Scope*, Newsletter of the Center for Immigration Studies (Fall 1990).

Unions and Communities under Siege: American Communities and the Crisis of Organized Labor, by Gordon Clark. In *Journal of Economic Issues* (September 1991).

Friends or Strangers: The Impact of Immigrants on the U.S. Economy, by George Borjas. In *Population and Environment* (Winter 1991).

The Labor Market as a Social Institution, by Robert Solow. In *Journal of Economic Issues* (December 1992).

Anatomy of a Public Policy: The Reform of Contemporary Immigration Law, by Michael LeMay. In *Administrative Science Quarterly* (March 1996).

The Case against Immigration, by Roy Beck. In *Immigration Review* (Summer 1996).

Tragedies of Our Own Making: How Private Choices Have Created Public Bankruptcy, by Richard Neely. In *Industrial and Labor Relations Review* (October 1996).

Does Training for the Disadvantaged Work? Evidence from the National JTPA Study, by Larry L. Orr, Howard S. Bloom, Stephen H. Bell, Fred Doolittle, Winston Lin, and George Cave. In *Industrial and Labor Relations Review* (April 1997).

The American Mosaic, by Anthony Carnevale and Susan Carol Stone. In *International Migration Review* (Summer 1997).

Immigrants Out! The New Nativism and the Anti-Immigrant Impulse in the United States, Juan Perea, ed. In *Journal of American Ethnic History* (Summer 1998).

Economics, Ethics, and Public Policy, Charles K. Wilber, ed. In *Journal of Economic Issues* (March 1999).

Unwelcomed Strangers: American Identity and the Turn against Immigration, by David Reimers. In *Annals of the Academy of Political and Social Science* (January 2000).

Young Workers: Varieties of Experiences, by Julian Barling and E. Kevin Kelloway. In *Industrial and Labor Relations Review* (April 2000).

A Stream of Windows: Unsettling Reflections on Trade, Immigration, and Democracy, by Jagdish Bhagwati. In *Journal of Policy Analysis and Management,* Vol. 20, No. 1 (Winter 2001).

Beyond Smoke and Mirrors: Mexican Immigration in an Era of Economic Integration, by Douglas S. Massey, Jorge Durland, and Nolan J. Malone. In *Industrial and Labor Relations Review* (January 2003).

Making Americans: Immigration, Race, and the Origins of Diverse Democracy, by Desmond King. In *Labor History* (May 2003).

Science at the Borders: Immigrant Medical Inspection and the Shaping of the Modern Industrial Labor Force, by Amy L. Fairchild. In *Industrial and Labor Relations Review* (October 2004).

L.A. Story: Immigrant Workers and the Future of the U.S. Labor Movement, by Ruth Milkman. In *Industrial and Labor Relations Review* (April 2007).

Black Americans and Organized Labor: A New History, by Paul A. Moreno. At EH.Net, Economic History Services (May 14, 2007). http://eh.net/bookreviews/library/1216 (accessed September 23, 2009).

NEWSPAPER, MAGAZINE, AND DIGITAL ARTICLES

"Illegal Migration Turning into a Human Onslaught." *Houston Chronicle* (February 16, 1975), Section 3, p. 25.

"Achieving the Potential of Bilingual Education." *Christian Science Monitor* (September 28, 1979), p. 23.

"A Bilingual Future for the United States: 'Se Hable Espanol?'" *Texas Observer* (twenty-fifth anniversary edition, December 28, 1979), pp. 23–26. (Reprinted in the *Buffalo Courier-Express* [April 25, 1980], p. 28.)

"The Simple Truth of Immigration Reform." *Texas Observer* (June 15, 1984), p. 4.

"Immigration Policy Sends Blacks Back to South." *New York Times* (February 1, 1990), A:22. (Reprinted in *The Social Contract* [Summer 1995], pp. 270–271.)

"Strangers at the Gate." *New York Times Magazine* (October 6, 1991), p. 18.

"If You Don't Cook the Figures, You Will Find That Immigrants Cost Us a Lot." (With Virginia Abernethy.) *Washington Times* (November 24, 1995), A:22.

"Wrong Data." *National Review* (October 27, 1997), p. 4.

"Corrected Census." *Texas Observer* (October 9, 1998), 2–3.

"Cornell U's Vernon Briggs on Immigration and the Economy." *Investor's Daily* (August 27, 1999), A:6.

"Why Clinton Should Veto H-1B." *Ithaca Journal* (September 4, 2000), 11A.

"Immigration Economics." *New York Times* (January 20, 2001), A:22.

"Guest Worker Plan to Hike Jobless Rate." (With Lawrence Harrison.) *Boston Globe* (March 22, 2004), A:11.

"Immigration Harms U.S. Workers." *San Diego Union-Tribune* (September 2, 2001), G:3.

"A Major Mistake on the Border." *Raleigh News and Observer* (September 3, 2001), A:15.

"Doomed to Fail: The Unintended Consequences of Guestworker Programs." ILR Briefs, ILR Digital Commons, 2006. http://digitalcommons.ilr.cornell .edu/impactbrief/2 (accessed September 23, 2009).

"Immigration Redux." *Texas Observer* (June 2, 2006), 1 and 16.

"Farm Worker Shortage a Myth." *Ithaca Journal* (February 2, 2007), 7A.

The Authors

Avner Ahituv is CEO of Kibbutz Ramat Yohanan. Formerly he taught economics at Hebrew University and Haifa University, and he has published in the areas of human capital and labor economics.

Ernesto Cortés Jr. is on the National Staff of the Industrial Areas Foundation and the executive director of the Interfaith Education Fund. Under Cortés's supervision, the organizations of the Southwest IAF network have developed successful initiatives in the areas of job training, economic development, citizenship, and education. Cortés first encountered Vernon Briggs while attending graduate school at The University of Texas at Austin and, since then, his work has been influenced by Briggs's practical applications of economic theory.

William P. Curington is a professor of economics and senior associate dean for academic programs and research in the Sam M. Walton College of Business at the University of Arkansas. He holds a bachelor's degree in economics and history from The University of Texas at Austin, a master of labor and industrial relations from Michigan State University, and a master's degree and PhD in economics from Syracuse University. His primary areas of research are the economics of occupational illness and injury, disability, and employee compensation systems. Journals in which his publications have appeared include the *Journal of Human Resources*, *Industrial and Labor Relations Review*, *Industrial Relations*, and *Southern Economic Journal*. He was an undergraduate student in Briggs's labor economics course at The University of Texas at Austin and credits Briggs with inspiring him to pursue a career in labor economics teaching and research.

Michelle Bellessa Frost, formerly of Princeton University, is currently self-employed. Her research has focused on race and ethnic differences in the transition from high school to college.

Robert W. Glover is a research scientist at the Ray Marshall Center for the Study of Human Resources, Lyndon B. Johnson School of Public Affairs at The University of Texas at Austin, where his research focuses on various aspects of work and learning, especially apprenticeship, industry training practices, and school-to-career transition. Vernon Briggs introduced him to the field of labor economics and human resource development. Briggs's enthusiasm for teaching and genuine concern for workers and the less fortunate in American society motivated Glover to choose the field as a career. Vernon Briggs has been his mentor, teacher, colleague, and friend.

Seth D. Harris is deputy secretary of the U.S. Department of Labor. He is currently on leave from New York Law School, where he served as a professor of law and director of Labor and Employment Law Program, while also serving as research associate of New York University School of Law's Center for Labor and Employment Law. Harris writes about the economics of labor and employment law with a particular focus on the Americans with Disabilities Act. He was a senior policy advisor to both Secretaries of Labor under President Bill Clinton, and is one of Vernon Briggs's most appreciative students.

V. Joseph Hotz is the Arts and Sciences Professor of Economics at Duke University. He has published extensively in the areas of labor economics, applied econometrics, and the evaluation of social programs.

Christopher T. King is director of the Ray Marshall Center for the Study of Human Resources and a lecturer at the University of Texas at Austin's Lyndon B. Johnson School of Public Affairs, where he holds the Mike Hogg Professorship in Urban Management. He has written widely on education, workforce development, and social policy and has served in policy positions in federal and state government. He has a BA in economics from the University of Texas at Austin and an MA and PhD in economics from Michigan State University. He was a student in Vernon Briggs's labor and manpower economics classes at the University of Texas in the late 1960s, where he was inspired by Briggs's passion for and commitment to improving the lives of people lacking adequate access to economic opportunity.

Ray Marshall holds the Audre and Bernard Rapoport Centennial Chair in Economics and Public Affairs at The University of Texas at Austin. From 1977 to 1981 he was U.S. Secretary of Labor. His current research interests are education, labor economics, and immigration, and he has written widely on these subjects. He has served on a number of commissions and boards and currently chairs the board of trustees of the National Center on Education and the Economy and is a founding board member of the Economic Policy Institute. He and Vernon Briggs were colleagues at the University of Texas during the 1960s, where they worked on various projects related to minority representation in apprenticeship programs and authored a number of publications on that subject. They also coauthored a labor economics textbook.

Philip L. Martin is a labor economist and professor in the Department of Agricultural and Resource Economics at the University of California, Davis (UCD). After graduating from the University of Wisconsin–Madison, he worked at the Brookings Institution and at the White House on labor and immigration issues. He has worked for the World Bank, International Monetary Fund, and United Nations agencies such as the International Labour Organization and United Nations Development Programme. He is the author of numerous articles and books on labor and immigration issues. Martin's research focuses on farm labor and rural poverty, labor migration and economic development, and immigration policy and guest worker issues; he has testified before Congress and state and local agencies numerous times on these issues. Martin is the edi-

tor of *Migration News* and of *Rural Migration News* (http://migration.ucdavis
.edu) and received UCD's Distinguished Public Service award in 1994. He and
Vernon Briggs have crossed paths many times since the late 1970s.

Larry Nackerud is a professor in the School of Social Work at the University of Georgia. His teaching and research focus primarily on social welfare
policy, including courses and writings on immigration and political refugee
policy. In the late 1980s he studied for his PhD at Cornell in the College of Human Ecology, and Dr. Briggs served as an external member of his committee.
It was Dr. Briggs who inspired Dr. Nackerud to select political refugee policy
as the focus of his dissertation.

James T. Peach is Regents Professor of Economics and International Business at New Mexico State University (NMSU), where he has been a member
of the faculty since 1980. He is also co-director of the Office of Policy Analysis
at NMSU's Arrowhead Center. Peach is past-president of the Association for
Evolutionary Economics, the Western Social Science Association, the Association for Borderlands Studies, and the Rocky Mountain Council on Latin
American Studies. His research interests include demographic and economic
change along the U.S.–Mexico border, U.S.–Mexico economic relations, energy economics, and the economics of sports. Peach and William M. Dugger
are coauthors of *Economic Abundance: An Introduction*. Peach first met Professor Briggs in 1964, when he took Briggs's labor economics course at The
University of Texas at Austin.

Marta Tienda is Maurice P. During '22 Professor of Demographic Studies and Professor of Sociology and Public Affairs at Princeton University. She
has published extensively about race and ethnic inequality, the demography
of higher education, and the U.S. Hispanic population. She first met Vernon
Briggs in 1972, as an auditor in his introductory economics course at The University of Texas at Austin.

Charles J. Whalen is executive director and professor of business and economics at Utica College and a visiting fellow at Cornell University School of
Industrial and Labor Relations. He served as a resident scholar at the Levy
Economics Institute of Bard College in the mid-1990s, taught in China as a
Fulbright Scholar in the late 1990s, and worked as associate economics editor
at *BusinessWeek* in the early 2000s. He has written extensively on worker insecurity and economic stabilization, as well as on the history of economics and
its relevance to understanding contemporary employment challenges. He first
met Vernon Briggs while studying as an undergraduate at Cornell in the early
1980s, and Briggs's influence continues to animate his teaching and research.

Index

The italic letters *f, n,* and *t* following a page number indicate that the subject information of the heading is within a figure, note, or table, respectively, on that page. Double italics indicate multiple but consecutive elements.

About the Institute

The W.E. Upjohn Institute for Employment Research is a nonprofit research organization devoted to finding and promoting solutions to employment-related problems at the national, state, and local levels. It is an activity of the W.E. Upjohn Unemployment Trustee Corporation, which was established in 1932 to administer a fund set aside by Dr. W.E. Upjohn, founder of The Upjohn Company, to seek ways to counteract the loss of employment income during economic downturns.

The Institute is funded largely by income from the W.E. Upjohn Unemployment Trust, supplemented by outside grants, contracts, and sales of publications. Activities of the Institute comprise the following elements: 1) a research program conducted by a resident staff of professional social scientists; 2) a competitive grant program, which expands and complements the internal research program by providing financial support to researchers outside the Institute; 3) a publications program, which provides the major vehicle for disseminating the research of staff and grantees, as well as other selected works in the field; and 4) an Employment Management Services division, which manages most of the publicly funded employment and training programs in the local area.

The broad objectives of the Institute's research, grant, and publication programs are to 1) promote scholarship and experimentation on issues of public and private employment and unemployment policy, and 2) make knowledge and scholarship relevant and useful to policymakers in their pursuit of solutions to employment and unemployment problems.

Current areas of concentration for these programs include causes, consequences, and measures to alleviate unemployment; social insurance and income maintenance programs; compensation; workforce quality; work arrangements; family labor issues; labor-management relations; and regional economic development and local labor markets.